MW01141703

THE
INVISIBLE
BEAST

Cassi Eve

ISBN 978-1-64114-042-3 (Paperback)
ISBN 978-1-64114-043-0 (Digital)

Copyright © 2017 by Cassi Eve
All rights reserved. No part of this publication may be reproduced, distributed, or transmitted in any form or by any means, including photocopying, recording, or other electronic or mechanical methods without the prior written permission of the publisher. For permission requests, solicit the publisher via the address below.

Christian Faith Publishing, Inc.
296 Chestnut Street
Meadville, PA 16335
www.christianfaithpublishing.com

This is a true story. To protect the identity of certain people, some names have been changed. '

Printed in the United States of America

Contents

Preface

Dean Mack,

You changed my life. Before you, there was just me. I thought I had my plans. My path I had set before me. Then suddenly you were there. This amazing, handsome, rugged Australian man . . . full of life, laughter, and love. You had a way with people that's hard to describe. You could win anyone over with your jesting, teasing, and charm. I could not pretend you had no effect on me because, truthfully, your eyes saw into the depths of my heart. And although I was young and fickle, and against the advice of others, you took a chance on me. You reached for my hand and made me your wife. You challenged me, encouraged me, lead me, taught me. Taught me patience, kindness, friendship, and compromise. Taught me how to listen without judgment, love without fear, and live without worry. You taught me how to enjoy moments, make memories, and seize the day. You taught me faithfulness, loyalty, and strength. You are the strongest and most loving person I've ever known. I am so sorry, my love, that you suffered so much. I am so sorry you had to leave the boys and me before you wanted to. Thank you for fighting so hard to stay here with us. As the doctor said, it is the ultimate act of love. I am so happy you are free now. Healed. Restored. I'm going to miss you, your voice, your laugh . . . You've been my everything for so long.

Until we meet again,
Cass

My name is Cassi. I am thirty-three years old. I got married at twenty. I had two children by twenty-two. I was widowed at twenty-seven.

I have moved countries four times.

I have drawn near to God and I have run away from him.

I have known true friendship and betrayal. Great love and indescribable loss.

And I have found this to be true.

Beyond brokenness.

Beyond death.

Beyond the excruciating agony of loss.

Beyond the torment of watching your love slowly die.

Beyond utterly catastrophic events in life.

When all seems dark.

When all seems lost.

When life is dead

and purpose forsaken.

When you cannot imagine being anything other than broken and bitter in a life of misery.

I promise you.

There is

Hope.

And I pray

that in these pages, you will find it.

May you find strength for yourself here. That you may take whatever good lies in these pages as treasure. For your life. May you find comfort in knowing you are not alone. Not alone in your grief. Your mistakes. Your anguish. Your pain. Your despair. I have walked those shadows. I too have traversed those murky waters. Those foreboding mountains. And I have come to this moment to write the words before you now. So that you may read them.

It was all for you.

This

is my story.

THE MAN WITH EYES
THAT SAW ME

In the beginning, there was darkness. Brokenness. It was in my heart.

At the young age of sixteen, my heart had already been ravaged by the dogs of rejection and abandonment. Imprisoned by walls of Pain and bars of Loneliness, they hounded me constantly.

I longed for love. I did not know what true love felt like or how to get it, but I craved and thirsted for it. That craving drove me toward the shadows. I lived off the remnants I could find, scavenging the dregs and the crumbs to sustain me.

I was lost. The ground beneath me was loose gravel. Uneven. Slippery. My arms and legs were scraped. My clothes were dirty. My lips were cracked. The crumbs I ate only made the pangs worse. I kept going though my heart was wilting. I wandered, looking for signs of life. Signs of love. Signs of hope.

And then I saw one. In the face of a man.

He was handsome, yes. Extremely handsome even. But that wasn't it. It was the kindness in his eyes. The purity of his interaction. The freedom in his voice. His strength and integrity shone like a light. His face showed no sign of worry. Only virtue. Peace. All the things I longed for, this man possessed.

His eyes were piercing blue. Not aggressive. Rather, authoritative but gentle. Unrelenting yet understanding. For the first time, I felt seen. He saw me. Not as I was but as I was meant to be.

He planted in me a seed. A seed of hope. A seed of truth. That I was not meant to be a beggar. I was not given an appetite for love that I would suffer without it. There were forces stronger than the walls and bars that surrounded me. That the parched desert soil of my soul would one day know the sweet, transforming shower of spring rain. And that the desperately unyielding hunger for love that consumed me would one day be fulfilled.

The weeks and months passed. God began to show Himself to me. I felt Him when He was close to me. He started to show me He wasn't mad at me. That, actually, He longed to spend time with me. He wanted me to know Him. He wanted to free my heart from its prison. I let Him, and so He did.

He took me by the hand out of the prison of Pain and Loneliness. He ushered me into a new place where the dogs could not get to me. He washed my hair. He washed my hands and feet and gave me new clothes. He made me new from the inside out. The tears would come like a healing rain when He spoke to me tenderly. When He showed me in little ways that He cared and He was there. Listening. Loving. And in Him, my heart began to blossom.

I never expected to see the man with blue eyes again. But I did. Three years later. In he walked. Into my father's house. He was the same. But I was different.

I discreetly studied his frame, aware of each gesture and movement. Each word. His thick Australian accent was intoxicating. His laugh a beautiful boom. His dark hair fell past his shoulders. He stood head and shoulders over me. He was rugged and beautiful. That was just the beginning. I stared at him, carefully following the lines in his face. Whenever he caught my gaze, I quickly looked away. Shyness and embarrassment swept over me. I felt naked. I was sure if he looked into my eyes, he could read my thoughts.

Quietly aware of him, I sat next to the fire. He came and sat next to me. My heart stopped. Flushed, I sat as still as a statue. *Breathe, Cassi, breathe.* He shared fascinating stories of his travels through Spain. Turkey. Scotland. I was captivated but so self-aware. *Act naturally, Cassi. Oh my gosh. Is this happening?*

He was so laid back. Conversation came easily. He was living in Atlanta, working with a ministry there called Blood and Fire. They ran a homeless shelter and rehab. They helped crack addicts get clean and off the streets. He was completely inspiring, his selflessness, living so completely for others. *How could someone be so . . . so good?* There was nothing not to love about him.

He rolled out his swag as he continued to entertain us with stories of the outback. Shooting kangaroos and rabbits. Riding motorbikes. Camping in the bush. Wild boys. Wild pranks. He had many adventurous tales to delight and enthrall us with. Right at that moment. Looking into that joyful, handsome, tender face. So free. So alive. Wholehearted. *I would go anywhere with this man. He could roll me up in that sleeping bag right now, and I would go. It doesn't matter where. He could tie a string around my finger, and I'd live in a barn.*

Little did I know I would be asked to live up to my promise. To follow this man to the ends of the earth.

After his visit, we wrote letters. He wasn't forthcoming in any of them. I couldn't tell if he liked me. Ten months later, in he walked again to my father's house. Dean Mack. I secretly wished someone would inform me prior to his visits. Being prepared would be preferable.

He was on his way to Australia, staying in California for a couple of days on each side of his trip. The chemistry between us was unnerving. He made me shy. My usual bubbly and outgoing self was completely hidden under awestruck bashfulness. And once again, I tried to act natural but only succeeded in stoic awkwardness.

He left for Australia and came back. I wanted to get the chance to talk again. Just the two of us. That I might be a slightly more coherent and lively version of myself.

The night before he went back to Atlanta, we finally sat down without agenda or distraction. We were in the living room. He sat on the couch in his relaxed, albeit intense, manner. I sat in a plush chair adjacent, resisting the urge to hold a cushion around my tummy to partially hide behind it. We talked about the things we'd like to do and see. I told him about my dreams. Walking through crowds of children with dark-colored skin. They were reaching out to me.

"Well, is that just going to be a mission trip for a couple of weeks, or is it something you could give your life for?" His eyes were alight with the passion of a man who had left everything for the poor.

What am I willing to give my life for? I'd never thought of it that way. My plan was art school. Maybe Europe. *Give my life for missions?* It had never occurred to me. I sat on it for a moment.

"I . . . don't know." I averted his steady, questioning gaze.

He told me more about Atlanta. Leaving his hometown of Esperance. Selling his car. Leaving behind his surfboards. Friends. All to answer the call. Go to Atlanta. Sleep in an old, rundown brick building. Serve the poor. Eat with them. Hang out with them. Pray for them. Help them. Love them. Live with them.

Who does that? Could I live like that? Could I be like that? Am I that good? Am I too selfish to give up a life for me? The life I want? But . . . what is the life I want? Dean seemed so free. So fulfilled. So undeniably joyful. *Isn't that what I want?* The wrestle inside me began. *Do I want God's will for me? Or my will for me?*

Our conversation was deep and intense. I was slowly getting used to staring into the steady gaze of those heavy, magnetic eyes. One by one, everyone went off to bed. We talked until well after midnight. As we spoke, I noted his questions were deliberate. Thought out. This wasn't a casual conversation.

Those questions got me thinking. And I pondered them for days as they echoed in my mind.

"Is it something you could give your life for?" What am I giving my life for?

Three days after he left for Atlanta, I checked the voicemail on my cell. "Hi, Cassi. This is Dean. Dean Mack. Yeah, just giving you a call to see how you're going. Give me a call."

WHAT? DEAN MACK?! Dean Mack is calling me? And wants me to call him back? He likes me! Oh my Lord, he likes me! AHHH! DEAN MACK LIKES ME!

Elation. I beamed. *I know now. I know for sure. He likes me.*

We talked on the phone every night for hours. About everything. Except about how we felt about each other. He read the Bible to me. Encouraged me. Told me God had given me gifts. He told me amazing things about God I never heard before. He was so patient with me. He was so good at pointing to God. In my complaining or criticism, he gave me humble silence. And in the silence, I heard God's voice. And God's words changed me. My heart softened. Tears came. I cried without knowing why. I did know God was doing something deep. Healing. Molding. Refining. Making me more aware of Him. Making me aware He was with me all the time. Loving me all the time.

Confession

One evening, Dean called. He sounded different. Hesitant. Pensive. He asked if he could tell me how he felt about me. I was sitting on my bed in my room, holding my breath. I was hanging on to every. Single. Word. As this incredible, inspiring, God-loving, passionate, generous man told me how much affection he had for me, I went to another level. Another plane. A place of complete jubilation and ecstasy. Where you hear the most marvelous words you could imagine.

He saw something in me. Something I couldn't see. Something others couldn't see. A depth. A beauty. A compassion that would only surface with time and trial. Something unearthed in the heat of the desert after being worn by the wind. And parched from every earthly comfort. Something exquisite. Precious. And rare.

The relationship blossomed. The love of God shone through Dean's acts of kindness. He was gracious. I was honest about my flaws. The hesitations of my heart. He was amazing. So pure. So devoted. Such a "good" Christian. I felt I paled in comparison. So underserving. He had already done many incredible things. *What had I done?* He was twenty-six years old and a virgin. I was nineteen and not. In my mind, he deserved someone far better. Someone more . . . like him. And I told him I thought so.

"No, Cassi. No. That's what grace is for. That's what grace means. It means receiving something you feel you don't deserve. Cassi, the blood of Jesus has washed you white."

My sin . . . is gone? Forgotten? Hot tears brimmed my eyes and spilled down my cheeks. On my knees, I wept and wept. *But I don't deserve this. I don't deserve him. He's too good. He's too amazing. Lord, I'm sorry. I'm sorry for everything. I'm sorry for the things I've done.* My sin reminded me of who I had been. Fickle. Flirty. Foolish.

YOU ARE LOVED. YOU ARE ADORED. YOU ARE SO CHER-
ISHED. YOU ARE BELOVED. YOU ARE CLEAN. YOU ARE
WHITE. YOU ARE FORGIVEN.

In awe, I laid on my floor, letting my sobs rise and fall with my tears as Jesus swept over me. As He washed me clean. As He broke the power of the memories. As He unlocked my chains and set me free. *Is this who you are, God? This is who you are? God, you really are good. God, you are so, so good.*

Each day seemed to birth new hope. More life. More promise. My heart was coming alive in ways I had never before felt. My spirit soared. Dean invited me to come to Atlanta in October. To spend our birthdays together and for me to see the ministry.

And so I went. To see the man who stole my heart.

ATLANTA

On the plane there I was okay until the last hour. Nerves took over. My stomach dropped. Palms sweaty. My heart in my throat. *What am I going to do? What am I going to say? Oh my gosh. Oh my gosh.* Overwhelmed. Excited. Anxious. He was at the airport when I arrived. In his usual jeans and T-shirt. As ruggedly handsome as ever. I tried to act casual. I couldn't make eye contact. My heart threatened to flutter out of my chest and fly away.

He drove me to the ministry center where he volunteered. Atlanta seemed a maze. Dean was confident behind the wheel. We sat in the car somewhat awkwardly on the drive there. Unsure of how to act. How to be. *I'm in love with you, but I've never even given you a hug. Help me, Jesus.* We pulled up to an old brick warehouse. Dean explained to me it was one of the only buildings that didn't burn during the Civil War. It was a rough area. The old industrial area. Getting out of the car, I felt self-conscious and out of place. But everyone I was introduced to met me with warm eyes and a welcome embrace. Faces alit with the joy of God. I was starting to recognize it. Dean seemed more at ease in this environment and around his friends, which helped me relax. I got to meet many of the other volunteers and some of the people living in the shelter.

I got the tour. The café area. The kitchen where they made meals for the homeless. The area where they kept donations of clothing and other items. They had tarps up for privacy for people who were living in one section of the building. The place where they did worship nights. Then he showed me his room. It was a large room that two of them shared. It was drafty. The asbestos ceilings were crumbling. There was dust and pieces of it on his bed. It was a simple setup. A bed, a nightstand, his Bible, and some other books. There was no heating or air. With each new discovery of this man's life. I was more enamored. Amazed. *What a beautiful sacrifice. To be so far from home. So far from family and friends. The ocean, which he loved. To be here. To live a life of love and service. Could I live here? Could I do this? Could I do what he was doing? Live a life of sacrifice? A life of service to others?* I pondered these things in my heart.

On the second night I was there, they had a worship session. It was a large area in the old brick building. Right in the middle of the room. All the musicians set up in sort of a large circle, facing in. Dean had his electric guitar. It was bright red with flames and glitter. The worship started. I was trying to focus on God, but all I could think about was Dean. The questions, for which I sought answers from my own heart. I could see it coming. An intersection. Dean was lost in his melodic adoration of Jesus. Free. His eyes were closed. His heart played the guitar with his fingers. It was breathtaking. Everything about this man was just "wow". And the questions continued to press. *Could I do this? Could I lay down my own desires? My own ambitions? What would that look like? What would that mean?* And as I watched Dean, I knew. *If it means I get to be that free, that joyful, that full of life. Then yes. Yes, I can.* And the answer brought the peace.

For my birthday, we took an hour's drive on Dean's Harley to a little town outside Atlanta. Motorcycles made me nervous, but I managed to try to enjoy the ride. Mostly because I got to wrap my arms around Dean and lean my head against his back for the journey. We arrived at some kind of Oktoberfest thing. Lots of people. Some really cute old buildings and then a large grassy area and pond. The October sun glowed, cascading its rivers of golden beams as Dean and I laid in the grass. He laid on his back and I next to him on his right, my head resting on his arm. With his left hand and my right, we touched, completely unaware of the people walking past. The activity all around us. He traced the shape of my hand with his finger. The magnetism filled my blood with warm syrup. I looked at his profile, studying his features. The lines of his face. Every freckle.

Every eyelash. *Gosh, you're beautiful.* I could hear his heartbeat. The heart I loved. The heart that was mine. Our hearts were being knit together in that moment.

This. Us. Yes.

On Sunday morning, there was a worship gathering of sorts in the same building as the shelter. It was red brick with massively high ceilings and lots of windows. The floor was concrete. It was drafty. There were plastic chairs placed out in haphazard rows. In the back on the left, you could see tarps and mattresses where the homeless slept. It wasn't fancy. It felt industrial and old. The musicians were at the front and started to play. Dean was playing his red electric again. The room filled with people. There weren't lots—maybe fifty. I had never seen such a diverse group before. There were black people, white people, upper middle class people, and homeless people. Addicts and ministers. Volunteers and victims. Little kids and old people. Babies who hadn't lost their first teeth yet and addicts who had lost theirs to smoking crack. As the worship began, I looked around the room. I stood toward the back. There were people standing to the side, talking. Some sat. Some stood. Some raised their hands. The children danced. They ran around. A little girl ran toward me. She had dark skin. She was probably four. She had the most gleeful grin and confidence. I instinctively bent down and put my arms out. And this little girl I had never once met or spoken to before ran straight into my arms. I swung her around in circles. She squealed and I started laughing. I put her down, and she started running again. Other children came up and danced with me. I had never been in such an atmosphere of complete freedom. No one was telling anyone else to be quiet. No one told the children to sit down. Everyone was free to just . . . be. And do. To just be God's children and delight in His presence. And whatever that looked like was fine. It was perfect. Tears filled my eyes as I surveyed the room again. Seeing people so free. So joyful. The most incredible freedom filled my heart. And pure joy ensued. I couldn't stop smiling. And the laughter poured out. *So this is what it feels like to be free. Praise you, Jesus.* I raised my hands. Tears of joy continued to pour down, washing off my makeup and making my mascara run. *I don't even care. You are so good. Oh God.*

You love your children. Thank you for this place. Thank you for these people. Thank you for bringing me here. I could see such beauty in it all. And I could see why Dean was here. It was so worth it. So worth the sacrifice. There was no comparison really. *I could do this, Lord. I want to live for you. I want to lay my life at the altar. My desires. My aspirations. Have your way with me, Lord Jesus. I want what you have for me. I want to be a part of what you do. My heart is yours. I'll hold nothing back. You can have it all.*

After the gathering, lunch was served. Fried chicken. Large round tables were laid out, and everyone who needed a lunch found a seat. Most of them were staying in the shelter. I found a seat at a table with about seven black homeless men. Most of them were ex crack addicts and had to eat their chicken with less than half their teeth. I chomped into my chicken, looked around the table, and couldn't hide my smile. *This is awesome.* My heart was still swollen with joy from worship. I felt right at home. As right as rain. There wasn't any place I'd rather be than eatin' fried chicken with these homeless guys. And I smiled so much my cheeks hurt.

The following day, Dean took me to a café for breakfast. Every place we went to in Atlanta had a style all its own. Chic in an earthy, contemporary, and unassuming way. Simple and confident. Eclectic. Breakfast and a walk. We had this feeling, both of us. This feeling that individually, God could use us to do good things. We would touch many people. But together, we would do great things, and we would reach many more. We didn't know what it would look like or how it would work. We just had this sense. This knowing. That God had great plans for us. Together.

We got some more time alone that evening. I was longing to be close to Dean, bursting at the seams with desire. We walked through the park that had been built for the Olympic Games. I wasn't paying much attention to it, just relishing every precious moment with my love. Holding hands. Talking. Listening to his stories. Family. Church. Travel. At one point, he stopped walking. I turned and faced him. He was more than a foot taller than me. I had to tilt my head all the way back to look at him. I was secretly hoping and willing him to kiss me. We had never stood this closely face to face before. It was quiet. I could hear the loud thump of my heart in my ears. The park was still and cool. We both wore jackets. His arms around me were strong and unmoving. I had been dreaming about this moment for so long. We stared into each other's eyes. From the night we first met, when I was a sixteen-year-old girl. To the night we met again, when we talked by the fire. To writing letters. To his next visit when he asked me those intense questions. To the hours and hours of phone conversations. And here we were. In each other's arms. Hearts brimming over. *Kiss me.*

Unexpectedly, he spoke. "I really want to kiss you right now." He averted his eyes a little. Paused. "But I really feel like I should wait till I ask you to marry me."

I had to wait a moment for it to sink in. *What? Wow. There was a lot of revelation in that statement. He's not going to kiss me right now? He's going to wait to kiss me? He's going to wait . . . until he asks me to marry him? HE'S GOING TO ASK ME TO MARRY HIM?*

I was both thrilled at the idea of the proposal as well as quite disappointed knowing I wasn't getting a kiss right then. This man perplexed me. Never had I ever known someone with such self-control. Here I was, in his arms. The woman he loved. Ready to kiss him. And . . . he wouldn't do it. I marveled. Although disappointed, it made me feel safe. Safe to know he was so strong. Safe to know he knew what he wanted and how he wanted it. I respected him. He was uncompromising. I looked into his eyes as I thought about what he said. There was so much love in those eyes. Love and passion. Devotion. Purity. Honesty. I leaned my head against his chest. *My husband. You're going to be my husband.* I was filled with sweet, delicious, warm syrupy joy. It poured over me. Head to toes. *I cannot wait to be Cassi Mack.*

On my flight home to California, I had new wings. New breath. New meaning. Everything was new. Everything was beautiful. There was hope everywhere. Life everywhere. Love and joy that was brimming over and flowing out. My heart was soaring. At glorious heights. I felt so loved. So loved by God. So loved by Dean. An incredible, prayerful, godly, handsome, gifted, playful, fun, beautiful man. Who adored me. All the longing I had done. All the waiting. The search-ing. The hoping. And now, at last, it's here.

Shortly after I got back from Atlanta, Dean started talking about taking me to Australia to meet his family. I was thrilled at the idea. We decided he would come to California for Christmas, and we would fly to Australia shortly after. The weeks flew by. Our love grew. We spent each night on the phone. He continued to love and encourage me. God continued to grow me. Heal my heart. Bless me. Talk to me. Guide me. Give me wisdom. Before long, Christmas was upon us, and I could see my love again.

We had a wonderful time with my family. Everyone loved him, as everyone always did. How could they not.

Vahley, Esperance, and the Back of a Holden

I was a typically ignorant American. Or perhaps more so than most. I thought Australia was a green, wet, marshy sort of landscape. When I thought of Australia, I thought khaki. Swamps. Kangaroos. Koalas. Crocodiles. That was about all I knew.

The flight there was easy. We had been given stand-by business class seats, which we got, so we were lapping up luxury I had never known in the air. Or land for that matter.

I leaned my chair all the way back, almost a complete lying-down position, and I wasn't even nearly touching the seat in front of me. We were served champagne and warm towelettes. We watched a movie and slept most of the flight. Quite comfortably.

Sydney. We got off the plane and entered the airport. It was busy. It's always weird when you travel thousands of miles and end up somewhere similar. At least it seemed so. We took a shuttle over to the domestic terminal. On the walk through the airport, I did notice something though. A massively enlarged photo of a man's face. It was an advertisement for something. I could see the pores of his skin. *Oh my gosh? That's not airbrushed! That's like real skin.* I blinked my eyes. I don't know that I'd ever seen an advertisement that wasn't airbrushed. *Wow. This isn't LA. Praise God.*

When we were on the shuttle, I was feeling that low-pressure headache of overexcitement, lack of sleep, and too much recycled air. I leaned over and asked a young guy in front of me.

"Excuse me, what time is it?"

"Hov ight."

Um . . . Is he speaking English? "Sorry, what?"

"HOV POSST IGHT."

Are we speaking the same language? Is he saying "half past eight"? Gosh, I thought Dean had a strong accent. If this is a sign of things to come, I'm in trouble. Wow.

The flight from Sydney to Perth was short and simple. Just the four-and-a-half-hour jaunt. My excitement was mounting again.

When I woke up and looked out the window, I was astonished to see nothing but red desert in every direction. *This is Australia? I don't see a single tree or bush. I don't even see water. What the? Isn't Australia like wet and lush? Gosh, I need an education.*

We got picked up from Perth by Dean's sister, Karen, and her husband, Matt. We piled in the car for the four-hour drive to their farm at Lake Varley, which was about halfway to Esperance.

This isn't a trip. It's a journey over many moons. I groaned within but tried to put on a brave face.

Dean and Karen talked mostly, catching up since the last time they'd seen each other. They were very close. She was stunning. She looked so much like Dean. Dark brown hair, piercing, steady blue eyes. Beautiful olive skin. She was tall. Sharp. A little intimidating. She was telling Dean about Lake Varley. Only it sounded like she kept saying "Vahley." Australians just opt to leave the *r* out of most words, I came to find out.

I stared out the window, taking in all the surroundings of this place. This entirely new place. It didn't take too long to get out of the city. Once out of the city, there were lots of trees. I was happy about that. There was so much red desert we had flown over, I wasn't sure what to expect. The sun was brilliant. It was summer. *Wow. December in Australia. It's hot. Gosh, this is weird.* The trees were different, but there were lots of eucalyptus trees, which I did recognize. The road was mostly straight. A hill here. A bend there. Blazing red dirt lined each side of the road. Outside of the red was green bush and scrub. And lots of paddocks. Sun. Light. Heat. Trees. Road. Red dirt. Space. Lots and lots of horizon. Lots and lots of space. We'd pass a farmhouse in the distance every now and then and some big sheds. Mostly the sheds were made of sheets of silver corrugated iron.

The first kangaroo I saw was dead on the side of the road. *That's a shame. I wish the first one I'd seen had been alive. Haven't we passed this farm already?* I was suddenly recollecting something Dean had said to me. "Western Australia is one of the most remote places on Earth." *Is that what he had said? If it was, then he wasn't lying. Gosh.* We had been driving for hours. And there was so much land. There were miles and miles and miles in between. Up until now, I hadn't thought I was much of a city girl. Looking at this, I felt very much a city girl indeed. No In-N-Out. No Target. No mall. No Starbucks. No on ramps or off ramps. Barely any traffic. Dean fell asleep on my lap. I studied his peaceful expression. My amazing, handsome man. What a dream. What an adventure. To be taken to the other side of the world by no other than Dean Mack.

I had no real idea of what Esperance would be like. Every step, I just lived in the moment, taking it all in.

We stayed at Karen and Matt's for a night at Lake "Vahley." I found out that the population of which was forty. You heard me. Forty.

I really am at the ends of the earth.

We drove along a dirt road for ages and then pulled into a "drive-way." It was another red dirt road that was like a mile long. There was a huge silver shed to the left. I could see a few guys standing around, watching us drive in. The shed was full of farm machinery and vehicles. And there were those big round shiny things—come to find out they are called silos. To the right, the land sloped down, and there was a nicely-sized cream brick house. Surrounded by fields. In every direction. You could see little fence lines. I could see what looked like sheep in the distance. *Oh my gosh. Dean's brother-in-law is a shepherd!* We parked, and I got out to look around. I walked up to the fence line. Land. Space. In every direction. The sky looked so big. Everything else was tiny. It was like being at the edge of the ocean. A vast expanse. I felt infinitesimally small. And, unexpectedly, very safe. The smell of the earth. The quiet. Peace. The warm sun. *I like it here. I like this. Dirt. Sun. Plants. Sheep.*

We had a meal and stayed overnight to rest. The following day, we got on the road to Esperance.

Finally.

We passed a sign that said "Welcome to Esperance." *We're here.* I quickly recounted the journey it took to get here. *Gosh, this is a big trip.* It was New Year's Eve. Esperance felt like a small country town. Lots of brick houses with corrugated iron roofs. The town center was a cross section with the post office, a couple of banks, and some retail shops. Hairdressers, shoes, some cafés. The ocean was easily visible in the backdrop. It was sweet and quaint. Not overly perfect. It didn't have that vainly immaculate sort of presentation. It was like homemade cookies. Deliciously imperfect. You could tell the town was more about the people in it than its facade.

We pulled up into Dean's parent's driveway. I was nervous but also exhausted, which dampened my nerves. Dave and Sue greeted Dean and I warmly with big hugs as we got out of the car. It was easy to tell they had been missing their youngest son by the emotion in their expression. Sue handed me a little gift. They were beaming. Overjoyed. They were so sweet. I loved them immediately. And I could tell they felt the same.

We went inside, and Sue boiled the kettle. I followed Dean's lead and sat at the dining table. They still had the Christmas tree up. The house was homey. I looked around the room. You could tell there had been many dinners and memories made here. Everything had a place. It was organized but full and warm. It almost had a farmhouse feel to it. There was a wood-burning stove in the corner. Big windows looked out to the front garden and driveway. It was simply charming and exquisitely humble. We visited with them for quite some time.

Dean asked me if I wanted to go for the scenic drive along the tourist loop, to which I eagerly agreed. I had heard so much about these beaches, I could not wait to drink them in. It was late afternoon. We drove toward the coast, which wasn't far. There was a pattern of small clouds painted in smoky lavender decorating the horizon. The sky was starting to turn that light bright blue when the sun is getting low. The long, windy road took us around and up to behold the crisp turquoise of the Southern Ocean and the rocky offshoots of the coast of West Australia. The only beaches I'd seen rival these were those in Mexico. *Stunning. This is just breathtakingly stunning. Wow. What a beautiful place. What a beautiful amazing place.* And suddenly it made sense Dean was from here. He was just as rugged and breathtaking as this coastline.

Dean turned off a small gravel road, which led to a little parking lot. There were long sets of stairs from there heading down to the most vividly aqua-colored water. I got out of the car and stood, taking it in. The water. The deeply pure turquoise and royal blue. The breeze. The sky with its hues of blue, lavender, and pink. The clouds with their purple tint. The sound of the waves. The birds. What a contrast to the seedy, overcrowded, filthy beaches I had grown up on in Southern California. This was so untouched. So pure. I looked at Dean. He had this oddly pained expression on his face.

"Are you okay, sweetie?"

"Yeah . . . I'm all right." He stared off in the distance.

"Are you feeling okay?"

"Yeah, I'm feeling fine." He looked down at his feet and then up again at the water. The sun made his face glow. *Gosh, you're good to look at.*

It looked as though something was troubling him.

"Is there something you need to say?"

"More like something I need to ask you." And with that, he looked straight into my eyes.

I looked away. My heart missed a beat. *Um, um, um. What? Is he thinking of asking me what I think he's thinking of asking me? Oh Lord, please not right now. I'm not ready to answer this right now. Oh my gosh. Oh my goodness. Oh please, Dean, not now. I'm not ready yet.*

He must have read my mind. Suddenly, the wind picked up, and a few moments later, he motioned to the car. We drove back to the Mack house.

Oh my Lord, is he going to ask me this soon? Of course he is! I should have known. How did I not know? Okay, so, think. Am I ready to marry this man?

At the house that night, they put on a BBQ. There were dozens of people. I was meeting them all for the first time. I studied him. The entire night, I hardly took my eyes off him. *Is this the one, Lord? Is this the one?* I watched him talk to people, tell stories. Everyone I spoke to told me how much they genuinely love him and what a great guy he is. It was obvious they all adored him. And what a beautiful family. He had a great relationship with them. Apart from his older brother, Paul. That relationship was harder to figure out.

Toward the end of the night, I knew. The peace came.

This is it. This is the one.

After the BBQ, Karen and Matt drove Dean and me out to the Duke. A popular little getaway spot at the beach an hour or so away. We left around eleven and wanted to try to make it there by midnight. Dean wanted to visit some friends who were staying there. Matt drove. Karen sat passenger. Dean and I cuddled in the back. Dean still hadn't kissed me. My heart raced at the thought of it. At the thought of him popping the question and finally getting the kiss I'd so long dreamt of.

We stared into each other's eyes.

Dean whispered in my ear, "What if I said I can't live without you?"

A huge gleeful smile crossed my face. I looked at him and whispered back, "I'd say, then don't."

And with that, he whispered, "Then marry me."

"Okay." I was jubilant.

And we sealed that promise with our first kiss.

And so we were engaged. In the back of a Holden. No ring. No plan. Not much money. None of that mattered. It didn't even cross our minds. This. Love. This is what it was all about. We were all in. And it was magic.

We had three weeks of adventures in Esperance. Church. Camping. Dinners. Stories. Cuppas. Visits. Surfing. Family history. Farms. A crash course in Aussie life, language, and laughter. At the end of our trip, Dave and Sue threw us an engagement party. Nothing but sunshine, smiles, and goodness. Beyond blessed.

Becoming One and
Cheddar Ruffles

I was working as a receptionist at a hotel during our engagement
as well as going to school. I often found myself lost in thought.
Staring at my ring. Impatient to start my life with Dean. One
typical day, I stood, as I often did, staring at my ring. Lost in a sea of
dreamy bliss. This feeling came over me. This knowing. This flash.
A dark cloud loomed ahead. A tragedy. Something bad. *Something is
going to happen to Dean when he is thirty.* Confused. *Lord, what is this?
Why would I think this? What is going to happen to my beloved?* It was
unsettling. I didn't like it. And I never forgot it.

Seven months later, we were married. July 20, 2003. It was an
afternoon backyard wedding. About eighty people. The sun shone glo-
riously. And all the elements played their part in its grandeur. Dave
and Sue came out from Australia. As did Dean's brother, Paul. Karen
and Matt couldn't come because she was in the late stages of pregnancy
with their first child. My dad performed the ceremony. We had afternoon tea laid out. Simple. Beautiful. It was perfect. I married Prince
Charming. The Australian, slightly more rugged version.

I laid my head against his chest that night as we went to sleep.

Now I'm really his. And he is really mine. Mine. A smile spread
widely across my face. *Is this really my life?*

Husband. You're my husband.

Our honeymoon consisted of five days in Puerto Vallarta and a
road trip up the California coast. Two glorious weeks, and it was back
home to start our lives as a married couple. Dean and I had been

married seven weeks when I vividly recall waking up at five in the morning. My very first thought was *sour cream and cheddar Ruffles.* And my next immediate thought was, *I've never thought about sour cream and cheddar Ruffles at five in the morning before. Something must be different.*

My body trembled, wilted, and froze as I held the stick with two lines. Dean walked past. "Honey, what's wrong? What's that? Wait . . . Are you? Are you pregnant?"

He grabbed me, and we embraced as I tried to find my breath and my feet. Then my big, rugged, handsome, Australian husband dropped to his knees and wept.

"I never thought I would be a father. I never thought I would be a father." He said, his face in his hands.

And so marital bliss ended abruptly with the onslaught of hormones brought on by the unexpected conception of a symbol of our love. The three-to-five-year plan got abbreviated.

The first year was a lot of fun. And a bit of drama. Learning to be a married couple is not an easy adjustment. I thought I had married a really laidback guy but . . . not so much.

"Sweetie, can you come here please?" he called out to me.

I walked into our bedroom. "Yes, hon?"

"The closet door."

"Yes?"

"You left it open."

Is he serious? I had picked up all my clothes and hung everything up. *This is the bone he wants to pick? The closet door? Wow.* I closed the door and left the room huffily. These tense moments occurred somewhat regularly. He had high standards. I ended up appreciating it, but at the time, it drove me crazy.

God continued to draw me close. Continued to bring illumination and revelation to me. He gave me a deeper and deeper passion for Him. And a deeper desire to belong to Him fully. I would spend hours reading the Bible, completely enraptured in the stories. Drinking in the knowledge God was pouring into me. Filling me up. Preparing me.

God dealt with my vanity swiftly. I watched as my cute, youthful figure blossomed into a fuller flower than I'd hoped. Disheartened.

Vessel. I'm a vessel for something greater. Something amazing. And so I learned sacrifice.

Nine months later (and seventeen days overdue), our first prince was born. Asher.

They took him by cesarean, which is another word for being a purse, opened, that four people are rummaging through.

It was like giving birth to my heart. Like having my heart on the outside of my body. Love like a flood. Smitten. Over the moon. We were captivated by every move. Every yawn. Every gesture. Adoration flooded our hearts. We would sit and study him. All his features. Just to watch him breathe, we were beyond content. Dean was besotted. Asher was so peaceful. So calm. Such an easy baby. He made the cutest faces. He slept well. He ate well. We sang to him. We read to him. We bathed him together. Dean and I would lay in bed with Asher in the middle and just delight in his every sound and breath and feature. Dean was such the doting father. Playing with Asher when he got home from work. Talking to him, teasing him, cuddling with him. And I got to watch. My heart swelled and sang joyously with each passing day. So immense was our love.

One night, I was nursing Asher, now five months, in my rocking chair when I felt an oddly familiar pang. And in a flash, I knew. I wasn't alone.

I froze. *What was that? Surely not.* Tests confirmed what I suspected. *Really? Wow. Um . . . I have a baby. What do you mean I'm going to have another baby? Fourteen months apart? I'm going to have two kids fourteen months apart?*

It took me ages to get my head around it. *I have my baby. How can I have another baby?* Thankfully, I had time to get used to the idea. Our second little prince was on his way. Maddox.

And so, here I was. We'd been married eighteen months. I was still getting used to being a wife. And now a mother of one with one on the way.

My poor body was still recovering from the long, heavy pregnancy with Asher. *Here we go again . . . Sigh. I so was not brave enough to plan it this way. God, I hope you know what you're doing.* But there was only more change coming.

You Can Go but You Can't Come Back

February 2005

When Asher was about eight months old and I was about three months pregnant with prince number two, we decided to make a trip over the pond back to Australia so Dean's family and friends could meet our son. As we were packing, Dean expressed concern. "Honey, I still don't have my green card. I just don't know how I will go leaving the country and coming back again."

We had been going through the process for more than a year. Dean had originally come over on a nonworker's religious visa, associated with the ministry in Atlanta. We were trying to get him switched over to a residency visa where he could live and work legally in the United States. But they make it so difficult. The hoops, the fees, the appointments, the lack of communication. The office was a good two hours away, and every time we went, there was one kind of hang up or another. We had finally assembled all the paperwork they had requested and had money for all the fees, but we were unable to get an appointment before our trip.

I assured him, "Sweetie, it's going to be fine. We will bring all the paperwork with us. I mean, we're married. We have a kid together. What are they going to do?" He was hesitant but relented.

We did the long flights again, landing in Perth and the drive to Esperance. We came and stayed for three weeks. Dean's parents were delighted to see their grandson. They were the same. Warm, loving, amazing. I loved how routine they were. Brekky at six thirty. Morning tea at ten thirty. Lunch at twelve thirty. Afternoon tea at three thirty. They would go for a walk in the morning after brekky and then usually in the evening after work. Sue would go to the shop in the afternoon around four for groceries and the paper. Dave would come home and stoke up the fire while Sue made dinner, which was served at six. After dinner, cuppas and sweets were served. Mum and Dad would read the paper and play a game of Rummy-Q. I marveled. It was all so established. So solid. So reliable. I loved it. I had never seen anything like it before, and I loved being part of it. Last time I had come to Australia, I was being introduced. This time, I was part of the family.

We drove the tourist loop again. Soaking in its magnificence.

"Wouldn't it be awesome if we could live here?" I looked up at Dean.

"It would, babe. Maybe one day we will."

Dean got to participate in some of his favorite pastimes: shooting, off-roading, surfing, camping, and bush golf. I had my first go at firing a gun. Which was also my last.

After our fabulous visit in Esperance, we stayed a couple of nights in Sydney sightseeing. We got on the plane to fly back to the States. We were satisfied with our first vacation as a little family.

Little did I know, everything was about to change. Forever.

We disembarked the airplane and went through to the customs room. There were two lines. One for American passport holders and residents, and one for foreigners. Dean usually went through the foreigner's line. He had been in and out of the country numerous times without trouble. This time though, we decided to go through the American passports' and residents' line together as a family. We approached the counter and presented our documents. I had mine and Asher's passports, and Dean had his religious nonworking visa. The man checked my documents but kept looking between the three of us and back at Dean's visa.

The man asked Dean, "Are you still working with the ministry in Atlanta?"

Dean and I looked at each other with uncertainty. *Why was he taking so long? Why was he questioning us?*

"No." The answer was "no."

"I'm sorry, sir, you have to go to secondary questioning."

What? What's going on? I was nervous. I could tell Dean was too. We were both exhausted from the trip, and this seemed ridiculous. Thankfully, Asher sat quite happily in his stroller.

We were directed to a room. There was a large sign with your rights written out. There were two women who started speaking to us. They were rude. They carried guns. They looked at us in disgust. As if we were criminals. *This is so strange. Why are we here? What's happening? Surely everything is fine. Surely we can go home now.* The atmosphere felt charged and uncertain. The bright fluorescent lights and tension wore on my already weary nerves. My pregnant belly rumbled. *I need a bath. And food. And sleep.*

They told us Dean was going to have to speak to the supervisor, whoever he was. They told me I had to leave because it wasn't "safe." They said they would call me when a decision had been made. They said he would probably come home. Or at least get thirty days to tie up his affairs and then have to return to Australia.

What? WHAT? This doesn't make any sense. God, what is happening? I kissed Dean, hugged him, and told him to call me as soon as possible. I pointed to the large sign. "Those are your rights, babe. Don't let these people push you around."

So I drove home. Pregnant. With my nine-month-old son in the back seat. Without my husband. My stomach was in knots. I was so tired. Angry frustration pulled at my weary mind.

About four hours later, I was sitting at home with the surreal reality of being on my own. Not sure what to do or think. The phone rang. I answered. Dean.

"They're putting me on the first flight back to Australia. They took my belt and all my things. They are holding them for me. Like they think I'm going to hang myself or something. There's been a guard assigned to me. I can't even go to the bathroom alone. I miss you so much, babe . . ." His voice broke. I could hear his words, but I couldn't process them. He couldn't talk long.

I just sat. On my couch. In my house. In shock. All our things all around me. Our wedding gifts. Dean's shoes in the corner. His jacket across the armchair. Signs of him everywhere. But no him. No Dean. Helpless, my head swam. Hundreds of thoughts rushed my mind like an angry mob.

What do I do? Do I try to get him back? Do I move to Australia? What on earth is happening? God, how can this happen? This man has selflessly served the homeless in this country for years, and they treat him like a criminal? The injustice! He's my husband! I'm an American citizen! We have a son and another on the way. How can this be?

Overwhelmed. The frenzy of phone calls started. Family. Lawyers. Friends with influence. Friends who knew people with influence. *Was he deported? Was he just denied entry? When can he come back? How long will it take? How much will this cost?*

I took solace in my time with Asher. He was still nursing. He was at a delightful age. All around us, the world swarmed with its enormous problems, deadlines, demands, worries, appointments, chores, and checklists. Asher was unfazed. His sweet countenance was just as cheerful. Calm. His big eyes swallowed me up, and we created a cocoon of comfort and happiness that the outside world couldn't penetrate. His wide gummy smile made me laugh over and over. I took comfort in his endless affection. We spent hours and hours together, enjoying blissful, brief, eternal moments.

It soon became apparent I was going to have to go to Australia. Getting Dean back to the States was going to take time. Months, maybe more. After a week or so, I started organizing our things. Organizing is not really my forte. What to sell. What to put in storage. What to bring to Australia. I then booked flights.

I tired easily as the pregnancy was progressing. Nursing Asher, carrying the baby, with the additional emotional strain of our circumstances as well as tying up loose ends and packing. I was wrecked. I stayed at my parents' house until the time came for me to fly out, three and a half weeks since we arrived back from Aus.

THE PONCHO, THE RUDE MAN, AND A REUNION.

There was no going-away party. I thought I would be gone a few months. We all did. No big send off at the airport. My little sister dropped Asher and I off at curb side. I had a stroller, a car seat, one VERY large suitcase, a carry-on, and a diaper bag. And a pregnant belly. Check-in was pretty straight forward. *Okay, security check.* I got in line. Asher was in the stroller. I got to the front of the line to go through the metal detector. The man looked at me coldly. "You can't push that thing through here. You have to fold it up and put it on the conveyer belt."

Are you freaking kidding me? Um, okay. I pull Asher out the stroller and fold it down. So I'm standing, with my pregnant belly, and holding my healthy ten-month-old son with the stroller folded on the ground in front of me. I looked back at the security guy.

"You gotta put it up there." He gestured to the conveyer belt.

You've seriously got to be joking. I looked blankly into his indifferent expression. *This guy isn't even going to help me lift up the stroller? Even though I'm holding a baby AND pregnant AND traveling alone. Really? Rude much?* I looked behind me to be greeted with the vacant gaze of an unmoving stranger.

So with my one free hand and all the strength I could muster, I heaved the stroller up onto the conveyer belt. I gave the security guard a look that I hoped let him know how I felt about him at that moment. I walked through the metal detector, which went off. *Awesome.*

The guy looked at me. "One more chance." With stern eyes and tight lips.

It was a threat. *Is he enjoying this?* Rage. With my one hand, I undid my belt buckle and put it on the conveyer belt. Walked through again. Green light. Get me the **** out of here.

The plane ride was interesting. Fourteen hours in between two business men with a breastfeeding baby. *Great.* I wore a black poncho so coverage wouldn't be an issue. But ponchos aren't soundproof. When I was feeding Asher, all you could hear were loud suckling and gulping noises amplified by awkward silence. *Yeesh.* Eating was interesting. How do you put a lap tray down while your ten-month-old is in your lap, which isn't particularly deep because of your overly protruding, robust unborn child? Messy.

The bathroom, another beauty. I never knew I was so talented. I held Asher in one arm whilst I undid my jeans' button and zip and pulled my pants and knickers down, all with one hand. I wouldn't recommend it. Getting them up was trickier. Lots of wiggling. Wiggling I didn't have the energy for.

When it came time to sleep, I called the stewardess over. There were little baby beds at the bulk head a few rows up from me. I asked her if she could talk to the people up there if they would mind letting my baby lie down in the baby bed, seeing as though they had no need of it. She declined. Instead, she brought me a padded duffle bag.

"What's this for?"

"It's for your baby to sleep in."

"Uh . . . huh? "Like on the floor?""

"Yes."

That'll be all, thanks. Yeesh. I'm not going to put my baby in a bag on the floor. You mustn't have children, sweetheart. So Asher and I stayed awake for the fourteen-hour flight. I couldn't sleep for fear of my arms relaxing and dropping him. *Okay, the goal is to survive this. It's not enjoyable. We just have to survive it.*

Arriving in Sydney was a whole new challenge. I had to get me, the baby, the stroller, the car seat, and all our bags from the international terminal over to the domestic terminal. *Lord, help me.* I had Asher in the stroller, and I got a luggage trolley, on which I stacked all the bags plus the car seat. Trouble is, how does one person push both a stroller and a luggage trolley? I was exhausted. And fed up. I shoved the wheels of each so they locked together. I had one hand on the stroller and one hand on the trolley. And then I leaned forward and got as much momentum as possible, heading in what I was hoping was the right direction. People had to get out the way. I was coming through and not in the mood to be polite. Praise God someone came along halfway through and offered to help me. I had to blink back tears. That simple act of kindness meant the world to me at that moment.

The flight to Perth was uneventful. All I could think about was being reunited with my beloved. Asher and I were walking on air when we made our way to the gate. Asher smiled widely when he saw his dad. Dean was awaiting us with open arms and a look of pure joy. We were trashed from the trip and the last three weeks of agony. But we were together again. That's all that mattered. And God had a very good reason for bringing us to Australia.

We just didn't know it yet.

It was nearly five years before I stepped foot on American soil again.

Finding Up Down Under

We moved in with Matt and Karen to start with. Their little cherub, Phoebe, was one and a half now. She and Asher played well together. Dean helped Matt as it was the season for seeding. I helped Karen. There was plenty to do on the farm. Lots of mouths to feed. We were cooking for our families as well as the workers. We had to load the food and kids up into the four-wheel drive and deliver the food to the guys out in the paddocks. Karen prepared lunch and dinner as well as morning and afternoon tea. Watching her work had me in awe. I soaked up her many techniques and gleaned from her wisdom daily. It was a crash course on farm living. There was enormous amounts of laundry and housework as well as taking care of the children. I would often look after the children as I found joy in it and seemed to have a natural knack as well. The nearest shops were an hour away. Karen and I would load up the kids and take our list to fill the fridge, freezer, and cupboards with enough good eats for the week. I enjoyed our rides. We always seemed to find our way into meaningful conversation. Confiding in each other. Getting to know one another better. Karen was wonderful for conversation. Our friendship and trust grew with the time we spent, learning from each other. Mostly me from her. She was excellent in all the things she did. I admired her greatly.

I loved getting outside when there was free time. The stillness of the farm helped to calm the waters within. I took deep breaths, soaking in the tranquility. The sky was so big here. GOD was big here. The landscape, endless. It wasn't hard to feel close to Him. He was all around me. The sun. The clouds. The wind. The rugged Aussie land.

The paddocks. The sheep. God was restoring my soul after the weeks of hectic chaos. The going to Australia. The coming home without Dean. The packing. And the trip back to Australia again. I tried to take the change in my stride. It was an adventure. Dean found it hard because he loved the States so much. This territory was a little too familiar for him. Before I'd left, I had lodged the paperwork with the American Consulate for Dean's green card. We would just have to wait.

Dean was keen to get to Esperance to find us our own place. After a few weeks on the farm, we were off. Dave and Sue made room for us to stay with them while we got established.

After being in Lake Varley for a couple months, Esperance seemed like a bustling center of commerce. The townspeople were genuine and down to earth. I loved how everyone seemed to know everyone, and life seemed uncomplicated. People made a habit of stopping for conversation. Unhurried, the highlights of the day for them were the people they ran into. Australians often make unannounced visits. Stopping in for a cuppa and a chat. I came to love their easy nature. Their open hearts and homes.

When it came to eating out, your choices were very limited. There weren't many choices in retail in general, which I found great frustration in. The stores opened late, closed early, and most were shut on Sundays. There was no running to the drugstore at eleven at night for cough drops. Not in Esperance. You have to think ahead and have things on hand. This city girl was in a small country town and coming to find out what that really meant. A lack of convenience, choice, and fashion.

We rented a big farmhouse on a few acres of land just ten minutes outside of town owned by family friends. It was one story with two large living rooms, four bedrooms, and a couple bathrooms. The floors were a very forgiving sealed cork. There were verandas all along the perimeter of the house and an established garden with plenty of personality. The house was tucked away from the road and surrounded by paddocks. The cows greeted us at the back of the house in the mornings as I hung out the washing. What a different pace of life. I came to love it. Its simplicity and poise. So different to the breakneck, fast paced, materialistic, celeb-obsessed world of Southern California. Laundry. Water. Fire. Cows. Sigh. *Praise you, Jesus. What a beautiful place.* The environment suited me better and also Asher. The calm.

With winter coming, the cold fronts moved in. We found the house was hard to heat. Dean would come home from work and chop firewood. We kept the fire going all the time. Water was limited. All our water to the house was fed from rainwater tanks. Every. Single. Drop. Was a raindrop. *Wow.* I never treasured water so much as now. It was the most gorgeous water to drink and shower in. Suddenly, my resources were finite. Never had I cherished wood and water in such a way. I'd been raised too removed from their sources. Surrounded by switches and bottomless taps, I'd taken them for granted.

The terrain was rugged and pristine. Harsh and inviting. Red gravel. White sand dunes. Turquoise beaches. Mines. Red backs. Dugites. Living in Esperance was going to be different to anything I had ever experienced. And I had a feeling it would change me forever.

We established a weekly routine. Shopping day, playgroup day, ladies' Bible study, cleaning day. Days we visited friends. Days we brought Daddy lunch. Dean and I enjoyed each other. He seemed relatively unaffected that, once again, my body was in full bloom in every direction. He made me feel beautiful. He worked hard. We started going to Dean's church. The one he grew up in. Their welcome was immediate. It was like walking into a big, warm, rug-ged Aussie family. They were huggers. I liked that. The people of Esperance were so refreshingly unconcerned about their appearance. I mean, not entirely. They looked after themselves well enough. But they weren't obsessed with . . . perfection. I had grown up around it my whole life. The comparison. Obsessing over flaws. Faults. Your value and importance. Your worth as a person, founded on your weight, shape, beauty, youth, dress size, and fashion sense. I found it both completely freeing and incredibly odd. Many of the older ladies have hair growing out their chins. Missing teeth. Big noses. Flat chests. Bad skin. Crooked teeth. Yet it's almost as if they were unaware of these "flaws." They didn't appear self-conscious. Rather, unfazed. It was so different to everything I'd ever known. It's like . . .

like they accept their humanity. They accept their flaws. An instead of obsessing about it, they just . . . carry on with life. And in it, they were so beautiful, their joyful and contented spirits shining through the wrinkles and unideal features. I decided to immediately adapt this attitude. I want to accept my flaws. I want to embrace my humanity. I don't want to pretend, obsess, and compare as I was so accustomed to doing.

And the freedom came. *I don't have to be perfect. I don't have to compete. My value is not in what I look like. I can just . . . be. And that is enough.* Liberation.

PAIN AND BIRTH

August 2005

Two boys are born. Fourteen months apart. Wasn't brave enough to plan it that way. That was all God's timing. I didn't understand it.

One born in the States. One born in Australia.

One brunette with brown eyes. And one blond with blue eyes.

One calm. One ferocious.

One content. The other demanding.

One the heart of a shepherd. The other the heart of a lion.

Maddox was born. I was determined to use the birth canal I was born with. Still, despite my protests and much to my disdain, I was once again strapped down and splayed open.

He was magnificent. A beautiful little cherub with striking blond hair. For the first three days, he wore a frown with one eye open. No, really. He had a distinct furrow in his brow. All of his features were from Dean's side of the family. One hundred percent Mack, that child. I searched his face. His limbs. Trying to find some sign of me. None. If they hadn't have pulled him out of me, I never would have guessed he was mine. All I could hope was he would develop some of my personality traits (which he never did). You try nursing a baby who's looking at you with one eye and a furrow in his brow. We were both unsure of each other.

The day after he was born, the nurses were nagging me to get up and about. Dean and I went for a walk and sat down in the courtyard. The sun was out, and it was warming up. Dean told me his shoulder was bothering him. We tried to think of something he may have done to injure it, but nothing came to mind. We passed it off with the classic Australian, "Ah well, you'll be 'right."

After three days in the hospital, we were back at home as a family. Now of four.

I tossed and turned, trying to sleep. I felt the Lord prompting me with this question: Do you want more children?

Gosh, this is so odd I should be feeling that I have to make this decision now when Maddox is only a few days old. I wrestled and wrestled with it over a number of nights. *Lord, if I only have the two boys, I will be happy with that.*

And with that, I fell into peaceful slumber.

Maddox was more of a handful than his older brother. And so, the battle of wills ensued. Dean was working for a builder, doing construction. He came home with more and more aches and pains every day. This shoulder. That shoulder. The knee. The hip. I tried to sympathize, but after months, I concluded I'd married a complainer.

We bought our own house. It was little. A two-bedroom with a big yard and shed. We put in a new kitchen, and Dean redid the bathroom with new tile, tub, and shower. It was a quaint, sweet little house, and I found happy contentment in it.

Looking after two boys who were so close together had its challenges. My Irish twins. Oh, but I had so much fun with them. Maddox continued to delight us with his growing personality. Cheeky. Stubborn. He loved playing with Daddy. Resounding laughter reverberated through our home. My favorite was the laughter. The delicious sound of my children being chased. Tackled. Wrestled. Tickled. Kissed. Then the raspberries would start. They would laugh until their cheeks glowed and they were breathless with delight. We made happy memories. We captured the light that was life and relished it.

But in the background, an underbelly of uncertainty brewed as Dean's pain worsened. These were my favorite memories. Standing at the stove cooking dinner. Listening to Dean and the boys playing. Dean's booming voice followed by raucous laughter. A house filled with laughter. Watching him with them. How they responded to him. He was such a good dad. I distinctly remember standing in the hallway one day, watching Dean make Maddox laugh. He was blowing raspberries on his neck, Asher cackling away as he watched. *Life could not get any better than this. I have everything I could hope for. My heart is full. My life is perfect.*

We celebrated Dean's thirtieth birthday at the house with a bunch of friends. Told some classic Dean stories. Of which there were many. The night was pleasant. For a moment, it crossed my mind. The thought about Dean. And being thirty. The sense of an impending darkness. A forceful disturbance.

I was still getting used to Esperance. Still trying to find my place. Trying to figure out who I was. A wife. A mother. An American living in Australia. A girl from the suburbs now in the country. I still felt very much in the throes of change. *Will the dust ever settle?*

Dean and I got along very well apart from the times I felt I disappointed him. That my cooking fell a bit short and my cleaning wasn't quite up to scratch. I would leave a basket of unfolded clean washing on the floor. It would be late. I'd get my pajamas on and turn out the light. Crawling into my delicious bed, ready to relish my slumber.

"What's this?" he'd say.

Oh my gosh, I'm so tired. Why is he asking me questions. It's eleven at night. I looked up from my pillow between heavy eyelids.

"That's some clean washing I need to fold. Don't worry about it, babe. I'll do it in the morning."

On the light would go. I would feel the washing basket drop onto the bed beside me. And then he would proceed to folding it all, whipping the clothes in the air to get the wrinkles out, followed by fitful folding. *Really?* You could feel the tension radiating from him. *How am I supposed to sleep like this?*

So up I would get. Now I'm wild with frustration as well and commenced folding just as huffily. Just as loudly.

Most of our arguments stemmed from this. My desire for his praise, and his desire to "help" me get better. I had to learn to not be so sensitive. He had to learn to be gentle. Over time, his efforts to teach me better methods did help me. But the process was painful.

Blood, Sweat, and Pain

One typical afternoon, Dean and I sat in the living room together. Chatting. He said something. "You know, I never could imagine living past the age of thirty. I think I would rather just be with the Lord."

He said it so casually that I was taken aback. *What?* I didn't know what to say. I felt angry actually. *What about me and the boys? You'd be happy just to leave us?* It was hard for me to see past how that would affect me. How it would affect the boys. It bothered me. I tried not to think about it.

One morning, I walked into the bathroom when Dean was having a shower. On the back of his leg was the biggest, blackest bruise I'd ever seen. I stared.

"Honey, how did you hurt yourself?"

"I don't remember," he reckoned.

Something's not right. You should know if something left a mark on you like that.

It was his sternum that became unbearable. Hardly pressing on it sent him through the roof. Months went on. The symptoms were so vague. So unrelated. His shoulders would flare up. The right one. Then the left. Red and swollen.

"Did you hurt it at work?" "Did you do it surfing?" "Did you hurt it moving the wood?" "Did you lift something else really heavy?" I would question him, searching for a cause. But we couldn't make any rhyme or reason out of it.

Then the night sweats came. He woke up drenched every morning. The sheets saturated. Then there was more bruising. Black bruises without explanation. Minor scratches that bled for hours. More pain. Sternum pain. Joint pain. It would come. For three or four days, he would hardly be able to move. And then it subsided. There were flus. The man who never got sick was suddenly sick all the time. He lost weight. He looked pale. He was still going to work every day but would come home weary and get in bed.

Dean was outside the house one day working on the fence. He came in with a small scratch on his shin. Although small, it had soaked his sock with blood. It bled for hours without stopping. It seemed odd that a little scratch would bleed so much.

There was a smell. An odd smell I started to notice. Distinguishable but hard to describe. Sort of . . . "off." And it didn't leave.

Something dark had taken hold. We just didn't know what.

This sickness has a name. But whatever that name may be, the name of Jesus is bigger. Stronger. Higher. More powerful. Every other name has to submit to that truth. To that knowledge.

Jesus.

The name above all names.

And my hope is in Him.

All the months and years God had spent pouring into me. Strengthening me. Teaching me. Guiding me. Was for this. For this moment. When I would be asked to put everything I learned into practice. When I would have to walk it out.

My Enemy Has a Name

A s Dean read Psalm 23, he thought, "God, I don't know what it's like to walk through the valley of the shadow of death."

I AM GOING TO SHOW YOU

And so a dark cloud settled over our home. An underbelly of uncertainty brewed as Dean's pain worsened. Dean and I watched a program on Australian television about country people who get sick and have to move to the city for treatment. They interviewed families. Husbands who took care of terminally ill wives. Wives who took care of husbands. My thoughts swarmed. *Having to take care of an invalid spouse. I can think of nothing harder. To be a carer. A giver. In a relationship that's supposed to be give and take. To only give. Not to take. God, how hard that would be.*

How could I know that is precisely what I would be asked to do.

Dean and I sat down one day and made a list. A list of all random symptoms that had plagued him for months, and he went down to the doctor with that.

They did a simple blood count. He came home from the appointment and got into bed. As had become his usual. I was at the kitchen sink. The boys played noisily in the living room. The phone rang.

"Honey, it's the doctor." I called.

He came to the phone and listened for a couple minutes.

"Thank you," he said flatly. Hung up the phone. And carried himself back to bed.

I was searching Dean's face for some indication of what the doc told him.

"Honey, what did he say?" I asked. I was on edge. We were so keen for answers. Some kind of answer to the mysterious affliction.

"He thinks I have leukemia," Dean called out from the bedroom in a matter-of-fact tone.

The word rang in my ears. The earth slowed down. Or maybe it stopped. leukemia. leukemia. Everything I knew about leukemia is that it was "leukemia." Period. That's all. That's it. End of story.

And so my enemy had a name.

Over the next few hours, I read everything I could find on this illness. This disease. This bloody awful hell of a thing. I wanted to know why. How. How often. Where. If knowledge is power, then I was going to become very powerful. I read. I searched. I researched. I looked at charts. I studied the statistics. I read until my eyes were burning. My vision was blurred. Exhaustion set it. The tears left me shaky and wilted. I had feasted on knowledge. Gorged myself on it. But the promise of power never came. The name still held the power. That savage demon of a name.

I laid next to Dean that night. Unable to sleep. Unable to close my eyes. *My Dean. How could this happen to my Dean? He's so strong. So young. How?* The invisible monster ate away at Dean as I tossed and I turned. I watched him sleep. *My boys. Oh, God. They need their Daddy. We need him. I need him. God. Not Dean. Please, God.*

A couple of days later, we were flown to Perth. We left the boys with Dean's parents. It was the first of many trips to come. They needed to take a sample of bone marrow from Dean's hip to get a proper diagnosis.

Royal Perth Hospital was busy. Lots of people everywhere. The building was dated and older looking but not too overly worn down and seemed clean enough. There were a couple of gift shops at the entry and then beyond that the cafeteria and café area with seating. There were three main elevators in the lobby, dinging and opening and closing for dozens of people at a time. There was a door to a large staircase just to the right of the elevators, which I made note of. Getting in the overly crowded elevator was something I was going to want to avoid as much as possible. How could I know this is a place I would come to know so well? This cafeteria would become part of my daily routine. I would become one of the people who traversed this hospital regularly.

We were given directions to the second floor to a room in which they did the blood and bone marrow testing for diagnostics. We entered the room, which wasn't very large. It was all open with maybe ten or so beds around the perimeter. I noticed across the room there were people who looked to be having dialysis and others getting transfusions of one sort or another. There were bright fluorescent lights, which I hate on the best of days. I tried to keep an outer calm as my insides felt like crumbling.

Dean seemed strong. There were two or three nurses running everything. One of them approached us and directed us to one of the beds. I sat in a chair next to Dean. They explained they would insert a rather large needle into Dean's hip to extract a bit of marrow, and it would be painful. Dean shook his head and opted not to have any local anesthetic, which he later regretted. I sighed to myself at my stubborn husband. As I looked around the room, I marveled at how this seemed to be so "ho-hum" to the other patients. A regular part of their lives. Reading a magazine or a book. It's odd to be in a room so full of foreign objects and activities where everyone seems so comfortable, and here I was about to fall apart.

When they were ready to do the procedure, they told me I should go for a walk. My queasy stomach was grateful not to have to watch or tolerate that stuffy, fluorescent room full of needles and bodily fluids.

I went back to the busy lobby but decided there was an over-load of people and energy. I needed space and air. I walked out the hospital doors and out onto the street. The sun was shining. It was a beautiful day despite being winter. There was a historic cathedral just outside the hospital. It offered benches and grass and some lovely gardens. I passed it with an appreciative glance and walked the opposite way toward the shops. It must be one of the oldest areas of Perth. The sprawling magnolia trees offered friendly canopies on each side of the road. The buildings were older looking and ornate with lots of molding and windows. Back in the days when there was more pride taken in architecture. There were sweet benches on each side of the road. I was just glad to be having some time on my own. Time to walk and breathe and think. Or try to think. Or try not to think. Or try to choose something good to think about. *God, what is going on? How did I get here? What are you doing? What are we doing? What are we supposed to do? Dean. Oh my God, not Dean. Not Dean. Please not Dean.*

After meandering around for a short while, they called and told me I could come back. I made my way back through the busy lobby and to the second floor to retrieve Dean who was looking rather sore. The room was still stale and stuffy and fluorescent but not as bad the second time around when you know what you're in for. They let us know there was an appointment for us to see the doctor the following morning to give us the results of the diagnosis.

Dean and I walked quietly back to the car. He was limping a bit. I could tell it must have hurt. No wonder. Getting a needle punched through your pelvic bone.

June 2006

Hello Friends and Family,

If you haven't already been made aware of what's going on, I'd like to let you know as well as give you all the latest updates.

After many months of strange bone inflammation and being sick on and off since Easter, we have been told by our doctor on Friday, June 16th, that Dean may have a type of leukemia or lymphoma. So, after a few days in and out of the hospital and doctor's office, the government paid for plane tickets for dean and I to go up to Perth to see a great Hematologist. Yesterday, we flew in and met with the doctor in the afternoon. They took Dean's blood and did quite a few tests (mostly to rule out things like

HIV and hepatitis). When those results came back, they said Dean's white blood cell count is back really low again, and that although there are no leukemia cells, the blood is abnormal looking. So, they had us come in today for a bone marrow sample. They had some trouble getting the sample, apparently, Dean's bones are literally dry! So, at this stage, they are sending off for the results on the bone marrow that will take until Wednesday next week. So until then, we wait! We are hoping to flog off the kids and get some time together at the movies and what have you. The good news is that for the last few days, Dean has been feeling really good.

Considering everything, we are doing great. Dean is just doing awesome. He's so brave. I am enjoying the peace, laughter, and joy that only the Lord can give when everything else is stripped away. To be in the midst of the chaos and the turmoil yet not be a product of it or tossed this way and that but to steadily move forward toward Him, my eyes upon Him, possessing the all freeing truth that to live is Christ and to die is gain. He will carry me through, my Jesus.

Much love to you all, and many thanks for your love, concern, and prayers for us.

Cassi

Tomorrow. Tomorrow we will have some answers. And at least, in the knowing, we can start this battle knowing what our enemy is. Although I felt I already knew.

The following day, we got up and got ready. One of those days that's awful and horrible, and all you know to do is what you've always done. Get up. Try to have some breakfast. Get dressed. Brush your teeth. All the while, you feel almost numb because your heart doesn't know how to feel. Your mind doesn't know what to think. You're hanging on to the here and now because it's all you can do.

It was June 26, 2006. Asher's second birthday. He was in Esperance, and we were here in Perth. On our way to the doctors to see if Dean really did have cancer. I don't know if I had imagined exactly what Asher's second birthday would be like. But it wasn't this. We wouldn't even see him today. *Be strong, Cassi. Dean needs you. The boys need you. Hang on, honey. Be strong.*

Dean and I were rather somber on the drive there. We walked into the doctor's office. It was adjacent to Royal Perth Hospital. It was a very full waiting room. I looked around, again so surprised at the number of people who seemed familiar with this place. I wondered how many of them were waiting for news like ours. Or how many had received their news already. Most of the people there were a lot older than us.

After a long and fairly agonizing wait, a lovely young Asian woman called us into her office. She introduced herself and asked us to sit down. I searched her eyes for answers. They looked sad. I felt her hesitation. She asked us a few questions about how Dean had been feeling and then finally she said, "I'm sorry to have to tell you this, but your diagnosis confirmed you have leukemia." I could tell she felt terrible being the bearer of bad news.

And there it was. Now we know. We know the name. That filthy word. That filthy, awful being from the pit of hell was upon my dear husband.

Dean and I nodded slowly as it sunk in.

"Yes, well that's what the doctor in Esperance told us he thought it was."

She seemed quite surprised and a bit relieved we took it so well. We walked back to the car together and decided to take refuge in some retail therapy.

As we walked, I studied Dean. His gait, his frame, his color. I could see the disease taking its toll. He was looking more pale and ashen. He was losing so much weight. My strong handsome husband was being eaten away by an invisible monster.

Jesus. I need you, Jesus.

The way I looked at Dean changed. It was hard to understand. It's like I already knew I was going to lose him. It didn't make sense to me that I knew. I didn't want to think that. I didn't want to know that. I felt guilty for thinking it. I was a believer in miracles. I had prayed for miracles. I had seen them happen. I have known people who have had cancer and survived. I had seen firsthand the power of prayer. How was it that I just had this knowing? How was it that I didn't believe he would get well? I wrestled my own thoughts and feelings. Fighting for truth. Trying to tell what was God's voice. What was my voice. What was logic. What was feeling. What was truth? Nevertheless, I knew. It might be months. It might be years.

The clock was ticking.

The thing was, Dean was so good. He was just so good. He was an amazing friend. He had so selflessly given himself to the ministry in his early twenties. When other people were starting to buy cars and houses, he sold everything and moved to Atlanta to work with the homeless and the crack addicts. He'd never been drunk. He'd never smoked a cigarette. He was hardly ever sick. *How could someone so healthy get this? Why would God allow this to happen to such a bright spark? One of the best among us? Why Dean? When he was so good?*

The questions gnawed at my swollen heart.

THE CALM BEFORE
THE STORM

W e went back to Esperance to get organized. We would have to go back to Perth straight away for Dean to start chemotherapy.

A week later, we were back with the boys getting settled.

We were incredibly blessed that a nearby church offered us accommodation near the city. A cute little three-bedroom house with a small front yard in Victoria Park. Only about a fifteen-minute drive to the hospital.

Some friends of Dean's, Byron and Diane, asked us out to dinner not long after we arrived in Perth. We shared some stories and laughs with them. It was nice to have an evening out having dinner. To feel like we were being social. To do something fun and normal. Something that didn't take place in a stuffy, stale room with fluorescent lights. Byron got a napkin and a pen and gave it to Dean and me.

"What are your monthly expenses?" He looked at Dean intently. "Write them down," he said, gesturing toward the napkin as he sat back in his seat.

Dean and I looked at each other.

He continued, "Dean, I don't want you to have to worry about your family getting looked after. Right now, you just need to focus on getting better. Your treatment is six months, right?" I felt a lump in my throat.

"Yeah," Dean said.

The look in his eyes was intense and resolved. I hardly knew them, but they had been friends of Dean's for years. There were no words. I was completely overcome with humble gratitude. At the gesture alone. I could have got on my knees and wept right there in the restaurant. But that would have to wait until later.

Dean took the pen and, on the napkin, jotted down some figures and came up with a rough number and handed it to them. Groceries, fuel, phones, and so forth for six months came to about fourteen thousand dollars.

They sent an e-mail out, and within three weeks, we had donations and pledges of more than seventeen thousand.

We were overcome. The support and generosity. Overwhelming. *God, you're so good. God, you're so amazing. Thank you, Jesus. Thank you, Jesus.*

One of the first things Dean needed to have done was have a PIC line inserted. They use an ultrasound machine and put this IV line in under the collarbone and straight to the heart. It has three or four lumens (places to attach a syringe or IV) so there could be literally four different fluids coming in at once. Dean was going to be having blood taken all the time. They would be giving him infusions of all sorts as well as administering the chemo drugs. This gave a "tap," if you will, to allow all of this coming and going without having to puncture the skin every time, which is risky business when you're immune compromised. After the initial shock of the diagnosis, Dean and I took on the sort of effervescent optimism of soldiers who are preparing for war. Soldiers who haven't seen the carnage. Or experienced defeat. Having yet to taste its bitter blood. We armed ourselves the best way we knew how. With hope and prayer and a positive attitude. Faith. That God would get us through. How could we know? How could we know how dark and desperate the days would soon become?

Dean was a champion. He had his first lot of chemo in the hospital. He flashed his beaming smile at the nurses. Teased them that they might be overcome with lust upon seeing his shirtless body. They rolled their eyes at the notion. "We've seen it all before, really." Unfazed but with a smirk. And Dean delighted in the stirring.

53

They explained that Dean would have alternating rounds of chemo. A lighter round and a more intense round with more severe side effects. The first round was mostly a breeze. The chemo itself looked so deceitfully harmless. So inconsequential. And one might think it so except the nurses treated it as death itself. They put on an apron, gloves, a face mask, and eye protection before even handling the outside of a bag. It would get hung up and then pumped straight into Dean's heart. And it's such an odd thing to watch. As it's death to the one and life to the other.

The boys were ten months and two years old now. They were too young to know or understand the brewing storm. They were delightful. They were a handful. They forced me to get up every morning. They needed breakfast, lunch, and dinner. They needed walks. They needed stories and songs. Trips to the park. Learning to go up the steps to the slide. Building sand castles. Their smiles were unbidden by dark thoughts. They struggled not with worry or doubt. Their laughter was wholehearted. And they were my medicine. They kept me sane. They made my days sweet, even when they were sour. I had not the luxury of falling in an emotional heap. The boys needed me. They loved me. They were life to me.

After the first round of treatment, Dean and I were happily satisfied with ourselves. This wasn't so bad. We had settled into our little Perth home. The boys were happy. And Dean was handling treatment so well. We were a family. The darkness was there. The uncertainty was there. But the sun shone on us. We felt blessed. We felt prepared. We felt good.

The second round of chemo proved to be much harder than either of us could have imagined. A battle storm would ravage Dean's body. And one just as fierce. My mind. Heart. Soul.

And we would be forever changed.

THE STORM

The great news was three homecare nurses were available to the Perth area to see outpatients. This meant we were able to get a lot of the chemo drugs and bloods administered and taken from the house, which was fantastic. It meant we didn't have to go to the hospital every day, and Dean could sleep at home in bed next to me. Not at the hospital. We would only have to go into the hospital for infusions, doctor visits, and if Dean was ever needing treatment for infections.

My parents came to visit, which was wonderful. My dad, Steve, and my stepmom, Ginny. They were a huge support for us. Having them there made the burden so much lighter. They helped with the boys and kept things cheerful. We leaned on them a lot. I loved having them. Something of mine. Something from home. They brought a familiarity. A sense of safety. That somehow everything was going to be all right.

The homecare nurses would come bearing their bait and tackle boxes full of potions and receptacles. Our mornings would be spent answering a myriad of questions on the status of each main bodily function and part. But they were kind. And strong. And weren't shy in nagging Dean to do right by his body. Diet. And meds. Dean was fairly casual about most "rules." A chemo diet was no exception. His lectures were lengthy and frequent.

"You're not *supposed* to eat sushi, Dean."

"You're not *supposed* to play football, Dean."

"You're not *supposed* to lay in the grass, Dean."

"Give yourself half a chance, Dean!"

Dean wore a smirk as they huffed and puffed through disapproving eyes.

The tidal wave of side effects came. Crashing over us with vehement ferocity. Pummeling us on the shoreline with a power and a weight that was crushing and debilitating. No air. No relief. Mouth ulcers. Fatigue. Diarrhea. Pain. The awful pain. The light was gone from his eyes. He filled out less and less of his clothing. He had to cinch his belt. Then the fever came. Hospital.

It was a lung infection. His body fought. His body was tired. Tired from fighting the cancer. Tired from recovering from chemo. Tired from this lung infection. But still he fought. He coughed. He coughed and wheezed. He coughed until he threw up. I held the bag as the ceaseless coughing caused him to puke bile. I nearly lost my stomach as the pungent stench hit my nose. I felt the warm bile settle in the bag in my hands. Surreal. *Since when is this our life?*

Dean got up the next morning and got in the shower. He started moaning so I went to check on him. *Was this my husband?* This gaunt structure. Bones protruding. His hairless, naked frame. His usually tanned skin, pale and sickly. Slightly bent over, he was trying to wash his leg. He was on the verge of tears. He was in too much pain to bend down. Helpless. *God, help us. Jesus, help us.* I couldn't process how I felt about what I was seeing.

I slowly walked over. I got on my knees. The tiles were wet. I took the sponge. And I started to wash his body. This aged. Spindly. Bald. Boney body. His legs. His feet. And then. Something unexpected. The most amazing feeling came over me. Dean and I had showered many times before as lovers. But this was different. This was . . . holy. Pure. Never had I felt this intimate. This vulnerable. *My sweet husband. My darling.* My knees were hurting. I was cold from the spattering water. But I didn't care. Joy came. Starting in my chest and slowly flowing out to all my limbs. *What a privilege. What a privilege this is. To be in this moment. With this precious man. The man who holds my heart.* And in my heart the words whispered . . .

LOVE IS PATIENT. LOVE IS KIND. THIS. IS. LOVE.

And it was painful and beautiful and awful and amazing.
After a few days in hospital, Dean was able to come home.

TEMPTATION IN THE TEMPEST AND THE CUP OF SORROW

W e started to find a routine in Perth. The neighborhood we lived in was charming. The houses were quaint and full of character. The trees were pillars of strength and flaunted their colorful blooms. Dean most of the time didn't feel up to doing much, and his tolerance for noise lessened each day. We fenced off the front yard so the boys could play outside. We went on walks. I tried to give Dean as much peace and reprieve from their boisterousness as I could. They were just getting into movies, so we often had one in the afternoons. Although a dark presence was in our midst, our life was peaceful. It was pleasant even. On Dean's good days, he would sit outside with us and rough up the boys. I took pleasure in watching as I always had. I took lots of photos. Somehow now, each moment was that much more precious. Every cuddle and kiss and laugh Dean had with them, I cherished it in my heart, trying to perfectly capture each moment to relish in the undetermined days to come.

So here I was, twenty-three years old. Living in a foreign country. Husband terminally ill. Two babies. Everyone needing me. Everyone. With all their needs. So many needs. Every day. Food. Naps. Meds. Laundry. Cleaning. Caring. Cooking. Crying. Consoling. Washing. Watching. Carrying. Hugging. Driving. Lifting. Wiping. Rinsing. Changing. Sorting. Folding. Closing. Scolding. Holding. Day after day. The routine set in. And it took its toll. And the lies came. Slow at first. And quiet. Fleeting. Faint. And then it grew.

You're so young. What are you doing here?

Washing the dishes. Dish after dish. Staring listlessly out the window. Into a backyard.

You're so talented. You could do anything.

Child approaches. Falls. Screams.

When did this become your life?

Dean yells, "What's happened? Why is he crying?"

My boy. He reaches his arms out to me. Covered in snot. Slobber. Fat tears rolling down his cheeks. Other child crawls down the hallway, banging toy against the floor.

"What's that noise? I can't handle that sound!" Dean calls out from the couch. He was too unwell to get up much of the time. His hearing was so sensitive. I tried in vain to shush the children.

Don't you want to have fun? Just go and have a good time? Do something exciting?

Took the boys out for a walk.

Visions danced in my head. People my age. Shopping. Dating. Dancing. Living so carefree. So happy. Nights. Lights. Fun. Food. Freedom. No kids. No sickness. No worries. Dressing up. Good times.

I began to feel the urge.

Run.

As if the visions themselves were pulling me up. Picking me up. Pushing me through the door. Putting on my shoes for me. Holding wide the door. Promising me a life of happiness. Freedom. Freedom from the endless chores. The endless crying. The endless needs. The monotony. The awful monotony. The exhaustion of it all. The day after day draining. Dull. Aching. Day.

I could feel it. In my heart. The compelling urge to run. Or maybe eat. Or drink. Find a lover. Anything. Anything to keep from feeling this overwhelming, crushing, awful, uncertain, grievous pain. The pain of my heart. Breaking. Watching the man I love waste away. And be so grumpy. With me. With the boys. Become consumed by illness. Cancer making a feast of his body while we all look on. I watch as my children want to play with him and he turns them away. Because he's too tired and sore and drained and exhausted and consumed. Here but not here. And I try to put on a brave face. As I watch it all. Helplessly. My innocent boys. So healthy and strong. Futures so incredibly bright. And they are so unaware that their dad . . .

And I felt parts of my heart I didn't know I had break. Slowly. Agonizingly. Piece by piece. Day. By. Day.

Dean got admitted to hospital again. Infection. Again.

It's difficult to describe what happens when you feel like you're losing someone you love. That they are fading. And you can't stop it. My heart wanted to protect itself. My heart wanted to distance itself. If I'm going to have to live without you, then I better keep steady. Better keep a distance. My heart felt like it was going numb. He was floating away. Or maybe I was floating away. But either way, we were drifting apart.

One night, I was up late talking to a close friend of ours, Phil. I tried to tell him. Tell him what it was like. The uncertainty. The fear. The feeling of losing him. My heart. Wanting to distance myself. And, like a true friend, he said, "Cassi, you can't do that. You made a vow."

And in that moment, my heart, which was a floating balloon. Drifting. Distancing. Suddenly. Hit the ground. Smash. A million pieces. And I felt everything. Everything I'd been trying not to feel. Crushed. Broken. Dean. Me. Our wedding day. His smile. His laugh. His voice. "In sickness and in health," I heard myself say. *I said that. I promised. I promised not to go. Not just that I would stay. But that I would stay and love. With my heart open. That I wouldn't try to protect myself from pain but I would bear the pain. For the sake of love. The struggle. In the worst of moments. Faithful. That I would be faithful.*

My heart and my stomach tore. I started heaving heavy sobs into a couch pillow. I couldn't catch my breath. A torrent of pain.

Waves of it crashing. I struggled to contain it. *Dean. I need Dean. Dean needs me.* Suddenly, I was keenly aware that Dean was at the hospital. It was midnight. The boys were asleep. I have to go to the hospital. I left the boys with my parents and drove into the city. *I'm coming, Dean. I'm coming, sweetie.* I managed to navigate the night roads though my face was still contorted with sobs. The lights were a blur. *I'm coming, darling. I'm not going to leave you, darling. I'm sorry. I'm coming, honey. I'm sorry.*

Park. Walk. Enter. I announced my arrival on Dean's ward.

"I'm sorry, darling, we haven't got any spare beds for you. They're all taken."

I smiled. "That's fine. I don't mind."

I entered Dean's room. Where my beloved was peacefully sleeping. *Hello, love.* I curled up onto the cold tiles next to his bed. Smiling. Happy. Content.

This. Is where I belong.

Peace.

Sleep.

Hi everyone,

Well, to be honest it has been a pretty tough week. Dean got out of hospital after round 2 of chemo on Wednesday. Only the home visiting nurse found he had a fever on Friday morning and by Friday night he was admitted to hospital again and on antibiotics. They are hitting him with some solid antibiotics that kill a muriate of bacteria. At this point though, Sunday evening, Dean still has a temperature, n dry cough, no appetite, lethargy, mouth ulcers, and some skin problems. There is a reaction happening on his back and some sores on his legs. The doctors are hoping for an improvement by tomorrow morn-

**ing, if not they will start treating him for what
it then must be, either a fungal infection or
something in the lungs, pneumonia related I
think.**

**I am just trying to get through some
days. I'm feeling strong at the moment. Dean
really needs us all right now, he's struggling,
it's the hardest its gotten so far. Bless you Jesus,
for it is in You I trust alone.**

Love,

cassi

Spending my time at the hospital with Dean meant being away
from the boys. When I saw them, all I wanted to do was pick them
up, squeeze them, and kiss them. Which, of course, I did. Inevitably,
they would be absolute angels for their grandparents and other care-
givers. As soon as I got home, chaos.

On the one hand, I felt so sorry for everything they were going
through. And I was so tired. So terribly exhausted. I wanted to come
home bearing gifts. Spend time with the children free of conflict. But
the whispers came.

YOU ARE THEIR ONLY PARENT RIGHT NOW. THEY NEED YOU.
THEY NEED YOUR LOVE. AND THEY NEED YOUR DISCIPLINE.

So I would come home to them and set the standard. It wasn't
easy. But I knew they needed it and would be the better for it.

The boys were growing. Boisterous. Loud. Lovable. And free.
Dean was courageous and optimistic despite being pummeled and
pumped with pills and poison. Me . . . Well, I guess I just took care
of everyone. I soldiered on. Finding joy where I could. Relying on
God to give me love on the days I was dry. To help me to be gentle.
Selfless. I came to the end of myself so often, I was daily coming to
Him. Praying for so many things. Pouring my heart out to Him. I
knew He heard me. I knew He was listening to every word. I felt as

though His ear was almost touching my lips. That He was listening even for my whispered prayers. And when my heart was too heavy to pray and all I could do was cry, He would wrap His arms around my waist and press His head against my chest so He could hear the cries of my heart. Though broken and hurting, I knew without doubt I was incredibly loved.

September 2006

Everyone!

My apologies for the lengthy delay in updating you! Well, we've just finished round 3 of what will be 8 chemos. Dean is doing quite well. We have done this round of chemo from home, and that should continue through the rest of treatment. Having Dean home has been great for everyone. He's been feeling a little flat, but he's perked up a little today, making phone calls, chasing up some different projects, talking about the future. He's had two lumbar punctures in the last week, but they seem to have gone by smoothly. With this round of chemo, we have had Dean taking these immune supplements daily and they have made a great impact! So we will continue with those for the rest of treatment.

We are doing well. The season has its challenges. And some days I am just looking forward to my pillow. But at the moment, I am feeling very strong and very certain, with a clear mind and a clear vision, my eyes fixed on Him. Dean is doing well also. He has recovered from infection completely. In fact, at the end of last month they gave us a week and a half off completely from the hospital and Dean was

feeling great, we couldn't keep up with him! So, we recieved some time to break, and now we are back into it, just taking it one chemo at a time. Every now and then, I'll realize that I'm trying to do it in my own strength, and I'll come to the end of my self and then I allow Him to posess my heart and He renews me and I carry on again.

Love to you all, we are blessed in this.

cassi

The Perth sun blazed through our front windows in the after-noons. I had the blinds closed, and I put a movie on for the boys. I was enjoying the tranquility. A rare moment when no demands were being laid upon me. Feeling emotional. Having a *"God, this is really all too big and too much for me"* moment. I put my face in my hands and started to cry.

I could hear Asher walking around doing something. I just sat, letting the tears come. Crying soft sobs. Pouring the contents of my heart into my hands. Letting God close enough to count them.

Finally, I wiped my face and looked up. There was my beauti-ful two-year-old standing a few feet away from me. Looking at me with the kindest expression of concern. And then I realized I was surrounded. Dozens of toys. Encircling me. My sweet boy had gone and gotten every toy from the toy box and put them all around me. In a flash, I thought of how I bring Maddox something to play with whenever he starts to cry. And here I was crying, and Asher is doing the same thing! Oh, I started to laugh! A great big belly laugh. I just could not stop. Asher looked perplexed now. I picked up my boy and squeezed him tightly.

Oh my God, you have really blessed me.

My guitar whispered to me. Offering itself up as a means for artistic expression and emotional release. I would put the boys down for a midday nap. In those days, they slept a solid three hours. At which time, I would go out in the front yard and sit on the grass.

Guitar in hand. Under the giant fire tree, I would sing my heart out. Sing and sing and sing to the Lord. Every thought, every feeling, every prayer, every cry. I sang it all. And He heard me. I knew He heard me. I felt Him so close. He heard my every whisper. And the songs just came. Worship songs. Songs of victory. Songs of praise. Songs of brokenness. And I sang it all away. The tears would come. And He would come to the hurting places. God would bathe my heart in peace. He would come and fill me. Heal me. So I was ready to pour out again. Ready to pour into my boys. Ready to pour into Dean.

I examined my heart. Therein I could not find the faith Dean would be healed. *Why? What's wrong with me? What's wrong with my faith?* I still had a great sense of struggle and guilt over it. *Isn't it just a choice? Don't you just choose to believe in the outcome you want?* I didn't want Dean to die. But I could not shake the inexplicable certainty I held that he would.

A hearse drove past. Would I be driving in its shadow one day? Its hungry cradle impatient to carry my lover away.

CASSI, IT'S NOT ABOUT WHO IS ON THIS EARTH AND WHO IS NOT. AS LONG AS YOU ARE HERE, I HAVE A PLAN FOR YOU.

I had relied on Dean so much. He was older. He had so much experience. He travelled the world. I could have leaned on his wisdom my entire life. Relied on him to hear from God. His decision making. His strength. His abilities. All of that was changing. I had to lead. I had to be strong. I didn't want to be. I didn't choose to be. But I had to be.

"If your cup is full of joy, drink it with thanks. If your cup is full of sorrow, drink it in communion with Him" ("Can You Drink the Cup?" by Henry Nouwen).

My cup sat before me. Full. Full to the brim. Full of sorrow. I was being asked to drink it. Steadily down. In its entirety. Every last drop. My Lord was there. He held the cup in His outstretched hand. His gaze steady. Kind. Like a petulant child, I stood. Stubborn. Frightened. My eyes questioning. My heart struggling to find the courage. My mind grappling with the knowledge of the inevitable

64

pain that would ensue. Perhaps I could tip it out. Or maybe gulp it down speedily. Holding my nose. Or maybe I could hide. Under the table. Anything. Anything to get out of slowly and steadily drinking down the contents of its liquid. Dark and potent.

TRUST ME, I hear Him say with His eyes.

My love for my Lord compels me. *I love you, my Lord, but must I?* I implore.

And in His eyes, I see His own memory. Of the cup that He wanted to pass over. He, like I, asked for another way. Any other way. Other than taking the cup. In obedience. And bearing the weight of its contents. And I saw He understood me. He understood my hesitance. He understood my frailty. He understood my weakness. For He had felt it too.

Oh Lord, that I would be willing. To take the cup of sorrow and drink it in communion with you. And so, inspired by His act of devotion and obedience, I took from Him the offered cup. And drank the sorrow down. Slowly. Aware of each mouthful. As it filled my mouth and senses. As the effect took hold. A steady tide of melancholy. Inundating my being. Entirely. I breathed it in. The aroma of suffering. Gliding down my throat. Filling my stomach. Every cell. Every limb. Permeated in agony. The beat of my heart. Swayed by its languor.

I trust you, Lord. That this pain is not in vain. That you have a plan. A plan for my good. That one day, this pain will be worth it. That you will sow for me my cascading tears. And reap for me a harvest of joy. As you have promised.

I saw before me a stretch of desert. Of unknown length or breadth. I knew not how long it would take to cross. Nor how scorching the heat would become. Nor how desperate for sustenance I would become.

But I did know there would be something on the other side. Something that would make it all worthwhile.

And I held onto that.

Surrender came. And peace with it. To walk beside Dean through this desert. To love him and serve him through it all. And then, when the time came, to give him over to the loving arms of his Savior.

This was my call.

Food, Fury, and Vows
across the Sea

D ean loved food. No. He really loved food. And he absolutely would not tolerate the hospital food. So I became
the hunter/gatherer. Everything had to be completely fresh
(due to his lack of immune system) and, of course, suitable to his
snobbish pallet. It was like feeding a pregnant woman. A pretentious
pregnant woman. A pretentious pregnant woman who was doing
everything by the book. But worse. And so I regularly came and went
from the hospital, trying to see to his whims, cravings, and vague
requests for "flavor" and "freshness." There was lots of face palming
and eye rolling on my part.

One particularly pleasant day, I had a planned outing for the
boys and me. I wanted to get Dean his lunch before we went. Heaven
forbid he has to have a hospital meal. There are about eight parking
spaces in front of RPH. About six of them are handicap spaces. I
always parked in the five-story parking garage at the back side of the
hospital. The spaces at the front remained primarily empty most of
the time. I also noticed that quite often, people who weren't handicapped took advantage of their vacancy and utilized these spaces.
The temptation was strong, especially when you were making a
quick trip. Parking around the back in the garage involved getting
a ticket, circling for parking, walking across the garage and through
the overpass tunnel, and of course taking the trouble to pay afterward. Temptation got the better of me and I decided to pull into

a front row handicap space just this once. There were about five of them empty, so I figured it wouldn't do any harm.

I'll be fifteen minutes, tops. It'll be fine. I quickly got the boys out of their car seats, walked into the hospital, and took the elevator up to the ward. We went inside and brought Daddy (Princess Fuss Pot) his lunch. Then, back down the elevator and out to the car.

As I went to open the door, an older woman approached me. Her face was flushed and grimacing.

"Why did you park in this handicapped space?" Her tone was sharp and brash. I was so surprised I didn't have time to process what was happening.

She continued, walking toward me. "My husband is terminally ill! We had to park two blocks away!" She gestured behind me.

Oh dear. All bad things. Okay. This is bad. It was obvious she wanted to strangle me. *I have no defense. What can I say? She's right. I mean . . . my hubby is sick too . . . but . . . she's right.*

I tried to acknowledge her and let her know I was hearing her. "mm-hmm."

"Don't you 'mm-hmm' ME! I've reported your plate number to the hospital! That's a two-hundred-dollar fine!" And with that, she stormed off.

Really, Lord? Ugh, I don't have the energy for this.

I buckled the boys into the car with tears rolling down my cheeks, feeling beat up. I slouched into the driver's seat, and I cried my way to our destination. *I'm sorry. I was wrong. But why did she have to yell at me like that? I'm sorry. Oh God.*

Days like these were hard.

Taking care of a sick person isn't easy. Taking care of them for a day is okay. It can even be really rewarding. Having the opportunity to pamper them. Make them feel looked after. And it can be nice to feel needed and strong. After a week, the novelty starts wearing off, and it can feel a bit like weary work. But when you start talking about sickness that goes on for months. Years. It's something else entirely.

The compassion I felt for Dean. The patience. The desire to serve him. All of that was there. But over time, I felt empty. Wrung of every drop, I brought my heart, a sponge, to Him. Crying out. *God,*

I'm empty. I'm so empty. I'm so dry. I have nothing left to give. Fill me, Lord. Give me your love for Dean. Give me your grace. Your compassion. I have none left. Help me serve my family, Lord. I want to serve my family. But I can't go on like this. I'm tired. I'm so tired.

The hardest part about taking care of Dean was his lack of expression of gratitude. I think he was grateful. He just didn't show it. He didn't ask me how I was. He didn't consider my needs. In fact, most of the time, he was very irritable. Angry. Difficult. Demanding. Shouting. And high maintenance. Hard to please. I felt like I couldn't do anything right. Watching it happen with the boys was the most heartbreaking.

Softly, I'd say, "Sweetie, you aren't well. The boys hardly get to spend time with you. Make the time you do spend with them count. Enjoy it. Let me be the one to discipline them right now. I have the strength for it."

"I'm their father!" he'd yell. "A son should fear their father! I don't care if I'm sick or not. As long as I'm here, I'm going to act like their father."

Some days, his stubbornness had no end. And my frustration over it felt endless as well. Because of my own childhood, the yelling and shouting made my stomach churn. When Dean yelled, intense anxiety would pour through my veins. My stomach would tie itself in knots. Pulling. Tighter. My insides would quiver and shake. The ground beneath me would start to shake and crumble. I had nothing to hold on to. What he was going through was horrific. It was understandable. He had no control over what was happening to his body. The cancer. The chemo. All the bloody side effects. The appointments. The biopsies. The scans. One thing after another. Another. ANOTHER. I expected he would get emotional. Teary. Vulnerable. Sad. I suppose I expected him to respond the way I thought I would. But that rarely happened. Usually, it came out in angry frustration. My beautiful, fun loving, passionate, playful, caring, and wonderfully jovial husband was gone. Replaced by a brash, angry, brooding, and ungrateful man who frightened me.

And so, in the valley of the shadow of death, a dark cloud appeared. *God, only you can sustain me. Only you can help me love here. Mother here. Grow here. In this place of darkness. Devastation. Fear. Death. And loneliness.*

All the chemo and meds left an odd smell. One of which, oddly, was asparagus. Which made it impossible for me to eat thereafter. Some of the chemo had to be administered over the course of seventy-two hours. They would put the pouches of clear yellow liquid into a small black backpack and hook it up to Dean's lumen on the PIC line. An electronic pump would whir every few seconds, pushing the poison drop by drop into his bloodstream. We would lie in bed at night. The pump a deafening interruption to our silence and calm. Like the tick of a clock. But haunting. Like the steady gallop of horse's hooves. Advancing. And its rider was poison. Poison that we were hoping would save us. Save Dean. It wanted our trust. But it did not earn my confidence. And so, even as we slept, the war was waged.

Memories of years past drifted through my mind. My years as a teenager. Lost and wondering in the desert. Depressed. Vain. Broken. Alone. Ashamed.

I walked the desert now, but this time, it was different. I wasn't alone. And I walked this pilgrimage with purpose. In a single direction. Toward Him.

God, as hard as this is—and wow, Lord, this is so hard sometimes, it's infinitely better than a life lived without you. I would prefer a life lived in darkness with you than a life in light's glory without you. Because there is no life without you. And you are the light in my darkness.

Australia was feeling more and more my home, but my heart stung for missing my family. For that ease that comes from being around those who know you so totally. Where you can just "be." Where there's nothing to be proven. Said. Done. Suggested. You just *are.* And you are loved for that alone. Dean's family was mine too. They loved me well. But I longed for mine. I would find myself going about my day. Unassuming. Not thinking of much of anything. Then, a melody. A memory. A smell. Suddenly. I was undone. My heart in pieces. The faces of my sisters. Brothers. Parents. Grandparents. My life in America. Family dinners. Inside jokes. Dumb traditions. And then, sobbing. Praying incoherently through my blubbering. *Oh God. God, I miss my family. I miss them so much.* Before long, completely sprawled out on the floor. Forlorn. Feeling a million miles away. No idea when I would see them. Or visit. *I thought I would be here for six months. Maybe twelve months. How long has it been now? Going on two years? Oh God. When will I see them again?*

That September, my little sister was getting married. I was desperate to go. I stared at the invitation. Thought of it many times. On my trips in and out of the hospital and taking the boys to the park. It was always in the back of my mind as the date approached. I was hoping by some miracle I would get there. I would get to witness my sister's wedding. *I mean, how could I not be there? How could that even be possible? Of all the years we had growing up, talking about boys and daydreaming about weddings, how could it be that when she actually got married, I wouldn't be there?* It was impossible to fathom.

The night before the wedding, still in Perth, I realized I had to sit down. Admit defeat. Shed the tears. Face the music. And write something. Something that could be read at the wedding. And so I did. I typed and wept. Until I was happy with the words that could, at least to some extent, depict my love. My joy. And my sorrow. I would later miss my brother's wedding also, for the same reason.

September 23, 2006

Naomi,

Many congratulations today on your special day. It is with a great sorrow and a heavy heart that I must congratulate you in writing instead of with a hug and with a kiss and with my eyes and my words. Naomi, my sister, my deepest and truest friend, my love for you is not just a fact, it's a verb, it's a growth that springs up from the inner depths of my heart, and it is part of who I am. We are like two trees planted close together, and over the years, we grew up next to each other. And the trees were so close that they grasped the other. They were

friends, and in the storms, they clung to each other. When one was weak, it would lean on the other, and because they had each other, they made it through and became two grown trees, intertwined, definitely separate but definitely united. And my heart holds your heart, and your heart holds mine and our love for each other knows no boundaries. My love for you surpasses the boundaries of country, of land and sea; and it will not weaken with time or old age; or with sickness and separation. My love for you grows, because we are still two trees next to each other, though miles apart, our hearts knitted together in the spirit. And so, although I may not be here today to kiss you and hug you and wipe away your happy tears, just think of us as those two trees, bound together in love and sisterhood forever.

Six months we were in Perth. (It ended up being our longest stint there, but we didn't know there would be more at the time.) There were blessings each day. Little kisses from God for us. A visitor. A text. A stranger who took the time to look into my eyes long enough to see my pain. The compassion of others. A kind word. A gift. A prayer. Lightened the load just enough. Made us smile just that often. Kept our sense of humor intact. And our hearts and spirits afloat. The weariness and pain of it all would wear off just that bit that we could carry on. It was all of those little things that did it. They were the water in the desert. The shade from the blazing sun. The stamina in our strained legs.

And then, one arbitrary afternoon, Dean called me after his doctor's appointment. He'd just finished his sixth round of treatment.

"Honey, I asked the doctor if it was necessary for me to do the next two rounds of treatment. He said eight is really just a random number they choose. We're going home, sweetie. I'm done. We're going to be home for Christmas." I could hear the giant grin he was wearing.

Overwhelmed, I fell to my knees with tears of relief.

God, thank you God. We're going home. It's over. Thank God. We're going home.

I rocked back and forth as the cleansing sobs came. *We made it. It's over. Praise God. It's over.*

December 2006

Hello to everyone. I hope this e-mail finds you all well and full of the Lord's joy!

Dean met with Dr. Hermann today, and we have decided to finish the chemo! We've done the 6 and have decided against doing 2 more. With each chemo, it gets progressively more difficult for your body to recover and this last round was pretty brutal. So we are through with chemo, and we will move onto the maintenance phase which just consists of a few pills each week and is much more manageable than this potent stuff that we've experienced so far. As you can imagine, we feel quite exhilerated that we are leaving this desert behind and moving towards greener pastures.

If you are led, please pray for Dean as fear and doubt present themselves and try to take hold and for me and the boys as we move again and transition into this next season. We will be moving back to Esperance next week sometime. And we are planning to come to the states early next year, we're looking at Feb.

Thanks to everyone of you,

praise be to Him,

cass

THE SUNSHINE, THE FARM, AND THE WHITE WATER RIVER

And so we returned. Back home. Back to normal life. Normal things. Normal duties. Dean still took a plethora of pills every morning, but he was alive. To help keep the body in remission, the docs gave Dean something they call "maintenance chemotherapy." One pill a day. And one pill once a week. The once a day pill was fairly mild. The once a week one was . . . not mild. There's just no other way to put it. We were told Dean should be on these for two or three years. Any longer than that, they do too much damage to the organs. He felt good. We were out of the city and out of the sterile concrete high rise of imprisonment. The life was returning to his cheeks. The smile to his eyes. He hit the ground running as he always did. Straight back to work. Back to projects. Cleaning out the garage. All the usual things he did that drove me crazy. And it was delightful. Dean became himself again. He went from bed-ridden patient to bossy husband overnight. We were living on the farm at this point. Three hundred acres owned by Dean's uncle. Everything about it soothed me. The cows. The endless horizon. The red gravel driveway. The drafty old farmhouse with uneven wood floors. The old broken down tree house. It was so beautifully rugged and imperfect. I adored it. I don't know the last time the outside of it had been painted. There was the odd snake here and there. But it was freedom to us. You could hear dozens of different bird songs. It was home.

The boys ran free out the back, squealing and hollering with joyful contentment. And no one within earshot to protest in annoyance. We had space here. Time and space. Time and space gift wrapped in an old farmhouse on a platform of red gravel and kikuyu. And time and space was just what we needed. Time to heal. Space between us and the awful memories. The brush with death that was more like a belly flop onto the side walk.

The emotions started to come. In a trickle at first. Then stronger. I had been so brave for so long. Soldiering on. The adrenaline of the battle fueling me for each day's tasks and demands. And as the smoke cleared and the shock wore off, my emotions started to catch up. I would be doing something like beating the batter for banana bread. Boys in the living room watching TV. Dean working on a project somewhere. And the tears would come. Suddenly. Forcefully. Whisking me away in a torrent of white water. Fighting the strength of its current, I would struggle to surface for air. And I would gasp just before being pulled under again in a flood of suppressed emotion.

Everything was fine. The clouds had parted. The storm had passed. But trying to return to normal. After everything. There was no going back. Only forward. And now we were different. We'd seen things. Experienced things. Had conversations. We were changed. Dean had this incredible ability to bounce back. Get stuck into it. His tough Aussie attitude astounded me. It was harder for me. I processed things slower. I felt more. Going back to submissive wife after I had taken the reins of the family, that was hard. And we experienced bumps as the pecking order was restored.

As the months went on, the tensions eased. The torrents of emotion began to subside. And it seemed as though the sun might continue to shine forever. We did camping trips. Dean returned to full-time work. The boys had their birthdays, turning two and three years old.

The only major issue was the mood swings. Dean's anger started intensifying. His tone with me became more and more brash. It started happening in front of other people.

I tried to approach him about it. I'd always been bad at confrontation, avoiding it at all costs and preferring instead to internalize the pain and suffer in silence.

"Sweetie, do you hear yourself? How you're talking to me? It's not okay." I tried being brave, but the tears brimmed over. I couldn't hide the hurt.

He listened. He sat for a moment. Thoughtful. He then walked across the room and pulled open the drawer of meds. He pulled out a pill box. The one he took once a week. The stronger one. And read the label.

"Yeah, I thought so. That makes sense." He handed it to me to read.

It said something to the effect of causing agitated or aggravated behavior and mood swings. We deduced that his anger issue did seem to be the worst on the weekends, which was when he took this particular pill. We decided to switch it up and have him take the bad pill on a work day so as to lessen the extent that he was around the kids and me when his mood was all over the map.

Not many weeks later, he came home to me after a day's work. He'd spent ages cutting a piece of tile to fit an electrical socket they decided to move. He'd shouted "FUUUUUCK!" and thrown the tile piece across the concrete floor of the unfinished house. The unfortunate electrician was still standing nearby and got the worst of it.

My heart ached for my poor husband whose moods betrayed his intentions. Whose body would not keep up with his will. His spirit, soul, and body were all operating at their own tempo and were completely out of sync. A man divided, battling his own flesh. Attempting to make his body submit to his will. His mind to his intentions. And his heart to his priorities. We would get times where they acquiesced. And our home would sing with joyous harmony. Other times, they would fall out of beat. Tear on each other. And the tune of our home would change to something more melancholy.

Taking his meds during the week helped. But I still noticed it. His irritability. Lack of patience. Explosive responses. I wanted to confront him on his behavior. But how much could I blame him? What was there to talk about? What resolution could be made? What could be achieved? They exaggerated his natural faults. How do you work through that? I didn't know how to. So I just tried to make everything perfect so he wouldn't yell. I walked on egg shells. Never knowing when I would inadvertently do something terrible. Knots formed in my stomach. Around everyone else, he was mostly personable and friendly. He almost seemed his old, warm, jovial self. There were only a few who were around us long enough to witness Dean's intolerance and explosive anger. And it helped me. Having people know, to some degree, what I was going through. It made it a little easier. It made me feel less alone. This particular issue made it hard for us to rekindle our marriage after the sickness. I was there. Serving. Loving. But my heart, a flower, hid. Protecting itself from the flames of his anger.

One day, in the kitchen, I said to Dean, "Honey, I would like us to pray for the faith for you to get off of this medication." I was referring to the nasty stuff. He looked at me, nodded, and continued to dry dishes. He looked deeply in thought.

Weeks later, at home, Dean was playing with the boys. He was glowing. Radiant actually. His laugh was filling up the house. The boys were shrieking their delightful squeals of pure elation. My favorite sound. I'd hardly seen this at all since Maddox was just a few months old. The sound of my husband and my children laughing. Bliss. I let the sounds wash over me. Giving me life. I saturated myself in the moment. And relished it.

I looked into Dean's eyes. They were a bright. Rich. Shining blue. They emanated joy. He was back. *Oh, my love. How I have missed you. You're here. It's you.*

"Babe, I feel so much better now that I'm not taking that medication anymore," he said offhandedly as he picked up Maddox.

Wow. That was fast. Okay, he's not taking the meds anymore. Those bloody awful meds from hell. Praise God. Well. That explains why he's so happy. I have my husband back. I have him back at last. Thank you, Lord. I smiled. *Now let's get on living.*

10 months was far too short. Sitting in the doctor's office. Dean was having some pain. He was losing weight. He had that ashen look. They did some blood work. We could hear Dr. Howarth on the

phone. "Fifteen! He's got a platelet count of fifteen? He's operating a bloody tile saw with a platelet count of fifteen."

He looked at Dean and shook his head. Hung up the phone. He looked over his glasses at us. "You're going to Perth, mate."

The invisible beast. It was back.

THE MASK

April, 2008

Hi everyone,

Sending out an update. We are onto medical adventures again.

Dean hasn't been feeling very well the last couple of months, up and down a bit. We went to the doc this week and he reckons the illness has come back. His blood results came back showing that his counts were all very low.

So, we are flying to perth on sunday evening. We will be there for a week to two weeks for testing and preliminary treatments. We will be getting the doc's recommendations for either another round of chemos or bone marrow transplant. If we do another round of chemos we are expecting to be able to do those from home, and flying back and forth, not having to relocate to perth. We are really glad about that because we don't want to move again.

In general terms we're going quite well. We've worked through our initial emotions, and are now feeling strong and ready to fight this thing. Our desire is just to walk in God's peace and strength and to see Jesus glorified in our lives.

love, cassi

And so off we went to Perth. In all my reading. All my conversations with the doctors. This is what I was learning. Getting remission the first time around is easy. Keeping you there is harder. Every time the cancer comes back, it's harder to get rid of. Now that Dean had relapsed, they would hit him with everything they had. The plan was two intense rounds of chemo. Remission. Bone marrow transplant. Radiation.

Dean and I decided to leave the boys in Esperance this time. I hated being away from them, but uprooting them was too much. I would stay in Perth with Dean for nine or ten days. Drive back. Spend nine or ten days with the boys. Repeat. Praise God for the people who were willing and able to be with Dean when I wasn't there. And those who looked after and cared for my kids when I couldn't. There were so many. Some days I didn't even know who my kids were with. But I always knew they were in good hands. Such was our network of friends and family in Esperance. A treasure trove of gems that was somehow opened up to us. They were each with their own radiance. Cut. Shape. And design. All exquisite. Esperance was ours to cherish. Appreciate. And we relished in its luster.

The regimen of poison began again. And all that came with it. The smells. The bodily fluids. The nausea. The headaches. The fatigue. The vomiting. The ulcers. The constipation. The pain. The listlessness. Steady suffering in many forms commenced. A serving of suffering that promised life on the other side.

May 2008

Hello Everyone,

My apologies for the lagging update! Just tonight we have finally got internet access here in Perth! The last 11 days have been pretty full on. On Thursday May 7th the doctors explained to us that Dean's blood counts weren't coming up and that they were probably going to go straight into the next chemo rather than give Dean a break in-between. The next day (while I was still in Esperance with the boys) Dean went into the hospital for platelets where he had a severe reaction. He has had some relatively mild reactions to platelets before, but this time was more severe. Dean's airways closed and his body broke out in hives. As he started coughing and the nurses and doctors gathered around him the look of concern on their faces sent him into a panic attack. His blood pressure and heart rate went off the charts as the nurses frantically pumped drugs into him to reverse the reaction from the platelets. In about 10 minutes his heart rate normalized and they had successfully reversed the effects of the reaction. After talking to Dean on the phone, the kids and I flew up on the evening flight to Perth to be together. There was much more to this scenario than I have written, for those that want that want to hear the full story of what the Lord did on that day, let me know.

Monday night Dean stayed in the hospital. They did lumbar puncture #4 and a bone marrow test. We are now living in a house provided by the leukemia foundation (we moved here on wednesday). On Thursday the doctors got back to us. The lumbar puncture showed that there are still some leukemia cells in Dean's spine, but they are getting fewer and fewer. The bone marrow test showed that Dean is not in remission yet which explains why his blood counts haven't been coming up.

Over this weekend we went to Karen and Matt's farm (halfway to Esperance) over Saturday night. It was really lovely to get away from the city for the weekend. The boys had a great play with their cousins and have now gone back to Esperance with Mum and Dad to spend the week going to school and swimming, the things they usually do. Dean has started his second round of chemo today. He's getting it here at home and we finish with it on thursday. This is the more intense round of chemo, so we are hoping and praying for no infection, that there will only be mild side effects and that it will put the disease into remission so we can move toward the next phase (radiation, transplant).

It's been an amazing week. Full of ups and downs. Some really hard days and some totally amazing moments between Dean and I.

Thank you so much for all the amazing emails and phone calls that we get from everyone. We are so blessed with this huge array of people that are loving on us and encouraging us in some of the simplest ways and its priceless.

Lots of love,

cassi and dean

Dean developed a lung infection. It always seemed to come to that. His lungs. When I was sitting with him, I noticed that his breathing seemed shallow and kind of labored. Lethargic. He was bald again. His exuberance was gone. He was a patient again. Hard to recognize. The physio kept coming in to try to get Dean to sit up and do some breathing exercises. I would come into the room. He wouldn't stir. He was awake. But there was no spark. Lethargic. His oxygen levels started to drop. They put him on a 5% oxygen mask. Then 10.

They put him on 15%, but his levels continued to decline.

When the 15% mask couldn't keep his O2 levels up, they moved him to the ICU. We had worked so hard to get Dean into remission, and now the hope of a bone marrow transplant seemed to be slipping away. The move into ICU brought the CPAP machine and pressurized mask. The mask was strapped to Dean's head with a series of Velcro harnesses to ensure it fits securely against his face. It completely covered his nose and mouth, with an airtight seal along the edge. It forcefully pushes warm air into the lungs, making the wearer feel claustrophobic. It looked like something you'd wear in a chemical chamber. No breaks. No food. No drink. They put in a feeding tube. Before Dean, the longest anyone had lasted in that mask was two hours.

They put the oxygen at 30%.

"Well, look. His oxygen levels are continuing to drop. His lung infection is getting worse. We are probably going to have to sedate him and put him on a ventilator. At that point, there will be no options left to treat the cancer."

Is this it, Lord? Is this when you're going to take my beloved husband? We were at the doorway again. *Is this where our paths part?*

"Do you understand what I'm saying? It's best to be prepared."

I hesitantly nodded. "Y . . . yes, I understand." And walked numbly back to his room.

Karen and Matt came to visit, and so did his parents. They brought the boys with them. We were all emotional. Karen and Matt were meant to be traveling. They considered canceling their trip considering Dean's condition. Karen went in to talk to Dean. Teary.

Even in his hazy, depleted state, he told her to dry her eyes quick and go on her trip. He wouldn't hear any talk of the worst.

The doctors approached me. "Mrs. Mack, this would be a good time to get your affairs in order."

"I'm sorry, what do you mean?" I heard the words, but I couldn't grasp their meaning.

What amazed every nurse and doctor on that ward was Dean stayed in that mask. Two hours. Three hours. Four hours. A day. Another day. They couldn't believe it. They'd never seen anyone tolerate it without going into a panic attack. I sat at his side. Sitting. Watching. Waiting. Praying for improvement. His oxygen levels started to plummet. Forty percent. Fifty percent. They were cranking the oxygen up, and his levels kept dropping. I watched the monitors as the numbers dropped. The minutes felt like hours, and the hours felt like days. There were no windows. Nothing to do. Except watch the blips. Listen for the beeps. Watching his temp. His oxygen. Pulse. He was burning up with temperatures. I had a bowl brought in with ice. Filled it with water. I took cloths and put them on his forehead, chest, and arms. He felt on fire. The mask started to give him a pressure wound at the bridge of his nose. He was such a brave soldier. *How can you be so strong?* Praise God he slept that night.

Nine days Dean spent in ICU. His oxygen levels kept dropping. They put the tank at 90%. They looked at me steadily. "The highest we can go is 100%. If his levels drop after that, there's nothing we can do."

I'm not sure what day it was. Each day seeped into the next. The doctors were coming by to let me know if they were going to sedate Dean and put him on a ventilator. I got there in the morning. The five-story parking lot I used every day was full. I had to park in another lot a couple blocks away. I walked from there up to the hospital and into the ICU. I spent the day with Dean. It was surreal. I was on edge. I waited for the doctors. The hours were painfully long. *Are these your last breaths, love? Will you come back to me again? Darling. Don't go. Please don't go.*

Every time I asked the nurse when the doctors were coming, she gave a vague answer. I didn't want to get up and go out at all. I could miss them. It was such an important day. They would be making a huge decision. I waited. And waited. At about eleven thirty at night, I figured they mustn't be coming. At least, for the moment, Dean would be staying where he was.

I wearily walked the couple of blocks down to the parking garage. I hated walking in the middle of Perth at night. During the day, it was airy. Mostly sunny. People everywhere. Shopping. Dining. Working. With the coming of dusk, though, came an uncomfortable tension in the air. A more sinister atmosphere. An uneasiness. I still had a lump in my throat. Emotionally exhausted. Waiting to know if Dean is going to live or die. *I need to get home to my kids. To bed.* I rounded the corner to the entrance to come to a locked gate. *Wait, what?*

I looked at the sign. "OPENING HOURS: 6AM–11PM."

Oh no. The parking garage I usually used was open twenty-four hours. *How am I going to get home?* I continued to read the sign. "IF AFTER-HOURS ASSISTANCE IS REQUIRED, THERE WILL BE A FEE OF $20."

Okay, twenty dollars. I can manage that. I called the number at the bottom. A man answered. "Yup, sure, we'll come down there. There's a fee though. It's one hundred twenty dollars."

My stomach dropped. The tears swelled. *What?* I looked closer at the sign. Someone had scratched the "1" away. The tears fell. I tried to find the courage to speak. Thank God I had enough cash in my wallet. "Yes, okay, thank you."

I hung up the phone. Stood there. Raw. Battle weary. Suddenly, a car piled with teenagers with all the windows down, music blaring, sped past me.

"Stupid whore!" Something came flying at me. I tried to duck out of the way but didn't quite make it. I looked over to see a large plastic cup with its contents on the sidewalk and some on my clothes. Immediately after, another car sped past. I quickly hid behind a small brick planter. Sat. Pulled my knees up to my chin. Buried my face. I couldn't hold it back any longer. Sobbed.

About ten minutes later, the men with the keys to the garage arrived.

"Were you out seeing a movie?" They asked.

A movie? I couldn't respond.

I gave them the money. They opened the gate.

Get me home. God. Help.

85

Love Stronger
than Death

To everyone's astonishment, including mine, Dean took a turn for the good. His O2 levels improved. They slowly started to drop the oxygen back. Eventually, he was ready for the 15% mask. They took him back up to the ward.

He lived. He was given back to me. He was mine again.

As bad as the lung infection got, the docs decided against radiation. Transplant only. Radiation would damage too much lung tissue. Dean had to spend a number of weeks in the hospital to regain his strength. I left once he was settled and stable to be with the boys in Esperance.

July 30, 2008, 8:14 PM

G'day All!

I hope this email finds you well. Wanted to get out an update, people have been getting anxious!

Well, Dean has now been home for four weeks. He was in the hospital with his lung infection for 5 weeks. He actually came home early and surprised me. You can imagine my shock at coming home and finding him in the house!

It took quite a few days for him to acclamate to being out of hospital. No more morphine, no more temperature control, no more getting waited on hand and foot - welcome to the real world! So, that was a bit tough. To add to my joy, my sister arrived from california the same day that Dean came home from hospital!

So the last four weeks have been so much fun. We've been motor bike riding and lunching, and partying and going out exploring, chasing kangaroos, in short having a BLAST. My sister got a good dose of west australia. She stayed for four weeks, I dropped her at the airport last night.

Dean and I even went away for 2 nights to Denmark (a small town about 5 hours away in a wine growing region) to celebrate our 5 year anniversary.

Dean has gained about 10 kilos (22 pounds) since he's been home, he's looking great. He has been in a bit of pain, we're unsure if it is muscular or bone related. Our GP here in Esperance says that it could be the disease. He has an appointment next week to meet with the hematologist in Perth. After that, we should get the schedule for the transplant and the okay for the donor.

Blessings to you all! Thank you again for all of your care and concern. We (especially Me) have been so blessed the last month with time at home together as a family and Dean feeling so good and my sister here as well, God totally answered the prayers for a break for us.

Will be in touch,

Cassi, Dean, and Boys

August 13, 2008, 11:12 PM

Hi everyone,

This is Dean writing the update this time and glad to be, thats for sure.

Well I have been home for 6 weeks now and loving being with my little family and friends and beautiful Esperance.

I spoke to my Hematologist last Thursday and he had just got back from holidays and is still getting his bearings on everything but he did say that my donor is now medically fit, but that he needs 4 weeks notice because he lives out in the country over in New South Wales, Australia. So thats all good news. He is a perfect match as well.

I guess this is fairly obvious but I have never asked him some of these questions.

I have been doing a little bit of work just to keep a bit of a challenge and goal ahead of me (you know guys especially have to have that achievement thing happening). I even achieved a dream that i had while i was on oxygen in ICU, of going for a surf once again, so i braved the cold waters and paddled my new board out and paddled and paddled. I didn't get a wave but it was fantastic to be in the salt again. It's funny how something small like that can really make you appreciate what you have.

i will find out more soon and keep you updated. Thank you all for your prayers and amazing support, of which i have found much strength and comfort, I can assure you. None of it goes unnoticed in the heavenlies. Blessings -dean

September 15, 2008

Hello All,

Well here we are. We checked him into the hospital on September 8th and Dean has been getting chemo since Tuesday the 9th. Yesterday was the first day he started to feel a bit average because of it. The good news is that they looked at his bone marrow and the disease is in remission.

Tomorrow evening they will be doing the bone marrow transplant. It's very straight forward. We are very hopeful and looking forward to a fast and speedy recovery. We are praying that the bone marrow will be well matched to Dean's body so that there are no graph mismatches. Dean is doing well. The next couple of weeks will be tough going with pushing through all the side-effects of the chemo and waiting for the marrow to settle in.

I've been very blessed with my step mom coming over from California to help me with the boys for a couple of weeks. The boys are doing well. A little bit out of sorts with being away from home and Dean being in the hospital again, but mostly good.

Thanks again to everyone! Our love to all of you.

Much love,

Cassi and Dean

The marrow had to be taken from the donor and put into Dean the same day. They collected it. Put it on ice. Flew it to Perth. Brought it to RPH and administered it into Dean's veins that very night.

The nurse brought in a small cup with a few ounces of pink liquid, instructing Dean to drink. It didn't look harmful at all, and I said so. The nurse informed us this pink liquid would destroy Dean's bone marrow, making way for the new. Dean told me receiving the bone marrow transplant reminded him of what it means to become a Christian. Everything in us has to die. Has to be killed off so we can receive his blood. His promise of new life. And we are made new.

I'm not sure what I thought a bone marrow transplant would entail. I suppose I imagined something gory. Where they cut into your bones, take something out, and replace it with something else. The procedure itself was far simpler than imagined. Drink this, and we'll pump you full of that.

It arrived. It was late. Nearly midnight. Dean was asleep in bed. I was in the chair adjacent. Watching. Waiting. Praying. Unsure of what was to come. The lights were all off. The room was dark. The ward was quiet. There was just a bit of light glowing from the hallway. The nurse came in. I had never seen her on that ward before. She had an air of calm. Her steps were light yet decisive. Her movements were sweet and proficient. She hung the bag full of the coveted contents. The promise of new life. She quietly took Dean's obs and made preparations. She wore a lanyard. It had letters sewn into it. The light was low. I was curious and strained to see what they were.

WWJD.

Wow. Lord, you're here. I could feel Him. In this very room with us. So near to us. *Thank you, Lord. You haven't left us. You're right here.*

She continued to fiddle with the lines, ensuring everything was in properly and flowing through. She leaned forward. The necklace she wore dangled freely. Its pendant fluttered. It caught the hallway light and flickered brilliantly into my eyes.

A gold cross.

Jesus. Mesmerized. I couldn't blink. My steadfast gaze beholding the symbol of hope. Of love stronger than death. My eyes were satellites staring into space desperately searching for signs of life. A sign of something greater at work. That we weren't abandoned. Unforsaken. The images downloaded to my heart. With each illustrious beam, He spoke.

NO! YOU ARE NOT ALONE! I AM WITH YOU. I HAVE NOT LEFT
YOU. I LOVE YOU.

Lord, you're here. In this dark little room. You're next to me. You're all around me. You're making sure everything goes right. The tears cascaded unbidden. *Thank you, God. You see it all. You know our pain. Thank you, Jesus. Thank you that you love me. You love Dean.*

The match between Dean's marrow and the donor's was as close as you can get (apart from a sibling). The risk involved is that the new marrow (which is a new immune system) could possibly see the new body (Dean's body) as foreign and therefore try to destroy or get rid of it. Turn against it. The benefit is you have this strong, new immune system that's going to fight cancer cells. The docs said a good indicator of how well the transplant has taken is what sort of skin reaction you get in the days following the procedure.

Dean turned purple. Deep. Dark. Purple. As though his entire body was covered in a dark purple bruise. It looked beyond awful. *Oh, my Lord.* It wasn't the sign we were hoping for. Confusion. I'd been so hopeful it would go well. The possible outcomes swarmed my mind like flies. Pestering. An incessant buzzing that refused to quell. *God, where are you? What is happening? I thought you said this would go well?*

WEEPING MAY LAST THROUGH THE NIGHT, BUT JOY COMES
WITH THE MORNING.

God, I want the morning.

They'd never seen a skin reaction that bad before. They took a skin biopsy. They seemed to love that. See something interesting. Casually cut off a piece. And then delight in a frenzy of hypotheses.

Dean was determined. He ate and drank well. He set his sights on getting out. Getting up. And getting back. To Esperance. Our city of hope. Well, town anyway. Head down, tail up, powered through. His spirit seemed unrelenting. And I grew to admire it more and more. His insides were solid iron. Half the time, I felt like I was falling apart. Dean was rock solid.

After about a week, Dean's skin calmed down. Started to look more normal. They put him on drugs called immunosuppressants.

They would suppress Dean's new immune system so that his side effects would be minimized. The problem areas would be the skin, gut, and liver. We found ourselves on a tightrope. On the one hand, there was the cancer. To fight the cancer, you need a strong, healthy immune system. On the other hand, you had the graft versus host disease (GvHD). It's the term describing how a transplant (in this case, Dean's new immune system) attacks (or rejects) the recipient's body. Treats it as a foreign object. This wasn't a rock and a hard place. It was glacier against granite.

The nurses at the BMTU were absolutely lovely. They were patient and sensitive. They always asked me how I was. Their demeanor was kind and their tone sincere that I would nearly burst into tears. The lump in my throat was almost a permanent fixture, blinking back the emotion. Trying so hard to keep it together. To be strong for Dean. Strong for the boys. The nurses said to me all the time, "It's harder for the carer."

And what a relief that was to hear. Someone was acknowledging me in all of this. They told me, "With the person that's unwell, they are just trying to make it through. They are so absorbed in what they are going through, they just focus on that. The carer has to watch it happen. And manage all the other aspects of life."

And it was so true. I was Dean's source of love. Strength. Emotional support. Encouragement. Meanwhile, I'm trying to wade through my own feelings. Pay bills. Raise kids. Keep everyone updated. Run the household. It was an enormous task. The nurse's words gave me strength. Affirmed my plight. I wasn't crazy. What I was doing was really. Really. Damn. Hard. Everyone's focus is usually on the sick person. Understandably. But as the carer, you get a bit lost in it all. Lost in doing everything for everyone else. It's lonely. There's no time for you to have needs. For you to be sick. For you to take time out. Everyone is counting on you. You have to carry on.

October 5, 2008, 6:05 AM

Greetings!

Hello all you beautiful people! Writing to update you on Dean's recovery and fill you in on the details of the last 3 weeks (since the transplant).

The actual administering of the new stem cells (marrow) went very well, quite boring actually. Dean slept through it and I spoke to the nurse, for the half hour that it took, as she was overseeing the procedure. I think she was a christian, actually, she had this lovely little gold cross necklace on and it kept catching the light and shining into my eyes! (One of many signs that God has been giving us here and there to remind us that he is always right there.)

Dean was good for the first 3 or 4 days following the transplant, but the effects of the chemo (that he recieved before the transplant) hit him on the 5th day and from then on it was pretty rough. Diarreah, vomitting, nausea, headaches, backaches, fevers, chills, infection, the lot! About a week post transplant Dean got a rash and it got so bad that he was red and purple more than anything else. It didn't bother him much, but it was a symptom of graph versus host disease (GVHD) very early on and quite severe, so the doctor told me he was quite concerned. GVHD is actually benificial in a mild form because it's a better guarentee of remission of the leukaemia, but can be very harmful and fatal if it is severe. So, when the doctor said he was concerned, it really made me take a step back and think,

"God, what are you doing?!" I had really felt like God had told me to just hope and believe "unabashedly." Like really hope for the amazing. And so I was confused. And that night I went home and I was having this talk with God and then he said to me, "You can still hope and believe Cassi. I haven't changed. I am still good. My word is still true and my promises are still true. You can believe me and my promises OR you can walk in doubt, worry, and concern. You can't do both. It is one or the other. You have to choose to believe in me and my word despite everything around you that says, 'nope, it's not reality.' Your reality is either my word and my promise, or everything around you that you can see."

And I was like wow! Okay, so I have to choose what I am going to believe, my eyes or my God. It was just really full on! It was like okay, Cassi, here in the face of your worst fears coming true you can either allow the fear to consume you or you grab that fear demon and step on its neck and say "I believe in God's promise and that his promises for me are true!" And so, That is what I did. I said, "Well, God, if I believe in you, you said that you gave me a future and a hope, that your plan was to prosper me, and that your plans are for good and not for evil. And you said that I could even walk on water (do the impossible) if I keep my eyes on Jesus, and you said that surely goodness and love will follow me all the days of my life and you said that you heal all my disease. And you said that the name of Jesus is above every name, so that must include the names of leukaemia and graph versus host disease. Okay,

God, I'm standing on your word, I'm standing by your promise and that's all I'm standing by." On one of the boy's cd's is the song "I'm standing, standing, standing on the promises of Christ my savior, standing, standing, I'm standing on the promises of God." And that song has never meant more to me than it does now! Mate!

Well, the next day Dean's rash started to improve, that was Wednesday. Today is Sunday and Dean is home (in our Perth house)! It's really amazing. They are going to see how he goes tonight. We have to be at the hospital in the morning for them to have a look at his medication levels in his blood, etc. It has been 4 weeks and it is amazing for a MUD (much unrelated donor) transplant recipient to be looking at getting out of the hospital.

Do, a huge "Thank you!" To all of you that have been continually praying for us, we have been so strengthened and encouraged by the saints! Bless you! Now you can all rejoice with us.

The next step is getting back to Esperance. God willing that will be next week!

"For the word of God is living and active. Sharper than any double-edged sword, it penetrates even to dividing soul and spirit, joints and marrow; it judges the thoughts and attitudes of the heart." Hebrews 4:12

Thank you God for the powerful weapon of your word, which is Life.

Many blessing to all of you, cassi

STIGMATA

Shortly after the transplant, Dean took my advice. He went to a naturopathy clinic. I'd been pleading with him to do it since the initial diagnosis. We found one in Perth where they do the super immune boosting injections. The boys and I remained in Esperance while he went to Perth for a week and received their regimen. One week of injections every day. At the end of the week, his immune system was crazy strong! In fact, his immune system was so strong his GvHD symptoms skyrocketed out of control and became completely unbearable. The experience was so demoralizing for us. To come to a place where we COULDN'T strengthen his immune system. Or else we would actually hurt him. Couldn't suppress it too much or we risk relapse.

Trapped.

We took one day at a time, trying to keep looking up. Looking to Him.

Our friends and family were our backbone. They were beyond amazing. More of a community than I had ever known. These people cooked for us. Gave us money. Watched our kids. Brought us all kinds of gifts. Trips. Blankets. Cards. Groceries. Flowers. Gas. Books. They stood by us. Prayed for us. Encouraged us. Cried with us. Laughed with us. Stood by us. Kneeled with us. Their hearts broke in unison with ours when bad news hit. They experienced our joy when we got good news. They walked the journey with us. They made sacrifices. They went out of their way. Spent time. Spent money. They poured love on us. In so many ways. At so many pivotal moments. Kind acts of every variety. Thoughtfulness I'd never witnessed, much less received. It was humbling. It was overwhelming. We found ourselves being in awe frequently of the generosity of so many around us. Some knew us well and others hardly at all. But all gave. They carried us. They lifted us. They strengthened us. They were life to our family. They were the steel toe in our boots. The thrust in our engine. And when the flames of our hearts burned low, they kindled, fed, and stirred them.

March 2009

Hi everyone,

As always, I hope this email finds you well! Well, we are on the road again. Dean and I flew up to Perth yesterday. Last week Dean went to get his routine blood test done and it came back with low platelets. Over the last three weeks he has been feeling quite fatigued and has had some random joint pain. Then, last week his sternum became sensitive and his shoulder bones started to hurt as well. So, the doctor decided to re-do his blood test, which showed low platelets again. Right there and then he punctured Dean's sternum and drew some bone marrow to have it sent to Perth for testing. On Friday last week we rang him and he told us that it was, in fact, the leukaemia.

So, Monday we met with the doc and he typed up a letter and got us organized with plane tickets, we packed. The boys are with Dean's parents back at home so they can stay in school and swimming and in their routine. The vague plan is that I come up here with Dean to get him settled into hospital and find out what our options are and what the doctors want to do, and then fly home. The boys and I will stay in Esperance and just come up to see Dean as often as we/I can. But we will just take it one week at a time.

We arrived at the hospital yesterday, we knew they had no beds, so, we just showed up at emergency with a letter and Dean's blood counts. We waited in the hallway at emergency for a couple of hours and then they got us into an assessment area, where we finally saw a doctor. And then just before I left, around 6pm last night the hematology reg came and saw us. She was really lovely and I felt like they really care about Dean. Our Hematology Dr. is semi retiring, so we will have a new Doctor. We haven't met him yet, hopefully we will today. We are hoping for a room for Dean today and to get to talk to the doctor about what they want to do.

In it all we are doing quite well. The main thing is that Dean is in a great Deal of pain. As of yesterday on 90mg of morphine he was still wincing in pain every time he moved.

But we know that God is so much bigger. So, we are believing for God to heal him.

Love, cassi

March 23, 2009

Hi guys,

I'm sorry I haven't written sooner. A lot has happened in the last couple of weeks.

They started Dean's chemo a couple of days after we got to the hospital. And the chemo went from Thursday to Sunday. Dean had to share a room for the first week with three other patients. That was really difficult for him because it was always noisy and stuff.

We met the new doctor, Dr. Wright. He is a bit more matter-of-fact than our previous doctor. Dr. Hermann was like a loving grandfather to Dean. Dr. Wright is a very good doctor though. And I appreciated his honesty. He said it doesn't look good for Dean because the leukemia is being very stubborn. Basically, they have got to get Dean into remission, which the doctors have told us may be difficult. Then once that is accomplished, to look at our other options. Maintenance chemo would buy Dean some time but would not cure the disease. Another bone marrow transplant would be very risky but is the only medical chance at long-term cure of disease. This is what they have explained to us.

They checked for leukemia cells in the spinal fluid, which they found. They have given him four lumbar punctures in the last two weeks. He can only have two more because beyond that (he will have had twenty), you risk damaging the brain.

They decided to skip the first round of chemo, which is a bit lighter, and go straight to the really intense round. They have to treat the disease aggressively because it has come back so aggressively.

This has resulted in a very difficult week for Dean. His mouth is swollen and full of ulcers. His throat is the same. He hasn't had much sleep or been able to speak, eat, or drink much. The pain has been excruciating for him. His blood counts have bottomed out, and he started to run a temperature yesterday. He has some sort of bug (infection) in his blood. They know the grouping but not the specific kind. They are treating him with antibiotics, but they aren't working as of yet. I drove up to Hyden (halfway) from Esperance yesterday afternoon. I got to Hyden around seven thirty. We had some dinner, and a little while later, the nurse rang us and said Dean was under the close watch of a doctor because of high temp, low blood pressure, high heart rate, and slightly low oxygen. So we decided to grab a cup of tea and keep driving to Perth. Mum and I arrived in Perth at about one last night.

When we got here, Dean was stable. It was a bit of a rough night, but he pulled through. The doctor came in this morning and said the next three days are crucial for Dean. There are lots of things that can happen. They started using some language I didn't like. He said the long-term doesn't look good, but now we are talking short-term.

Praise God, we had a prayer meeting on Sunday, before I left, and we are all praying and believing for a miracle. I am putting my hope in the Lord. All my trust, all my hope is in Jesus. My God is my rock, my strength, and my refuge—an ever-present help in times of trouble.

When Mum (Sue) and I arrived at RPH that night, seeing Dean was unbearable. I'd seen him sick. Really sick. Lots of times. This was different. This was on a whole new level.

They had tried multiple times to get an IV into his hands. He had white bandages with blood stains on the back of each hand. On his head was a white cloth to help keep him cool as he was completely burning up. His lips were cracked and pealing. The inside of his mouth was dry. When I came in to see him, he slowly opened his heavy eyelids. But only for a moment. His body shook with each heartbeat. As though he were swinging his sword which was clashing with that of his adversary. I stood there, taking in the enormity of his suffering. The excruciating suffering. Looking at him made me think of Christ. The bandages on his hands with wounds like stigmata. And I had to watch. Watching it. Watching it happen. That was the worst part. It's torture actually. And I could bear it no longer. I cried out. *GOD! I can't do it. I can't watch this. This recurring nightmare. Over and over and over. Please, God. Have mercy! Make him well or take him home! It's too much. The suffering. It's too much. The torment of watching it.* My eyes burned hot. *My love. My love. My love. My Dean. Oh God, Dean. Please, God. God, help me.* The sobs seized me as I convulsed with emotion. My hatred of this wretched fucking faceless bastard called cancer. *I can't do it, God. I can't do it anymore. God. God. God. Please. No more. Please.*

Mercy. Mercy. Mercy.

April 17, 2009

Hello everyone, sorry if you've recieved this email twice or if I have failed to send you my last few updates. I'm trying to get my recipients list accurate.

Dean's mouth has healed and his lung infection is all but gone, but he is weak and frail from these last few weeks in hospital.

We had a meeting with the doctor yesterday. I believe we saw a really soft side to him and I commend him for his courage and honesty in our conversation. Dr. Wright explained to us that the leukemia cells in Dean's body seem to be chemo resistant. He called them "bastards," which I thought was quite fitting and funny. He said that he was impressed with Dean's recovery from this past round of chemotherapy, and he commended Dean for his strength. Then he explained to us that the bone marrow sample taken a couple of days prior was a bad sample, and so they could not determine if Dean is in remission. He said that his hunch is that Dean is not in remission because his bone marrow is not making enough white and red blood cells. (They have taken another sample today and we should know how close Dean is to remission sometime early next week.)

He then spoke to us about having another bone marrow transplant and he has strongly recommended that we not go down that path. He said there is a 60% chance they will kill Dean in the process and a 0-10% chance that it will do any good. He said that he didn't want to do it, and it sounded as though he wouldn't even if we wanted him to.

So, he explained to us the maintenance chemo option, which would involve tablets and injections, much of that could be done in Esperance. Th goal would be to prolong Dean's life by slowing the growth of the leukemia.

With that said, we are probably going to pursue the maintenance chemo option. It will be good to get the results back from Dean's bone marrow sample because it will indicate what stage the disease is at. We are hoping to combine it with some holistic medicine at an immune clinic here in Perth.

So, in short, the doctor has said, as far as his expertise is concerned, that Dean has a matter of months to live.

I think this time is very important. We have by no means given up, but I believe the time has come for us all to pull together and love on Dean like never before. He really needs it.

As you can imagine, this has been a very difficult couple of days for us, especially for Dean.

I would like to put together a list of people who have it on their hearts to intercede, fast, and pray for Dean and our family and those who want to be kept up to date with our decisions and frequent updates on his condition. Please respond to this email and let me know if you would like to be included in this list.

I praise and thank the Father that he is giving us the strength and grace to walk through this. We have decided not to let the fear of death or presence of this illness hang over us like a dark cloud. We have laid down the burden that is too heavy for us to bear. We are going to rejoice in everyday, be grateful for the time we have together, and trust in the Lord. We pray to live each day full of righteousness, peace, and joy in the Holy Spirit. "For all Dean's times (years) are in your hand, Lord."

Much love and many thanks to you all,

Cassi

What you don't hear in these e-mails is my doubts. My fears. My struggles. The questions that plagued me. The feelings that haunted me. The things I struggled to admit to myself. The things I didn't want to think. The feelings I didn't want to have. Yet there they were.

Right before we left for Esperance, they checked to see if Dean was, in fact, in remission. As I had said in my e-mail, the doc didn't think he would be. I was particularly raw that day. The doctors prognosis confirmed what I'd felt for a long time. I wouldn't have Dean for long. Didn't know how long. But it wasn't going to be as long as I wanted. We wouldn't grow old together. The very idea made my heart almost too heavy to carry. My eyes were full glasses of water. Ready to spill over at the slightest disturbance.

As Dean was getting his marrow drawn, I did a bit of shopping. After an hour of relatively unfruitful retail perusing, I went back to the ward. Dean and I waited for the doctor a short while. The doctor was due to arrive to give us the results. He came in and sat on the edge of the bed. He then told us incredibly Dean was, in fact, in remission. Dean and I were elated. Progress! Hope. After so much bad news, this was a shot of adrenaline to the heart. And we were soaring. I kissed Dean. I had to walk. I left Dean to get himself organized and ready to leave. I just had to get outside and look into the sky and thank God. The Hay Street Mall was only down the block. It had become a frequent and pleasant escape for me over these months and years. God used the sun to caress my upturned, smiling face. My heart was a brownie with a molten center and my face its candle atop. I walked into Café 54 on cloud ten. Walking on air. Raptured in amazement. *Wow.* Beaming. Radiant. Joy. I ordered my chai latte and sat down in a booth. Wonderment. *Music. I hear music.* It was a song I'd never heard before. I listened intently. It almost sounded like . . . like a worship song. Then words. "Ooooooh praise Him, ooooooh praise Him, He is holyyyyyy, He is holyyyyyy." *Am I hearing that? Is that really playing?* I looked around at other customers to see if they could hear it too. *Heaven must have opened over me. It's a portal! I'm hearing the song of my heart being played in heaven!* Eyes wide. Ears drinking in the melody. Each. Exquisite. Note. I was raptured in musical euphoria. I studied my surroundings, trying to discern if this music was playing in heaven or on Earth. *That's really playing! That is actually playing in the café. Are these guys Christians?* I walked over to the café owner. We were on a first-name basis as I had been there so frequently. I couldn't hide my glee.

"I love this music! Are you guys Christians?"

"Yeah," he smiled back at me. "This is our pastor." He gestured to the man acting as barista. *Wow!* I tried to describe to them my morning and my awe when hearing the song. How it blessed me! Wings.

The joy of the Lord is our strength. And He filled me with strength that day.

I was going to need it.

When I got back to the hospital, the doctors said to us, "Getting the results back that Dean is in remission is really encouraging, but the reality is the cancer will come back and Dean probably only has about six months." That was sobering. *Where do we go from here?*

I got in the driver's seat, and Dean laid down in the back of the car. He was overcome with emotion. "What are we going to do honey? What do you think about what the doctor said?" I could hear he was crying, which he rarely did.

I was feeling strong. Resolve. "Babe, we are *not* going to let this be a dark cloud over our heads. We are going to go home and live life. And do that to the fullest. They are doctors. We can be grateful for them, but they don't have all the answers." Back to Esperance we went.

And then the worst began.

HE SET ME HIGH
UPON A ROCK

Dean and I came back to Esperance and to the farm. Days after we arrived, a longtime friend of Dean's contacted us about a house. Johnny Daunt.

We arranged to meet him at his beautiful four-bedroom home he was intending on renting out. We went inside for a cuppa. The kitchen's window displayed the glory of West Beach and her islands. You could hear the waves in their applause of the shore. The house was red brick. Spacious. But cozy. Lots of warm dark colors and big windows quenching the rooms' thirst for light. I was a bit distracted looking around so I almost wasn't paying attention to the conversation.

John's Australian accent was particularly thick. His demeanor casual. Kind. Very "no worries." He was a surfer. A builder by trade. Living on his own. "Yeah, I think, ya know, if you guys want the place, then you can have it. It's too much room for me, and I don't really need to rent it out. So, yeah."

Dean reacted, "Are you serious, mate? Ah, gosh, yeah, that'd be awesome!" His face was alight. He looked at me. "Whad'ya think, sweetie?"

I was trying to figure out what was going on. *Wait . . . is he saying we can live here? Is he saying we can like . . . move in? And we don't have to pay rent?*

I nodded my head, pretending like I understood.

When Dean and I got in the car, I attempted to clarify.

He was emphatic, "Sweetie, he's letting us live there rent free."

He looked at me with those glowing blue eyes. Sometimes they shined like the blue licks of a flame. It was so refreshing to see him excited about something.

"Wow, babe. That's . . . That's amazing . . ." I trailed off.

I paused. I was amazed by the outpouring of generosity of which we were regular benefactors. I looked out the car window. I loved the farm. It was home to me. I loved the paddocks. The space. The earthiness. The fact that we were out of town. It felt free to me. I pondered. *Dean is so excited about this though. And, I mean, it's free. How could we turn it down? Why would we want to? I'll miss the farm.*

I looked out at our future view. His eyes pleaded at me for the green light.

I grabbed his hand. "Yeah, babe. Let's do it."

"Ah, sweetie!" He started up the car. *Blessed. Wow. A new place. A high place.*

"For in the day of trouble he will keep me safe in his dwelling; he will hide me in the shelter of his sacred tent and set me high upon a rock" (Ps. 27:5).

Dean's GvHD symptoms became extreme. We were still trying to get the balance right. Keeping the immune system strong enough to kill the cancer cells but not so strong that it would kill Dean. The days and weeks were riddled with agony. The bottom of his feet were shedding. Skin just flaking and falling off. Even sliding on his socks was incredibly painful. The inside of his mouth was shedding and raw, sensitive to anything remotely spicy. He could only eat the most mild and bland foods. Foods that weren't very hot or cold. It robbed him of the culinary experience he enjoyed so much. And there were beginning to be concerns over his liver function. Because of the worsening GvHD, they upped his immunosuppressants. Dr. Howarth got Dean on an experimental stem cell treatment to see if it would make a positive impact.

Around this time, Dean and I resigned as members from the church we had gone to for years. It was a difficult decision. It was complicated. We loved everyone there so very much but felt it was our time to move on. We tried to do it wisely. Gently. Still, there were many who took offense to our leaving. I lost the closest friends I had. Virtually overnight. An outcome I did not anticipate.

Feelings of utter aloneness took over.

Jesus. It's me and you, Jesus. I have no one else.

Dean was trying to work a bit. He was dealing with many different ailments. His mouth. His feet. Pain in certain joints. He struggled to put on weight. Most days he would spend lying on the couch staring out the window at the ocean. I wanted to reach him. I didn't know how. And so I stuck to the things I did know how to do. I cooked for him. I did his washing. I tried to keep the house tidy. I looked after the boys. Those things were all tangible. I could check them off a list.

The steroids he was on made him so amped and irritable. On eggshells, I would go about my day, fearing his outbursts. Trying to make everything perfect. Do everything right so as not to trigger an episode. I always seemed to do something though. I didn't know how to make it better. It was the medication. I knew he didn't want to be that way. What was the solution? Where was the ray of hope? I would fantasize about jumping on the back of a horse and riding away. Into the horizon. I combated the overwhelming urge by picturing myself nailing my feet to the ground. *Stay, Cassi. Stay.*

He became more isolated. Talked to people less. His anger worsened, emanating from him like a thick vapor. No matter where I was in the house, I could feel it. Mealtimes mainly consisted of Dean waiting for one of the boys to forget their manners and then erupt in anger. I would sit silently while my stomach ate away at itself, shoveling food in my mouth. Hoping it would slow the growth of the anxiety threatening to engulf and strangle me. Everyone on edge. We ate in strained, fearful, angry silence. I fought back tears that threatened to garner attention. All the time and love poured into preparing a meal, which was joyless and traumatizing.

I didn't have paddocks or fields to wonder across for introspection. Like at the farm. The ocean became my open space hiding place. Where I took my tears. The aches of my heart. My fears. Prayers. Doubts. Wonderings.

And so I ran away from home. Every day. Into the arms of God. Where I could wilt into His embrace. Where I would run to Him and He would carry me. Where I would vent to Him and He would listen to me. Where we asked each other the tough questions.

There in the sand, I would lay them down. My heavy heart burdens. Adding salt and water to the ocean. Tears I would bring. My offering to God. Who pools together the collective suffering of us all. Creating a sea. Where suffering becomes beauty. And pain becomes grace.

Fever. Dean lay in bed. Burning up. Complaining of being cold. I stood in the bedroom, staring at him. Pacing. *God help me.* Whenever Dean started running a temperature at home, we would inevitably argue. It began a battle of the wills. He would never want to go to the doctor. Never wanted to go to the hospital. Never wanted to get seen to. Stubborn. Stubborn as anything. Dr. Howarth had specifically told me to get him straight to the hospital at the first sign of a temp.

I left the room and called Dr. Howarth. We had his personal cell. I explained. He insisted we come to the hospital straight away.

They took some chest x-rays. Pneumonia. He was admitted and was able to return home after a week.

My internal struggle continued as Dean's overall condition continued to worsen.

Lord, is this my life? Is this what my life is going to be? Caring for an angry man? Married to a man who can't be a husband in almost any way? Who is always sick and never gets better? It was the yo-yo that became unbearable. Almost dying. But then lives. Almost better. But then gets sick again. Going to the very edge each time.

The uncertainty.

That was the worst part.

As my friendships in Esperance diminished, the loneliness took its toll. Christmas was approaching, and I was desperate to spend it with my family. Dean and I knew it would be a risk for him to fly over for a couple of reasons. Immigration. The last time, they had sent him straight back. We still didn't have his visa issues sorted out. And of course, his health issues. Dr. Howarth was concerned. The fact that he was only just recovering from a bought of pneumonia. That his immune system was so weak. He would be exposed to so much on the flights and at the airports.

It was going on five years now since I'd been home. Maddox was four and a half now. My mom had never even met him. It's something I struggled to comprehend when I took the time to think about it. *I've missed both my siblings' weddings. My mother hasn't met my son. Nor has my brother. Or my grandparents.* I never could have imagined it.

I told Dean I couldn't go any longer without seeing them. I had to go. The pull was too intense to bear any longer. The time was now.

The decision was made. We bought tickets. We were to spend Thanksgiving, Christmas, and New Year's with them. It was something to look forward to.

Even still, the dark cloud that had hovered over us for so long seemed to descend upon us now. The days were darker. Gloomier. It felt as though the presence of death itself was amongst us.

Dean had a way of putting things that made things seem better than they were.

October 3, 2009

Hey everybody,

Just wanted to say g'day and thank you all for your continued support and prayer. An update on me is everything has been great, especially seeing the fact that I am alive and well. I still have some pain and side effects from the GvHD (for those that don't what that is, it is the transplant cells that are killing off the leukemia are also partially rejecting my body and I am on medication to get that balance right until the cells fully accept my body). Graft versus host disease. I have been working a bit and keeping pretty active. I still

have an off day every now and then but, all in all, am living life pretty normal. I would like to ask you to keep praying for us and also add on prayer for our trip to the United States, which we are booked to go on November 23, which isn't far away. My immigration visa still has not come through. It is yet again another huge step of faith to overcome, but I believe the Lord is in it and is gonna shine forth once again in our lives to the glory of Him again in what seems an impossible situation. I have an immigration lawyer working on it directly and has being doing a great job hurrying it along. I don't know what the current hold-up is, but it needs to be accelerated whatever it is. We are coming over for two months and a long for a real long break that is well deserved by Cassi and the boys. I am currently also receiving a trial treatment where they inject stem cells into my blood to help the GvHD, specifically my mouth ulcers, which still plague me. Thank you again and God bless. dean

A few days before we were due to fly out, Dean and I sat in our living room drinking in the sunshine and our cups of tea. He pulled his shirt down at the neck, revealing his collarbone. "I have this pain here, sweetie. I don't know what it is, but it's really sore."

I know what that is. I could see it in his ashen complexion. I could smell it. I had been in the midst of the invisible beast long enough to recognize it.

It was back. That evil, faceless plague. I knew it was back. But there was no way I could tell Dean. It would break his heart. I couldn't tell anyone. So I endured my knowing alone. This time, it took hold. And this time, I couldn't see it letting him go. The nightmare. It went on. Third-time relapse. A death sentence, short of something completely miraculous. I could feel a tremor. Like the beginnings of an avalanche. My insides quaked as I felt the shift.

To the Place I Once Called Home

The flight over wasn't much fun. Dean was always pretty uncomfortable on airplanes, mostly because his legs were so long. It was worse now. With his body in the condition that it was, he was in agony. We landed in LA. We prepared ourselves mentally to go through immigration and customs. Hoping for the best. *This is it. It's in God's hands now.*

The boys and I went through the American citizens' line, and Dean went separately through the tourists' and foreigners' line. The boys and I went through and waited in chairs outside. Tick, tock. My eyes were swollen and heavy from the long traveling hours and lack of sleep, feeling pretty rough. The boys were playing on all the empty seats around us. They were restless from the flight. Time dragged. Everyone else from our flight had come and gone. We waited. And waited.

Eventually, someone came up to me. "Ma'am, I'm sorry, we have to hold your husband for questioning."

You've got to be fucking kidding me. Here we go again.

"All right, boys, come on. Daddy's going to come a bit later." What could I do? There's nothing I could do. Frustrated and in a haze of jet lag, I left resigned.

My dad met us at the airport, and we had our joyous reunion, dampened by Dean's absence. I was elated to be on the ground. On the drive to their house, I drank in the sights. The hills. The palm trees. The blue sky. The chaos. The traffic. The surge of a million memories. Seeing my home with new eyes. The eyes of a foreigner. A country girl. So much life had passed since the last time I was in this place. And then I remembered I always knew I would leave. And I had. I had left. And now I returned. And I was different.

We got to my dad's house. Jubilance. *Oh my gosh, I'm actually here. I'm in Southern California. Wow. It feels like a lifetime.* Things had changed. My little brother who was only fifteen when I left was now twenty, married, and heading into the Air Force. My little sister, Naomi, was now pregnant with her second child. I was meeting her husband, Mark, for the first time. My siblings were grown up. That was surreal.

Immigration held Dean for about twelve hours. They didn't let him take his meds, which is really dangerous. When you're on drugs like steroids, you can't just not take them. Your body chemistry goes completely out of whack, and you can actually die. Dean took a taxi from the airport to my dad's house in Temecula. The taxi driver got lost. It took hours for him to get home. When he finally did, he was beside himself. Irate and exhausted.

"I got so frustrated that I was ready to charge at one of the security guards and take a bullet." Thoughts like that would have come from not having his meds.

After hours of looking into it, they found Dean had actually been granted his American visa. The one I had applied for four and a half years earlier. It had been approved six months after I applied for it. Apparently, it had been lost in the mail.

All these years . . . We could have come back . . . All these years, I haven't even come to visit my family . . .

It was time we would never get back.

Thanksgiving was a perfect reunion. We were all overjoyed. For them to see us and us them. For them to see Dean and hug him after so many years of our e-mails and updates. Oh to be home! Among my family again. My grandparents and parents and sisters and brothers celebrating and feasting together. It was an exciting time of celebration for all of us. The California weather lived up to its reputation. We had plenty of sun. I hugged and kissed my siblings over and over. I clung to them. Sat on them. Kissed them more. I got to hold my grandma's hand. I got to look into their eyes. Blessed in bliss.

Dean was so happy to be there. He had always loved the States. Even though he couldn't do much, he was bound in wonderment. That darkness though. That dark power was still working its way through Dean's body. Causing him pain. He was on the couch a lot of the time we were there. His ankle was very sore. The pain worsened. Daily.

A couple of weeks after Thanksgiving, Dean and I were crawling into bed. My parents had done up a lovely guest room for us. He was taking another lot of pain pills. We were way beyond following instructions on a bottle.

"I'm just going to keep taking 'em, sweetie. It's just too much." I looked over at him in the dim light, and I watched as he filled his palm with pills and threw them into the back of his throat. We got settled into bed. The silence punctuating the uncertainty hanging in the air.

"You're just going to have to keep going with the boys, and I'll fit in where I can."

I could hear it raining outside. Like the sky was crying the tears I couldn't at that moment. And then I knew. Then I knew for sure. I don't know how I knew. I can't explain it. I just knew. The way you know winter is coming. There's no stopping it. No slowing it. The cold will steadily approach. The trees will be barren. The darkness will encompass. *He's going. I'm going to have to go on without him. Oh my Lord. My God.* The anxiety in my chest tightened like a vice grip. The avalanche was getting closer. The tremors, stronger.

I went to Doug's house. I had to drop something off. He lived just next door. Doug is one of the most kind, jubilant, and generous of men I've known. We got to talking. He loved talking about the things of God. As though he were aware of the uncertainty that swelled and swarmed my heart, he smiled at me with radiant confidence and said, "Yeah, because we can trust Him."

The words pierced through the doubt clouds in my heart, letting in the light. Tears welled. *Jesus. I can trust you. But if feels like my whole world is falling apart.*

January. Time to go home. The journey was horrendous. Dean was no longer able to put on a brave face with the pain. His temper was explosive.

The next six months of my life were a living hell.

THE PRECIPICE

We saw Dr. Howarth. He was trying to surmise the reason behind Dean's worsening ailments and pain. He was thinking it was the GvHD. We were all hoping it was GvHD. Better that than the filthy demonic other. I listened to them talk. I knew it wasn't the GvHD. I knew. But I couldn't say anything. I didn't have the heart. I didn't want to be the one to say it. It was too horrible. Too awful. And so they upped his immunosuppressants. Increased them dramatically. Unfortunately, there was nothing left of Dean's immune system to fight the cancer now. And so it spread like wildfire.

Daily, I witnessed the slow, torturous, violent murder of my husband. His collarbone. His knee. His ankle. He was in excruciating pain. Dr. Howarth started doing cortisone injections. Two a day. Morning and evening. The injections left black bruises. He was covered in them. On top of that, he was on over 110 milligrams of Oxycontin a day. That's enough to kill a normal person. Still, that savage rabid dog called Pain would not be subdued.

February 2010

Hello all my beautiful friends and family!

It is time to write another update from the Mack family. We got back to Esperance about ten days ago after spending an amazing nine

weeks in the States visiting family and friends. I thank the Lord for that awesome time. What a blessing!

My reason for writing is Dean has been rather unwell for the last couple of months and is suffering agonizing pain on a daily basis. The pain goes to different parts of his body, from his ankle, to shoulder, to elbow, to rib, and so forth. We got some crutches for him at the hospital today because he was unable to walk with the pain in his ankle. We have been in to see the doc, and at this stage, we don't know what the cause of the pain is.

I want to thank you for so faithfully praying for Dean and our family. Today, the Lord was speaking to me about being in the eye of the storm, safe in his arms. And he brought me to the scripture. "Do not let your heart be troubled, nor let it be afraid." I rejoice in the faithfulness of God and His companionship. And I am beginning to see that partaking in the sufferings of Christ really does bring us closer to Him. The Lord has given me renewed strength, and I believe He has done the same for Dean, as much as he is suffering. As helpless as Dean and I and the boys may feel against this enemy, I thank God for the courage to stand against it in Jesus's name.

Blessings to you all,

Cassi

Dean's belligerent shouting boomed regularly. Anything would set him off. The boys and I would cower to other areas of the house. Nausea ate a hole in me while Anxiety seized my heart and throat. The stress. If a toy were left on the floor as he crossed the room, he would kick it against the wall as hard as he could. And shout. If I made the slightest mistake, he would ream me. I bought the wrong food. Or put things in the wrong place. Or didn't do this right or that. He would shout into my face. It was more than I could bear. Crushed. I couldn't do anything right. My strength depleted. We were careening toward an apex. I could feel it. Tremors. Quakes. The thunder of an approaching avalanche. The vice grip cranked tighter. Little by little. Anguish. Oppressive pain. Uncertainty.

The doctors wanted to run tests to see what was going on with Dean. I knew. I knew it was the cancer. *Get him to Perth, dammit.*

Dean was so brave. When people would ring to see how he was going, he'd say, "Oh yeah, not doing too bad. Thanks, mate. You know, I'm alive and well, so I'm grateful for that."

I wanted to grab that phone from him and yell to that person, "WE'RE IN FUCKING MISERABLE HELL!"

He'd have a laugh and a chat. And then it was back to our reality. A reality where Dean was ferocious. And mean. And unkind. Brash and hurtful. And no one knew what we were going through. No one understood. There was no fixing this. There was no changing it. It wasn't his fault. He didn't mean to act that way. He couldn't help it. We were reaching a precipice. A ledge. A cliff. A fall. Destruction. And the reality was Dean and I were going through such different things. He was dealing with pain and the idea of death and leaving his family. And I was watching him suffer. And it was killing me. *God, I can't watch it anymore. Heal him or take him home. I can't live like this anymore. This isn't life. It's not life for Dean. Or me. Or the boys. We can't go on like this. God, have mercy. Mercy!*

I went for my daily walk to my ocean refuge with God. *God, my heart isn't even here. I don't know where it is. It's not with the boys. It's not with Dean. It's somewhere adrift at sea perhaps. In search of a better life.*

WHAT ARE YOU GOING TO CHOOSE? YOU HAVE A CHOICE. LIKE ESAU HAD A CHOICE. ESAU CHOSE TO FORFEIT HIS INHERITANCE. HE CHOSE THE BOWL OF SOUP. YOU CAN FORFEIT YOUR INHERITANCE FOR RELIEF IN THIS MOMENT.

OR YOU CAN PERSEVERE THROUGH IT AND RECEIVE WHAT'S
IN STORE.

I collapsed in heaving sobs. *I don't want to be like Esau. I don't want the bowl of soup. I don't want to lose my inheritance. I want what you have for me. God, help me. Change my heart. Put my heart with my family. Make me want to stay. Change me, Lord. Change me.*

I went to church that week. Burdened. Heavy. Broken. During worship, I fell to my knees. All I could do was weep. I travailed with writhing sobs. Face in the carpet. Sobs violently squeezed my rib cage. Agony clutched my stomach as pain strangled me. My nose was running over my face and the carpet, which was drenched in my tears and slobber. I didn't care. The claw of anguish had its jagged claws deeply clenched in my heart. *I can't imagine not being broken. I can't imagine I could ever be whole again. God, I know you can do anything, but I can't fathom that this anguish could ever end.* My chest heaved as my insides shook like a bag full of broken glass.

God, if you don't want me to be a broken shell of a woman the rest of my life, you better do something about it.

WEEPING MAY LAST THROUGH THE NIGHT, BUT JOY COMES
WITH THE MORNING.

The darkness closed in.

Broken. Pain. Torturing pain. Unrelenting. Death. *Death is coming. Death is here. There's no escape. There's nothing I can do.* Pain. Anguish. Broken.

I called my parents.

"Daddy, it's too much. I can't do it anymore. I can't take it." I didn't bother trying to fight back the tears. They knew I was at breaking point. My dad said he would fly Ginny out to come help whenever I needed her. I knew it would be soon.

Doc ordered some tests. They were doing a blood count to see if Dean had relapsed. I was at our friend's house for dinner. Dean was going to catch up with me after he met up with the doc. *Answers. We will finally get some answers.*

I was at the kitchen bench chatting when he walked upstairs. He looked at me. We locked eyes, and he walked over to me. He pulled me into a strong embrace and whispered into my ear. "It's the cancer. It's back." He was shaking. I was shaking. We held onto each other desperately. As though an F5 tornado threatened to tear us apart. The avalanche. It began.

We stood and cried into each other's shoulders. *Oh, my love. My precious love. My beautiful sweet husband. I knew it. Oh God, I knew it. Oh, my Lord. Oh, Lord. Oh, honey. My poor sweetie. This is it. I know this is it. I know this can't go on.*

"I feel like I'm in a sinking boat, and I'm all alone," he whispered to me. He knew. He knew this was it. This is the end of the road.

Oh, darling! I know, I know, I know. Oh, honey, I know. It's not fair. I'm so sorry! I wish I could do something! I'm here, sweetie, I'm here. Lord! Why, Lord, oh why!

Preparation Continues: Swearing and Honesty

Back up to Perth. We had to fly. I was starting to get really bad with flying. I would just come undone. My blood would run cold. It felt like ice in my veins. Fear and Panic gripped me. I didn't like any of it. I didn't like where we were going. I didn't like what we were having to do. I hated leaving my kids behind. I hated what was happening to Dean. And I had no control. I had no control over any of it.

We got to Perth, and they started Dean on chemo. Ginny flew over to be with me. I was beyond grateful for her help and presence. Someone to vent to. Talk to. About nothing and everything. Cry to. Have fun with. She kept me sane when I was on the verge of going over.

My whole body came out of rhythm. I couldn't sleep. Couldn't eat. My appetite was gone. My body hurt all over. Aches. Pains. Crying spells. Bursts of laughter. Loud sighing. Extremes. Lots of extremes. And swearing. I hadn't been a big swearer, pretty much ever. But those swear words started to fly. Loud and clear. I wasn't holding back either. It was the only language I could find that described how I felt. And what I thought.

I was listening to worship music one night as I drove up to the hospital. Singing. Praising God. One hand in the air. All of a sudden, I was completely overwhelmed. Caught up in this jubilant praise. Joy. Joy came over me. It surrounded and filled me. A smile took over my face. And I saw it all so clearly. *We win. Either way, we win. We have the victory. If Dean gets cured of this cancer, then praise God! We win! If Dean goes to be with the Lord, then praise God, we win! We know exactly where he is going. After all, isn't that the first peace and certainty we get as Christians? That we know we have the hope of eternity. The victory is ours! We can't lose!* Tears of joy were streaming down my face. I continued to sing through my laughter. I was worshiping God! I was so full of elation and joy that I could hardly concentrate on driving.

The doctors came in the mornings. They had Dean on their "light" chemo. They gave it over the course of a few days. The side effects came but weren't extreme. I felt like they were giving us rhetoric. *I know this disease. I've read about it. I've seen it. I've smelled it. I've lived with it. I've watched it come. I've watched it go. I've been through two relapses and a bone marrow transplant. I know this disease gets harder to cure every time. Now, at relapse number three, they are giving him some light chemo? For what? Who are they kidding? Are they trying to buy him time? Are they trying to give us false hope?* I went along with it to start with. A day after the chemo finished, his collarbone became hugely inflamed. *It's already back. I knew it. I knew this was going to accomplish nothing.*

I caught the doctors before they came into Dean's room and spoke to them in the hallway.

"Please don't give us false hope. I need you guys to be real with me. I know once you've hit three relapses, chemo isn't going to help. I'd like the truth. Tell me if I'm wrong, but I feel like I'm going to have to say goodbye to my husband."

They couldn't look me in the eye. Just nodded and said, "Yeah, okay. You're right."

They found the leukemia had spread through Dean's entire body. It was in his organs. His bones. It had actually broken his ankle. They couldn't believe it. They thought Dean must have had an accident or an injury. No. The cancer was literally eating away his bones.

I knew I had to try to talk to Dean. About him actually dying. It was so hard. Because it wasn't hypothetical. This is real life. In real time. This was happening now. But how? How do I open my mouth and say everything I'm thinking and feeling to him? How do I be that honest? I had a muzzle of manners and sweetness. I didn't want to hurt Dean. Or upset him. But the pressure was mounting, and my words, like a geyser, were demanding release.

The boys were still in Esperance getting looked after. Dean's parents and some other families had put their hands up to help look after them while I was in Perth. I hated being away from them.

I was staying with one of Dean's younger cousins who was going to Bible school and her roommate. My days were spent at the hospital with Dean and my nights there. Every time I turned on the TV, there was a funeral or a widow. Every time. I knew. I just knew. I was being prepared. Prepared to stand with my boys and bury Dean's body. And somehow carry on afterward.

While Dean and I were in Perth, people volunteered to move our house. They put all our things into boxes and into Dave and Sue's garage. I had no home. I had no idea what the future held. Except one thing. Dean was going to die. That's the only thing I knew.

I could see my life like a beautiful dollhouse. Hanging by a thread. And I held my breath. Because any moment now, that thread would break. And my beautiful dollhouse. My life. My family. Everything. Was going to shatter into a million pieces.

I sat in Dean's hospital room. *I hate this place. I hate the smell. I can't wait till I never have to come back here again.* My disdain for the hospital grew exponentially each day. I stared numbly out the window. Dean was sitting up in bed watching TV.

My husband, oh my love. Things between us were getting tense. I felt I was being prepared for him to go. I think he knew it too. He just couldn't accept it. And even if you do know you're going to die, your will to live doesn't disappear. I didn't know if he felt like I was giving up on him. I couldn't change what I felt I knew. It's the only thing I knew. I hardly knew a thing except Dean was going. And God would help me to carry on afterward.

I walked over to Dean and sat down on the bed beside him. I leaned over and lay my head across his chest. My head resting on his heart. I was surviving. Pushing through. Battling on. Keeping it together as much as I could. I spent so much energy just trying to hold it together. So I let it out. My heart was bursting at the seams with unshed tears. I cried over him. My tears pouring onto his chest and running down his ribs onto the sheets. He placed his hand on my head and gently stroked my hair. *My love, my love. How am I going to live without you? Oh my love, my darling. My heart. How can a heart break this many times and still beat?* The tears poured.

I sat up and tried to dry my face. I looked into those blue eyes. Suddenly, sitting there in the bed. Bald and frail and sickly. He was transformed before my eyes. And I was looking at the Dean I married. On our wedding day. In his tux. With his long hair and dark olive skin. Radiant with joy and life. Youth and love. So handsome and carefree. Unaffected by the sands of time. By the dark shadow of pale death. He sat before me as if not one day had passed since we said our vows.

Tears in his eyes, he said, "You brought me so much joy, Cassi."

I smiled. "You changed my whole life." My heart swelled and squeezed as more tears fell.

We held our breath and our gaze. With tears full of love running down our cheeks. We completely understood each other. And we felt it. Hearts that didn't want to say goodbye. Hearts that wanted more laughs. More adventures. More memories. More time.

Time acknowledged the importance and halted for us at that moment.

Praise God. He knows how much I love him.

THE MAN IN THE
WHITE COAT

Dean's liver counts were getting exponentially worse every day. It was failing. They told us he would most likely slip into a coma in a week or so.

They sent the palliative care doctors in to see us. An older man walked in. He had stark white hair and wore a white coat. He was composed. His demeanor was gentle, and his face was kind. His eyes, wise. A middle-aged man was with him as well as some younger people who were students or something. Ginny was sitting next to me on the bed. Karen was in a chair next to the recliner Dean was in. The man looked at Dean. "Now is the time, Dean. This coming week is important. Think about the legacy you want to leave behind. Write the letters you want to write. Make the calls you want to make."

Dean had turned his head the other way and was looking out the window. Completely tuning out what the man was saying. I was silently pleading.

Dean! I'm begging you, please listen! You don't have much time! Listen to the man! I started sobbing. Because he wasn't. He didn't want to have that conversation.

Dean said something about being healed and getting a miracle. The man gave a thoughtful expression. "I've seen many people through the door to the other side. I have never been through that door. I have seen many people of faith go through that door. People who were waiting for miracles. People who thought God would heal them." His tone was sensitive. He was trying to open Dean's eyes. I continued to weep loudly. *Dean. Please listen, Dean.*

The old man looked up at me and then walked over. He stood beside the bed. Looked into my face. I tried to dry my face and compose myself a bit so that I could hear what he wanted to say to me.

"I'm getting this funny feeling," he said to me with a peculiar expression and paused. "I don't usually get this feeling." Hesitation. "My wife's first husband died of a brain tumor. He was thirty-five. She was left with two sons. They have grown into strong, successful men. You have boys. They are young. You will keep the memory of their father alive. And they are going to do well."

I was crying soft sobs, hanging on to every word. I felt like God Himself was speaking to me.

"Come here," he said. I got up from the bed and stood in front of him. He embraced me. And spoke. "The Lord bless you and keep you; the Lord make His face shine on you and be gracious to you; the Lord turn His face toward you and give you peace."

I sobbed into his soft white coat. I felt his compassion for me. His arms held me tightly. It felt like the Lord Himself. He knew. He knew what I was going to have to do. And so did I. His words were preparing me. He was imparting strength.

He looked back at Dean. "You need to speak with your wife. Tell her you release her to fall in love and get married again. Cassi, whether you plan to stay in Australia or go back to the States, you should talk about that too. We'll leave you to do that now."

And everyone left the room.

We were alone.

Finally. Finally, we could talk. We could have the conversation we have been avoiding for so long. I longed for it. I longed for the honesty. To say the words that gnawed away at my throat.

I sat beside Dean on the bed. We were both quiet for a few minutes.

After a while, Dean spoke, "If you want to move back to the States, if that's where you think you and the boys will find happiness, then you should do that. And, of course, if you meet someone, I release you to get married."

Thank you, God, we are having this conversation.

"But is it just me, or am I going to be around a lot longer than everybody thinks I am?" He gave me that boyish grin. *Oh honey, I wish that were true. Can't you see you aren't staying here, honey? You're going. You have to go, and I have to stay. I'm so sorry. I'm sorry. You can't stay. I'm so sorry, my love.* I wanted to find the courage to say the words aloud, but I could not.

The hospital chaplain came in. I had grown quite fond of this one over the last number of weeks. She took me aside so we could talk. I explained a huge relief swept over me when they told me Dean only had a week to live. And I felt awful for being so relieved. As though I wanted him to die. I just wanted it to all be over. The suffering. The almost dying and not dying. The pain. The struggle. The awful uncertainty. The yelling. The watching it happen. The living in the shadow of death.

"People can only take so much uncertainty," she said to me with kind strength and knowing eyes. "At some point, you have to know one way or the other so you can move forward." She was one of the few who understood me. Who understood my love for Dean but my inability to go on.

I hugged her and cried into her hair.

A Time to Die

They flew Dean to Esperance the next day. I drove. Ginny was with me, and my dad was on his way. One week. They said at the rate his liver was failing, he probably had about a week before he would slip into unconsciousness.

The avalanche gained momentum.

Something amazing happened to Dean in those last weeks. It started before we left the hospital. He'd been so angry. So belligerent. So hard to live with. And then, a sudden change. He was come over with this incredible sweetness. A gentle kindness. An almost angelic disposition. You could be in the same room as him, looking at the same thing, but the look in his eyes was magic. Otherworldly. He was on another plane. Seeing things differently. With childlike joy and appreciation. One of the cleaners at the hospital came in. A middle-aged Asian woman who wore a fake frangipani clip in her hair. Dean looked at her as though she were the most magical thing he had ever seen. And he told her so. Others. The people he spoke to. Encountered. He made such an impact. Telling them about Jesus. Inspiring them to fulfill their destiny. As though heaven had opened over him, ready to receive him. And he already shone with its luster.

We stayed with Dean's parents. Our things in boxes in their garage. I kept having that feeling in my chest. The one you get when you go down a big drop in a roller coaster. Your heart skips a beat. Pause. Then BOOM. Heart goes THUMP. Then a rush of adrenaline. I was holding onto Jesus so tightly, but the walls were closing in. The ground was shaking. I was at the edge of a cliff. Any moment, I was going over.

The first night we were back in Esperance, Dean and I went to bed together. He wrapped his arms around me. "I love you," he said, as though it may be the last time I'd ever hear him say it.

"I love you too," I said with the same tone. We squeezed together tightly. *Hopefully, I'll wake up, and he'll be cold. Wait, what? How can I want that? But I do. It's going to happen. There's nothing I can do. What kind of wife wants her husband to die? But I don't want him to die. I want him to live. I want him to live, but he's going to die. He's going to die.* My heart squeezed with Anguish and tormenting thoughts. Guilt and unrelenting sorrow. Tears poured out of my eyes. *When will I ever stop crying? Will my tears ever dry? I don't want to be sad anymore. I'm so tired of being sad.*

In the middle of the night, I heard Dean get up to go to the toilet. He clamored around, getting his crutches, and made his way down the hallway. I was listening for him to make sure he got there and back okay. CRASH. *Oh no.* I jumped out of bed and raced down the hall into the toilet where I found him on the floor. He was laying on the floor in his boxers. His tall gaunt frame barely fitting into the water closet. He was still holding onto his crutches that lay on either side of him. He'd fallen backward. His legs were bent and sprawled out on either side of the toilet. His head and shoulders were up against the back wall. His breathing was very labored. *Oh, my Lord.* I got down on the ground. The light was fluorescent and obnoxious. The tiles were frigid. His breathing was so loud and labored. He looked at me with eyes that were falling in slow motion. He was gasping. He took a few deep breaths and then exhaled and completely slumped over.

Lifeless.

Still.

Oh, my Lord. This is it. I'm saying good bye to my love. All I could think to do was hold him. So I wrapped my arms around him. Held him tightly.

Suddenly, his eyes flew open, and he took another loud, heaving gasp. He gave a few breaths and then. Completely slumped over again.

This is it. Oh my Lord, this is it.

I sat there holding him, trying to be of some comfort. Holding his head. Kissing his face. I was somewhat awkwardly bent over him. Trying to give him affection. But it kept going. Minute after minute. In what felt like eons. *Okay, maybe this isn't it.*

I got up and ran to get Ginny to help. She came in, and we managed to get the crutches out. Between the two of us, we gently pulled him out the toilet and into the hallway. Dean was on his stomach at this point. He was just too big and heavy for us to try to carry. Even thirty pounds underweight. He kept giving his heaving, labored gasps. We helped him slide along the hallway as he did an army crawl. Moving only a few inches with each pull as he was only using his arms. My eyes filled with tears. Awful. My darling to come to this. Unable to walk. Hardly breathing. Yet his determination shining forth. With each heave across the floor. Each drag, I heard his raspy voice saying, "God is good. God is good." Gasp. "God is good."

I don't know how long it took us to get him back to bed. Close to half an hour.

I tried to mentally prepare myself for a week of this torture.

But it wasn't a week. It was three and a half weeks. The longest. Most agonizing. Dreadful. Unbearable. Three and a half weeks of my life. Every moment was hanging at the edge of a cliff face. So high I couldn't see the bottom. Where my feet were not standing on the ground. But dangling. Toes barely scraping the dirt beneath me. And any moment, whatever it was that was holding me up, was going to let me go. And all that awaited me was a big, terrifying fall. And a whole lot of pain—if I survived. I nearly went insane. And I was going into that last stretch of agony as a woman battered. Bruised. At the end of her rope. Emotionally bankrupt. Physically distraught. Spiritually crumbling.

The first week went better than I thought. We actually laughed some. We tried to enjoy each other. Knowing this was goodbye. To end on a high. We got Dean outside as much as we could. We managed to coax him into a wheelchair and walk him out to the foreshore.

"So many memories," I heard him say under his breath. You could see them dance in his eyes as he gazed on the Esperance horizon. The backdrop of his childhood. Looking back on the many adventures. The stories he had once told me of. Fishing for squid at the jetty. Surfing in the bay. Practical jokes and pranks with his mates. The camping. Worship nights. The crazy motorbike stunts. His eyes lost in the bliss of savoring their aroma and aftertaste.

The second week, things turned.

To cope with the crushing emotional burden that I felt as physical pain, I walked. I walked for hours. Along the beach, by myself. I would walk. And walk. And walk. Thinking. Not thinking. Trying to process. Trying to plan. Trying to look ahead. Trying to get a glimpse of what my future held. Something to grab hold of. Something to hope for. I would try to imagine myself happy. The boys and I living in a cozy home somewhere. With a new life. A new home. A promised land . . . awaiting me somewhere. Far away from hospitals and poison. From silent illnesses that crush your family members and steal them away.

At night, I would crawl into bed next to Dean again. We would say our I love yous again. Pray that the torment would end. That he would be gone in the morning . . . but I would wake up and he would still be warm. And it was so disappointing. The idea of another day of torture. For all of us.

The incontinence came. Most mornings, I would wake up in a pool of Dean's urine.

He was so stubborn. About almost everything. In some ways, it was admirable. In others, deplorable. He was so unsteady on his feet. We wanted him to relent to getting a wheel chair for getting around the house as well as the long walks. He would hear none of it. So we had to deal with his falls, which were frightening and traumatizing for all of us.

During the day, I spent little bits of time with Dean, but it was becoming more than I could bear. Most of the time, he was out of it. His mind, fogged by the toxins in his blood, clouded his thinking. He would say bizarre things. Lost in a haze. Mostly unaware of what was going on around him.

And then, out of nowhere, moments of perfect clarity. He would look into my eyes. A frozen moment in time. Where we each saw each other. Felt each other. Knowing we were being torn apart.

Knowing there was nothing we could do. My life hung in the balance. I kept seeing my life, the dollhouse. Hanging by that thread. The fibers, unraveling. Getting thinner. And thinner. That little house was going to smash into a million pieces. At. Any. Moment.

They were giving him drugs to keep him alive. To prop up his failing systems. And what was offered to me to keep me going? Dean could not keep going on his own, yet somehow, I was supposed to? What dark elixir could strengthen my failing heart? My failing systems? The process was being dragged out far longer than it should have been. And to what gain?

I needed a plan. I wanted to pack boxes. I wanted to organize air tickets. One day, very soon, Dean would no longer be on this earth. And somehow, I was going to have to carry on. With my boys. For my boys. Somehow I was going to have to stand next to my boys and bury the body of their father. My lover. My best friend. And then keep going on this journey. Alone. So alone. No one understood how I felt. What I was going through. The focus was all on Dean. Trying to keep him alive. Believing he would somehow keep living. Why would anyone want him to keep living? His body was bruised and broken and crushed from top to bottom. He was living in excruciating pain. He couldn't do any of the things he loved to do. And the boys and I were trapped. Forced to watch. In slow, helpless agony. I couldn't watch it anymore. My boys couldn't live under the shadow of death anymore. It had to end. It was going to drive me insane. People looked at me as if I had given up on him. As if I'd deserted him. As if I'd hardened my heart and no longer cared about him. How could they know? How could they know what I felt? Thought? My desperate struggle to keep my head above the rising tide of grief. The excruciating sorrow that threatened to swallow me whole.

One day, I went for a drive. Had to get out of the house. Away from everyone. Everyone's opinions. Judging eyes. Prying thoughts. Unrealistic expectations. Silent demands. I sought solace along the tourist loop. The breathtaking drive Dean had taken me on all those years ago. When he had brought me to this incredible place. I needed to be alone. I needed space. Everything was out of control. A collision course that couldn't be stopped or fast forwarded. I drove. The sun was shining. Agony gripped. I cried. Cried out to God. *Lord. Lord. Oh, my Lord.* The tears flowed endlessly as I rounded each bend. The islands. The beautiful water. The glorious sky. The place where Dean nearly proposed. My inner turmoil bubbling over. Erupting from the deepest wells of my breaking heart. My heart. Needing hope. So needing something. To cling to. To hang onto. *God, I need you. Jesus, I need you.*

And then, everything slowed down.

I looked into the sky. I could see Dean. Standing on a rock. Young. Strong. Healthy. Larger than life. With his long hair. As he had been. He was running, jumping, exploring. In this beautiful place. Completely restored. Completely renewed.

And I could see God taking me back to America to be close to my family that I had missed for so long. He was setting us free. He was setting us all free. Dean would be freed. Free to live without limits. Free to do the things he loved. And I would be free to leave Australia. To make a life for myself and the boys. Elation swept over me. Deep joy started to bubble up. I started laughing. *God, you're so amazing! Lord, you're so faithful! God, you're so good! Wow! Lord, you are so amazing!* I was driving and smiling and overwhelmed. The heavens opened to me. All I could do was laugh and praise God. I was now looking at the islands and the sea and the sky, not with grief but hope. He gave me a glimpse. A glimpse of the awesome things to come.

I could see it all so clearly. *I know where he's going. I know he's going to be restored. I know he's going to a place infinitely better. With no more pain. NO more pain.*

Other people were trying to keep him here. Not me. *You have to go, Dean. I'm sorry, honey. You have to go. Let go. God is going to look after us. I know you want to. I wish you could. But you can't. You have to let us go. We're going to be okay.* I spoke to him in my heart. Reassuring him in my thoughts.

A friend of mine came to visit me at the house one day. Belle. She had actually come and lived with Dean and me a year or two before. She was one of the few who really knew. Who really knew what it was like for me. I adored her. She had two children but was only about twenty. She's one of those people who's easy to be around and be real with. She was no stranger to hardship. It had made her genuine. And tough. With a wonderful sense of humor. We chatted and arranged to meet the following day.

We met for lunch at a little place in town. I was eager to get out of the house of pain. She was a breath of fresh air. So many other people were such hard work to be around. They knew Dean was dying, and they would come in with such heaviness. Belinda wasn't like that. We chatted and giggled like schoolgirls. We told jokes and laughed about old memories.

"I want to buy you a new dress," she said with a big smile. *Shopping? Um, yes please!* It amazed me how she knew exactly what I needed. I didn't need a counseling session or a prayer meeting or a book or this or that. I needed a nice lunch, a good laugh, and a pretty new dress. I silently praised God that I was blessed to have such an amazing friend. We went to the dress shop. I felt like a woman for the first time in forever. I actually had fun. I tried on different dresses and shoes and jewelry. She bought me a dress, as promised, as well as a new pair of shoes and a necklace. I felt spoiled. Fresh wind beneath my wings. She was light in my awful darkness. And I wondered if she truly knew what it meant to me.

As the days wore on, the tensions mounted. Tensions between family members. The mounting pressure we were all feeling in our own hearts. Stretched to capacity. Stretched beyond measure. We all had different ways of dealing with our pain. We all had expectations of each other. Expectations we didn't realize we had. I wanted to be understood. I wanted everyone to understand I'd been watching this happen in slow motion for almost five years. Living with it. Every step. Of the way. *I'm weary. I'm at the end of my tether. I need grace. I need love. I need to just be accepted for wherever I'm at. I've slept on hospital floors. I've wept over this man's body countless times. I've massaged him, bathed him, comforted him, listened to him, fed him, cared for him. Everything I've had to give, I've given to this man. I have lived far away from my family for years. I've been grieving. Praying. Seeking. Following. Persevering. And walking. In this desert for so long. I can't remember what it's like to not be in the desert. It's all I know. And I'm so tired. I'm just so tired.* It was all I could do to just get up in the morning. To just cling to my sanity. A bit like Moses, when his arms were getting tired. My strength was depleted. It was only the Lord who could bring me through now. *I'm done.*

He was turning yellow. Bright alien yellow. The whites of his eyes were fluorescent yellow. He was completely bald with no eyelashes or eyebrows. In the last two months, he'd aged decades. Maddox asked Dean why he was turning yellow. He couldn't bring himself to answer. I was desperately hoping Dean and I would get to sit down with the boys. Tell them what was happening. I tried to be as honest as I could with the boys about what was going on. I wanted to talk to them before Dean passed away to try to prepare them for what was coming. It became obvious though. Dean's will to survive and his desire to stay made it impossible for him to accept he was actually dying. The idea of leaving us was too painful to contemplate. It was a conversation he couldn't bring himself to have. I would have to have it on my own.

I had spoken to the boys about heaven since they were babies. We had studied what the scripture says, read children's stories, and had many talks about it. Heaven is a very real place to them. I felt they would cope with Dean's death much better if they knew it was coming. I took them in one of the back bedrooms of the house, and we sat on the floor.

"Boys, we're going through a hard time right now, aren't we?"

They nodded.

The lump in my throat felt like a melon. I tried to keep my voice from quivering. "Daddy's been sick for a really long time, huh? You know how his eyes are yellow now?" *Oh God, help me do this.* "Well, Daddy is even sicker than before, and he's going to go to heaven very soon."

Maddox burst out crying. "I don't want Daddy to go to heaven!" He crawled in my lap. Asher was more reserved. He had more of a delayed and complicated reaction. Much like myself. I understood that. He was processing. I hugged them both. I was satisfied knowing at least now they could brace themselves for what was coming.

One day, I walked outside. Dean was in the shed, on his crutches, having a look at something. He looked up at me. Eyes like the most brilliant blue sky you'd ever seen. They shone at me. And he smiled at me with the sweetest, boyish grin. My heart sank deeper into the abyss of pain it was in. *You've been such a monster to live with. You've been so mean. And now, right at the end, you're an angel. Why do you have to go? You're leaving me. How am I going to say goodbye to you? Oh, babe . . .*

The idea of him leaving was easier when he was being angry and impossible. But this . . .

"Penny for your thoughts?" he said to me. Eyes like beacons, illuminating my heart.

I motioned to the car so we could speak in private. We never got any time alone. We were always surrounded by people.

I got in the driver's seat. He shuffled into the passenger seat, leaving the crutches up against the outside of the car. *It's time to be honest.* The words gnawed at my throat.

He looked at me with such sincerity and love. "Honey, I'm praying for a miracle. Will you believe for that with me?"

I wanted to say yes. To enter this place where the invisible monster is defeated forever, and we live happily ever after. But I couldn't. What I knew in my heart was I had to say goodbye. And I couldn't understand it. I didn't want to. But it was the only thing I knew.

I paused. "Sweetie, we've been praying for a miracle for four and a half years. I'm sorry, but I really feel like the Lord is going to take you home." My voice broke and tears fell. "I'm going to have to say goodbye to you and somehow carry on with the boys." My heart's vice grip cranked tighter.

He listened carefully. Nodded. His expression was understanding. Calm. "I have peace about what you said."

I grabbed his hand. We looked into each other's eyes. With love. With pain. With longing. Feeling powerful and powerless at the same time. He was the boat, going off into the horizon. I could still see him now, but these were fleeting glimpses. Stolen moments, haunted by the knowledge of imminent absence making them evaporate more quickly. Like the last sands in the hour glass that seem to run through with a quickening pace.

"I'm going to miss you so much . . ." I said as I squeezed his hand against my mouth. I could see understanding in his eyes. *Thank you, Jesus. Thank you that I can actually say what I think and feel.*

"Against all the odds, we stayed married. Most couples can't survive what we've been through. That's a miracle." We laughed at how true that was and we both felt a strong victory in being able to navigate such troubled waters and make it to the end holding hands.

We lingered in the car a little longer. I was hesitant to get out. These moments alone were so few and far between. By the time we got out, I felt relief sweep over me. *He knows I love him. He knows I don't want him to go. But he knows I know he's leaving. Thank you, God.*

Things were unravelling faster and faster. The boys and I moved out to the farmhouse. The place I had once loved. Hugged by paddocks and gravel. Traversed by cows, dogs, birds, and kangaroos. Lined with horizon in all directions. Dean stayed at his parents. I don't remember why this happened. It's a blur. I wanted it to be the four of us. I wanted it to be Dean and me and the boys at the farm together those last days. Maybe I didn't communicate it well enough. Maybe I should have fought harder for that. It was frustrating for everyone. We were watching a family member die. We took our frustration out on each other. I suppose that's normal. We all had so many thoughts, emotions, and opinions. I don't think we knew how to verbalize them or work them through together. Dean's family had theirs. I had mine. Thank God my parents were there. I needed them more than ever. We just kept trying to see the days through. Putting one foot in front of the other. Doing meals. Day to day life . . . waiting. Waiting for Dean to die. That's really what we were waiting for.

One night, he had quite a temperature. His liver was not functioning at all now. He was sweating and obviously very unwell. The doctor came to visit and said Dean was trying to fight something off. He asked us if we wanted antibiotics or something to give to him. I was so frustrated. Here we are waiting for the Lord to take Dean home and people are still trying to keep him alive. *STOP. STOP IT.*

"No. Don't give him any medicine." *What don't these people understand? WE HAVE TO LET HIM GO!* Why would you want to keep someone alive in that state? To me, it seemed selfish. *This isn't life. It's not even Dean. He isn't even himself.* He was already on that many different medications that he wasn't himself. There's a time to be born and a time to die. This was Dean's time. I was becoming increasingly annoyed with anyone who was trying to interfere with that process.

The next day, Dean was up and perky. *Oh my Lord, will this never end?*

My anxiety issues were intensifying. I could hardly eat. I was so overwrought with it that I was nauseous all the time. My long walks by the ocean brought me some consolation. Talking to God. Away from everything. Everyone. They were stolen moments out of the pressure cooker. I sought relief in the breeze. The salt air. My rhythmic steps. Crying. Numbness. Breathing. Walking. Trying. To. Keep. Going.

In the evenings, I would drown my sorrowful heart in a scalding hot bath. When it's hot enough, it gives you an adrenaline rush. Followed by a sense of calm. The beat of my heart would soften and steady. I would almost feel a sense of peace. And I could try to pretend. Pretend like my life wasn't about to shatter into a thousand pieces.

The nurse came in for her routine morning visit. It was June 16, 2010.

"Cassi, Dean is living without a liver. There's no reason he should be alive right now. You have to tell him to go. You have to tell him it's okay. You have to tell him you and the boys are going to be all right." She looked at me with serious and concerned eyes. She was forward. And I loved her for it.

Dean was lying down on the hospital bed we had brought into the living room. He was unconscious. I crawled into the narrow bed next to him and laid my hand across his chest. I looked at his profile. Listened to him breath. Tried to just enjoy being by his side. I couldn't escape though. The sickening and anxious feelings coursed through my body like thick poison. My heart, my stomach, my throat, my head all swarmed with uncertainty and lament. *God, help me.* I rested my head on the pillow next to his, with my mouth nearly touching his ear.

I whispered, trying not to weep. "You have to go, darling. It's okay. You can let go. The boys and I are going to be alright. We're going to be fine, sweetie. It's time. It's time to go now. I love you."

He didn't give any outward indication that he had heard me, but I knew my words would somehow get through.

The next morning, I woke up with unbearable Anxiety. It felt like it was inside of me, relentlessly shaking my core.

Dean was lying down in the living room in his hospital bed. He came into consciousness. My parents went into him. He was trying to speak. He hadn't been able to eat or drink for a number of days, and his mouth was too dry to get any words out. He kept trying and trying. My parents were straining to listen and understand. "It's okay, Dean. We are going to take care of Cassi and the boys. Don't worry, Dean. They're going to be okay." They sat with him and reassured him. I was so grateful they were there. So grateful they had the grace to bear it.

I was wrought with Anxiety. I could hardly stand. I couldn't even go into the same room as Dean. The avalanche. The cliff. The thread. It was all so imminent. My body could hardly stand the emotional strain. I felt like I was dying. The quakes. The trembles. They were intensifying. Like if I stood still too long, the gravity of all the turmoil would pull me by the ankles down into an abyss of death and darkness and defeat.

Later that day, my parents and I went out for a bite to eat. It was about five in the afternoon. My phone rang. It was my mother-in-law. "You'd better come home," she said. I looked at my parents. *Was he gone?*

We silently drove back to the house. I went into the living room. There were quite a few people there. A dozen or so. Dean's parents, brother, sister, aunty, and some other close family and friends. My Dean was there. Lying lifeless on the bed. Yellow. Bald. Still. Gone. *He's gone.*

The thread broke. I could see in slow motion as my dollhouse hit the floor. My life. Intercepted abruptly by concrete. Concrete in the form of an invisible beast. Bursting into an array of glass, wood, flooring, and siding. Exploding outward. The glass confetti flying in all directions. It would have been beautiful if it didn't represent the complete destruction of my life as I knew it. A house. A life. Reduced to splinters, shards, and dust.

And then relief. *Praise the Lord. He's taken Dean home. I know where he is. I know he's not in pain. I know he is restored.* A sweep of simultaneous relief and indescribable loss swept over me. The burden lifted. I knelt beside him, and slow tears streamed down my cheeks. *Is he really gone? Is this real? Is it really over?* Everyone was standing or kneeling around, grieving in their own way. I knew this day would come. I had known for a long time. It was finally here. The tie had been severed. I had done what I was called to do. I had a sense of accomplishment.

It is done. My love. Oh, my love. I'm sorry. I'm sorry it had to be this way. I'm sorry you didn't get to stay. I'm sorry for all the pain. I'm sorry for all the terrible suffering. My love. Be free. Be happy. I miss you.

The avalanche inside me was dropping huge sheets of ice. A ferocious thunder of snow. Coming for me.

The boys. The boys got dropped off, and I ushered them into the living room. I wish I had asked everyone to leave. I didn't think to do it at the time.

"Boys," I tried to keep my voice strong and steady, "it's time to say goodbye to Daddy." Asher looked stoic and unfeeling. I knew he would process it later, in his own time. Maddox broke down crying. "I don't want Daddy to die!" He cuddled his dad and kissed his cheek.

Asher awkwardly came over and gave a guarded "Goodbye, Dad." Watching my boys say goodbye to their dad at such a tender age was the pain of a thousand knives. Navigating my own emotions and grief felt like a task beyond me, how was I going to watch them go through this loss and help them navigate it? *God, my god. How I need you.*

Alone.

PLAYING ON THEIR FATHER'S GRAVE

They say grief comes in waves. Yes, grief does come in waves. It comes in giant smashing waves. And just when you come up for air, you get smashed by another one. And you can't tell which way is up. You're being pulled in every direction. Pushed and dragged at the same time. You can't breathe. And a sort of panic comes over you as you struggle against the mighty, crushing water. Only to find, as you come up exhausted and shaking from the struggle, you're pummeled again. And again. And again.

That night, I sat staring at photos of Dean and me together. I could hardly see them though because the tears wouldn't stop coming. I sobbed so much I coughed and gagged. My stomach muscles strained against the gut wrenching sobs that went on for hours. I made inexplicable sounds. My body shook and writhed. I was completely exhausted yet continued to cringe and wince and sob with the Agony. Unspeakable Agony that gripped me. The Grief pulled at every muscle, distorting my face. I was caught in the avalanche. I had fallen off that cliff. A tornado had come through. And it was all gone. Utterly ruined. Devastation. There I was. Surrounded by the broken pieces of my broken life. And I was trapped in the torrents of emotions, under siege by the carnage without and the turmoil within.

We started making arrangements for the funeral. I was feeling so many different emotions that it was difficult to distinguish them all. Let alone try to articulate them to anyone. Much less, actually understand them. I was fuming mad at Dean. I had so wanted to sit down with him and talk to him about what he wanted for his funeral. I wanted him to write letters to the boys. I wanted him to talk to the boys. He just couldn't accept he was leaving us. That didn't help me though. I was so angry at him. *Dammit, Dean.* Anxiety and the stomach knots were still compounding. Sickening. Oddly, it felt like I couldn't properly grieve until he was in the ground. Knowing he was just lying on a table somewhere still gave me a great deal of uncertainty. As though he might just sit up again and come home. The idea haunted me. The life we'd been living was so tormenting. It wasn't life. It was torture. My worst nightmare is it would continue, unending.

I booked my tickets back to America only shortly after Dean's passing. In the days that followed. It wasn't even a decision I had to make. I knew I had to leave Esperance. As it was, whenever I left the house, I felt I had no privacy. No room to navigate these emotions freely. I felt I was being watched and talked about. Living in a fish-bowl. It's not that people were being rude and judgmental—well, not all of them. They were genuinely concerned and I'm sure just wanted to know how I was coping. The last thing I wanted was an audience of onlookers with their opinions and suggestions. Well-meaning as they may have been. I could not wait to leave.

Tensions still ran high between family members. It was all so raw. We were all in so much pain. We were all so sensitive. And all of us could only see things through our own point of view.

My computer became my bedtime companion. I would fall asleep next to my laptop, listening to music, looking at photos. Wake up next to it. It was warm. It didn't judge me. It didn't give me unimpressive backward glances or silent disapproval. It was impartial. And always there. As such, it was a lifeline for me. And a place I could communicate with the few people in my life who actually understood to some degree what I was feeling. People I could be honest with. People I could swear to. Tell them how angry I was at Dean. Tell them how sexually frustrated I was being married to a man with terminal illness. How judged I felt. How misunderstood. How much I wanted a new life. I could tell them how much I fucking hated fucking cancer. And the fucking hospital. And the fucking drugs. And just fucking all of it. I loved those who didn't try to fix me. Preach at me. Give me a Bible verse. Tell me I shouldn't swear so much. They just loved me. They listened. They were empathetic and compassionate. They made me laugh. They laughed at my dark humor. They were there. I knew they were for me. They helped put me at ease. I didn't have many of these friends, but the ones I had became more precious than the rarest treasure. They kept me going. They kept me alive. They kept me sane.

I put together a garage sale. I sold most of our furniture and belongings for whatever price I could get for it. It felt good. It felt good to be packing and selling and doing something. Like at least I was moving forward in some sort of way with some sort of plan.

Anxiety continued to advance territory.

The day of the funeral came. It was drizzly and cold. It was fitting. Like Esperance itself was weeping for Dean. I wanted to get it over with. To do what had to be done. I was a broken pot trying to hold my shape. I couldn't fall apart here. Not now. *You're almost there, Cassi. Almost there.*

It was a full house, and the service was long. We wanted to pay him proper tribute, and that took time. I was happy with how it all came together. I wasn't at ease though. I can't explain what it's like, sitting in a room with your husband in a coffin. It's surreal. I was still falling off that cliff. Still midair. I felt at any moment, he would pop out of the coffin, and the nightmare would go on and on and on.

You thought this would end, Cassi, but it won't. You'll never move on.

Haunted. These thoughts, like bats, swooped.
I gave my speech.

Dean Mack,

You changed my life. Before you... there was just me...I thought I had my plans, my path I had set before me. Then suddenly you were there; this amazing handsome rugged

Australian man... full of life, laughter, and love. You had a way with people that's hard to describe, you could win anyone over with your jesting, teasing, and charm. I could not pretend that you had no effect on me, because, truthfully, your eyes saw into the depths of my heart. And although I was young, and fickle, and against the advice of others... you took a chance on me... you reached for my hand and made me your wife. You challenged me, encouraged me, lead me, taught me ... taught me patience, kindness, friendship, and compromise, ... taught me how to listen without judgement, how to love without fear, and live without worry. You taught me how to enjoy moments, make memories, and seize the day. You taught me faithfulness, loyalty, and strength. You are the strongest and most loving person I've ever known. I am so sorry, my love, that you suffered so much. I am so sorry that you had to leave the boys and I before you wanted to. Thank you for fighting so hard to stay here with us, as the doctor said, it is the ultimate act of love. I am so happy that you are free now. Healed. Restored. I'm going to miss you, your voice, your laugh, ... you've been my everything for so long...

Until we meet again,

Cass

Dean's parents got up to read what they had written for their son. They stood up courageously. Leaning on each other. A picture of grace and strength. And as they read, they began to thank everyone. The doctors. The nurses. Dean's friends. The church. Everyone.
Except for me.

A dagger in the heart. *Oh God. Could they not see? Could they not see what I gave for their son? That I loved him as much as I could. That I sacrificed my youth? My desires? My dreams? So I could stay by his side and take care of him? All the sleepless nights. The caring for him. Day after day after month after year. Did I fail? Did they not deem me worthy of acknowledgement?* The cracks in my heart threatened to give way to the mounting pressure of a flood of tears.

I SAW. I SAW EVERYTHING. I SAW WHAT YOU DID. I SAW WHAT YOU GAVE. I WILL ACKNOWLEDGE YOU. YOUR SACRIFICE. I AM PROUD OF YOU.

Then that is enough, Lord. His words comforted me as my heart ached. *That will have to be enough. And I suppose that's all that really matters.* I brushed away the tears that exposed me. As I was feeling half dead. And in shock. And agony. And torment. I also felt proud. I had served this man. I had done what God asked me to do. And I stayed till the end.

There is a reason grief comes in waves. If you experience the whole lot at once, it will kill you. Simply. If I were to feel all the emotion of losing Dean on that day, they could have dug a hole for me as well.

I was relieved when the funeral service ended and they put the coffin into the hearse. I knew this day would come. God had been preparing me for this day for a long time. My dad, Ginny, the boys, and I all went together in the car that followed behind. We drove in her shadow. She carried my love to his early resting place. As she had been so eager to do for so long.

Maddox said, "Mommy, is God going to give us a new daddy?"

Tears filled my eyes, and I turned away from him. I couldn't answer. *I hope one day, my love. I hope one day.*

We pulled into the cemetery. People were streaming in. Black jackets, boots, umbrellas, lots of familiar faces. The day was as dreary and bitterly cold as ever. We drove all the way in, following behind the hearse. *God, help me do this. This is where it ends. And something else begins.*

It was odd burying Dean. Maybe it's because I felt like I had lost him so long before that day. I had been grieving the man I had married—the fun, outgoing, healthy man I once knew—for a long time. Felt like he'd been gone for years. So the funeral . . . felt late.

They rested Dean's coffin on wood planks above the fresh hole that had been dug for him. There was a large mound of sand next to it. There must have been some prayers or something said, I can't remember. I just remember when the pole bearers started lowering him into the ground. Their faces strained by the agony of the mortal goodbye. Knowing you'll never see your loved one on this earth again. The dam of uncertainty that held my tears was nearly ready to give way. After Dean was lowered into the ground and they started putting handfuls of sand over the top of him, the dam could no longer contend with the pressure. Deep, heaving sobs surfaced. My dear friend, Cindy, hugged me as the reality sunk in. *He's gone. It's over. He's really gone. It's really over. He's not coming back. It's done. Dean. My Dean. My lover. My husband. The father of my children. That body I know so well. It's lying lifeless in a hole. In a grave. My husband is in a grave. Oh, my Lord. Dean is in a grave. He's gone. He's gone.* The claw of Anguish dug its nails in deeper and deeper.

People started to line up. They hugged me. One at a time. Offering their condolences. *Is this what people do at funerals?* I hadn't been to very many. So much love from so many people. All with such sincerity. I could tell they felt for me. It truly brought me comfort.

Praise God for the innocence of children. The boys were playing with their two cousins on the mound of sand next to the hole for Dean's grave. My stomach kept doing flips looking at them, afraid one of them might fall in. They were just being children. They weren't yoked with the burden of expectation. They didn't know you aren't supposed to "play" at a graveside. You aren't supposed to have "fun" and be "happy." It gave me hope though. *These children are playing on their father's grave, there must be hope for our future.*

Maddox came over to me. "Mommy, Daddy's not down there." He pointed at the coffin in the hole. "He's up there." He pointed to the sky. *Praise the Lord. My son knows. He knows where his dad is. His Daddy is in heaven. Not gone. Not lost. Just in another place. Another realm. A far better place. Far away from sickness and hospital walls. Where invisible beasts are not permitted.*

"That's right, my love. That's right." I squeezed him. *I have to keep going for my boys. They are my reason. My reason to keep going. For them. I'm all they have now. Oh, Dean. How am I going to do this? Why did you leave me? Why did you have to go?*

The mind tries to comprehend death, but it cannot. Our minds are not programmed to be able to understand it. We were never meant to endure it. *This is Dean's hometown? He was born here? He was here before? How is he gone now? How can he be gone?*

I had known he would be going for so long. I had seen it coming a long way off. And in the end, I ushered it in. I knew it was time. I knew it had to happen. But now he was gone, I was left with all the questions. *How? Why? Why, God?*

Transported

When I went into our bedroom, I was overcome with the urge to pack all of Dean's things away. I didn't want to wear my ring. I didn't want to see his clothes. I didn't want to see his shoes or his watch or his Bible. I wanted all his things to disappear. I found the feeling odd. When the hospital chaplain called to check in on me, I asked her about it.

"That's because you're not ready to deal with your grief."

That's not what I wanted to hear. *I've been grieving. I've grieved. I've been crying my eyes out for years. I'm so sick of being sad! I'm so sick of crying! I'm twenty-seven years old. I want to live my life without being sad all the time. I don't want to grieve anymore. I'm done grieving.*

There was certainly a finality with burying Dean's body. Everything had changed. My tie to Australia was broken. I was free to leave. Free to find a future for me and the boys. My parents and I decided it would be better if I were to fly back to the States with them rather than hang around Australia for a few weeks or months. At least, this way, they would be with me on the flight and could help.

I had organized a leaving party for me and my friends. I was saying goodbye to some of the best friends I'd ever had. Friends who had seen me through the worst times of my life. I wanted to go out and have fun. I really wanted to have fun. I'd done so much crying, so much grieving, so much taking care of everybody else. I wanted to have FUN. I felt torn though, as I knew it wouldn't be "perceived" well. "Oh, Cassi's only just buried Dean, and now she's at the pub." I could hear them say. The Gossip Tree flourished in Esperance. And many frequented her branches to eat her fruit of destruction and spread her nectar of poison.

One of the pastors in town, John Bayley, came to visit me. He had been a constant source of love and encouragement over these past years. Tonight was no exception.

"Cassi, there's going to be a lot of people trying to tell you how to feel and what to do. Dean's not suffering anymore. He's in heaven, having a party. You go out tonight and have a good time with your friends. And don't feel bad about it." I loved his radiant face and the unwavering love that shone from it.

Sweet freedom. They were just the words I needed. Permission to have fun. And not be judged for it.

I did go to the pub that night. We did karaoke and danced the night away. I had a blast. I was so glad I did it. Life is for the living. And I wanted to live.

Over the next days, my parents helped me pack and handle the logistics of leaving the country. Passports. Bank accounts. And so forth. As emotionally drained and mentally scattered as I was, completing tasks wasn't easy.

We said our goodbyes to Dean's family and as many friends as we could. Everyone was still grappling with Dean's death. It was a hard. I was so ready to leave. I couldn't ever imagine wanting to come back to this place.

This place where my dreams and love had died.

After a couple days in Perth, it was time to fly home. Where was home? I guess it was going to be California. We were boarding the plane. Waiting in line. There was a man in front of us. Asher struck up a conversation with him as he often does with strangers. The man was in his thirties and had a shaved bald head.

"You have a bald head," Asher stated in his blunt fashion.

The man was warm and friendly. "Yes I do," he said as he flashed a big smile.

"How old are you?"

"I'm thirty-two." He seemed intrigued by this inquisitive young boy.

"My dad had a bald head."

"Oh really, how old is your dad?"

"My dad's dead."

The poor man didn't know what to say. Hearing my little boy say those words triggered something. They rang in my ears. *My dad's dead. My dad's dead.* I was trying desperately to hold the tears back. I couldn't. The lump in my throat felt like an apple. The tears started pouring onto my cheeks and down my neck. *Not now, Cassi. Not here. Not now.* I tried to keep my composure. To put on my brave face. It was too much. *I'm leaving Australia. I'm leaving without Dean. I'm leaving him behind. Oh my God, Dean's buried in a hole, and I'm leaving the country. Away from my beloved. I'm leaving without him. Oh God. Oh God. He's dead. He's dead.* I shuffled down the aisle to my seat and put my bags in the overhead compartment. I kept sniffling and wiping the tears away, praying they would stop. But the wave had come. It was only just building. There was no stopping it. *Alcohol. I need alcohol.* I sat down in my seat, and one of the stewards came over.

"Miss, are you okay?" His sincerity and friendly demeanor was disarming and made it even harder to keep the torrent of tears from rushing.

I struggled. *What do I say? I'm not okay. I'm so not okay.* I was struggling to catch my breath to keep from sobbing.

"Miss, may I ask, are you leaving someone behind?"

How does he know?

I managed to nod my head yes. "My husband. My husband died two weeks ago." I could hardly get the words out. I could hardly believe them myself.

He gave a look filled with disbelief and compassion. "Is there anything I can get for you?"

Alcohol. "Um, Can I have a rum and coke, please?" I was a mess. Tear-streaked, mascara running everywhere, red, and flushed.

"I can't get that for you right now, but as soon as we get in the air, I'll get that for you, okay?" He was so nice. I nodded.

The Anxiety I'd been living with for months was peaking out now. Flying had become increasingly more challenging for me. Increasingly unbearable. Anxiety and fear would culminate in a frenzy of torture over me. The airplane their chosen scene for crimes against me. *Are we going to make it? I hate to fly. I hate flying. This is it. This is the last jaunt to my new future. My new life. Far away from death and pain and everything that's going to remind me of the hell I've been living.*

I'd been drinking steadily through the flight but hadn't managed to get to sleep. About halfway through, we hit some turbulence, as you always do on that flight going over the equator. Anxiety was getting more intense than anything I'd felt before. All I could picture was the plane crashing into the ocean. My palms sweating. A feeling like ice started in my chest and started running down my arms. A sharp pain in my chest. *What happens now? I feel like I'm going to explode or implode or something. Am I having a panic attack? I can't breathe. Oh God, I can't breathe.* I pressed the button for the steward. The same gentleman who had been waiting on me came over.

"Are you okay, miss?"

Tears were still streaming down my face. "Um, I'm sorry . . . I feel like I can't breathe."

"Okay, luv, why don't you come with me."

Praise God, the boys were asleep, and my parents were nearby in case they woke up. He led me down the back of the plane and sat me down. He put an oxygen mask on me.

I looked into his eyes, Fear permeating my mind. "Are we going to make it?"

He gave me a look full of empathy. Like he could see the desperate turmoil of my soul. He wrapped a blanket around me. Another stewardess came over. She was so pretty. She looked like an angel. She was an angel to me at that moment. She asked me about where I was traveling to and about my boys and things. She brought me some gourmet chocolates. I had to assume they were from first class. She rubbed my back and continued to ask me how I was feeling. She told me that everything was going to be okay. I still felt the threat of disaster, but I welcomed the distraction of conversation. My chest pains eased slightly. I don't know how long I was back there for. Every hour felt like a day. Eventually, I came back to my seat. I thought of every Bible verse I could that might bring me some solace or comfort. *You have me in the palm of your hand, Lord. You have me in your hands. Peace, Lord, I need your peace.* But adrenalin and panic coursed through my veins, prompted with each tick and tock. When our plane landed, I felt like I'd been given my life back again. I was completely drained and exhausted, but I was alive and on land. And that made me smile. I bid farewell to the stewards who helped me. *Thank you, God, for those people.*

We got in the car. Summer. I was transported. California in early July. Warm. Beautiful. Familiar smells. Familiar sights. Such a contrast to the Esperance winter I had just come from. Home. The driving. The honking. The speeding. The crowds. The pace. Culture shock. Even though it had only been six months since I'd been here, it felt like ages. I took a deep breath. And then there was that. The smell of home. *Everything is going to be okay. I'm home. Thank you, Jesus. You brought me home. I'm a mess. I'm broken. But I'm home.*

Home. Bed. Sleep.

I thought the worst was over.

I was wrong.

THE BUOY BOY

My dad had arranged for the boys and me to rent an apartment just over from theirs in Temecula. It was perfect. We were close. We would be able to spend lots of time together, and they would be able to help me out with the boys when I needed it. It was already furnished nicely. It took the boys and me a few days to recover from jetlag. Temecula was hot. We hibernated indoors for a good portion of the day, seeking respite from the blazing summer sun. Everything felt new. A new house. A new town. A new season. A new day outside of death's shadow.

Through Facebook, I had gotten in touch with an old friend, Cazador. He was an old flame, but we had been primarily friends for years prior to my marrying Dean. We had worked together in our teens. He had jet-black hair, considerate eyes, and playful freckles that contrasted his sharp attire. He was a hard worker with big aspirations and the drive and intelligence to see them fulfilled. I had always admired him, and despite being older than him, I looked up to him.

He was living in New York where he had finished university. We sent friendly e-mails back and forth. I enjoyed sharing with him. He was someone completely outside my world and my situation. Someone who knew me before the chaos and the carnage. Before the scars. I could relay the ups and downs of the journey I was on. Everything that had happened over the years. I could talk. And he heard me. And I very much needed to feel heard. Our conversations became more and more frequent.

"Cassi, you really need someone to look after you. You need someone to look after the boys."

His words brought such comfort. So much reassurance. *I do? Yes. Yeah, I do need that. I need someone to take care of me. I want a companion. I want a man in my life. Someone big and strong. Someone who can love me and do boy stuff with the boys. I've been alone for so long. I'm so lonely.* Loneliness pierced my heart like an arrow. I was desperate. Desperate for companionship. His words rang in my ears. *"You need someone to look after you."* Yes. That's what I need. I need someone. The seed was planted and dreams sprouted. My promised land. After all these years of hardship and pain and difficulty. To just have a normal life. A healthy husband. A whole family. Someone to share life with. Someone who could love me and appreciate me. Someone who was well enough to actually be a husband to me. Not a patient but a real husband. The idea was magnetic. And I pined for it. *Yes, Lord! Is this the man you're bringing into my life? To bring me joy and be a role model and father figure to the boys?* The sheer idea of it brought me hope and delight.

Cazador told me he was thinking about coming out to California. His parents were living not far from me, and they had come into some problems of their own. He felt he should come to their aid. With the added bonus that we could spend some time together in person. Our phone calls were lengthy. He gave me compliments. He made me smile. It felt it had been such a long time since I smiled.

"When are you going to come to see me?" He playfully urged.

"What? I can't leave the boys. You'll have to come out here and see me." We flirted like teenagers again. I fantasized about when I would finally get to see him. Sure, it was soon after Dean was gone. I knew people would have their opinions. They always did.

At night, I would dream about Dean. He is yellow and sick. He is chasing me. He catches up to me. He grabs my arm. *I knew it. I knew it would never end. I knew he would never die.* I would wake up breathless. Terrified. Tormented by the memories of his last weeks. His falls. His deterioration. His smile. His frailty. The unfairness of it all. The memories would hit me all at once. Each one, a brick. Smashing me. A tidal wave of grief. On the ground, I would bury my face in the carpet. Sobs. Hitting the floor with my fist. Screaming into a pillow.

Crash.

It should have been you.

Crash.

It's your fault. You gave up on him.

Crash.

Everyone wishes he was the one who lived. He was a better person than you.

Crash.

He would've handled it better.

I could see him. Images of him looking at me. Talking to me. On his crutches. In bed. Those eyes. Those blue eyes looking into me.

Crash. Smash. Wave after wave. Until I was spent. Squeezed of every last tear. Purged of every last sob. Head throbbing. Limbs limp. Exhausted from the high seas of grief. The relentless watery struggle. The current that threatened to take me.

My brother and sister came around often. I took such joy in my time with them. My brother was going to boot camp so we were gearing up to send him off. I loved going out on the town with my siblings. Drinks. Good times. *Fun! I want to have fun! Isn't that what you're supposed to do when you're young? Get out and have a good time. Dance. Take a chance. Live a little. Loosen up.* I was very inexperienced with alcohol. I would drink too quickly and wind up with a head spin. My mouth would start to go numb. I would have to sit. I enjoyed how relaxed it made me feel though. Anxiety would subside. I couldn't feel the claw of Anguish. Relief. Sweet lovely relief. Happiness.

In the meantime, Cazador texted me more and more frequently. He was charming and clever. He made me laugh. He made me blush. It was so incredibly delightful. And I relished every moment of the attention. I was naive. I let him into my heart. I told him everything. Someone I hadn't seen in nine years. My thoughts. Fears. My hopes for the future. My concerns for the boys. I trusted him. He was a buoy. Where I was treading water in an ocean of pain that threatened to drag me to its darkest depths. How could I know? That buoy I was grabbing would become a lead weight.

The phone conversations got longer and more frequent. They were the highlight of my day. I grew more and more attached to him. The idea of seeing him. The romance of it all. We started talking more seriously about his move to California.

He said he would be booking a flight within the month. *God, I feel like I don't need you anymore.* The thought frightened me. I was running. I was running from my pain. From the avalanche. I still heard it's growl within when things got quiet enough. I had given God everything. I had loved and served him as best as I knew how. I loved and served Dean as best as I knew how. And my life shattered.

I'll take it from here. I held God at arm's length and didn't want him any nearer.

Cazador called. "Hey, babe, how are you? Gosh, I can't wait to come see you. I need to rent a truck to pack up all my stuff and come out there. It's just . . . Well, one of my clients is behind on his invoices. So, yeah, I have to wait, babe. I have to wait till this money comes through."

"Oh, okay."

"Yeah, I mean, when this money comes through, it'll be no problem. It's just a matter of trying to get stuff organized until that happens. Like it's a bummer that it hasn't come through yet." He took a deep breath. "It just makes me a bit more stressed out because I can't start organizing things, you know?"

"Oh. Well . . . I mean . . . Do you need me to float you the money?" I was hesitant. But he wasn't actually asking me for the money. *I mean if he actually asked, I would say no, but I'm just offering.*

And if he's getting paid the money, it won't hurt surely. He'll just pay me back. That's no problem if I can help him out.

"Oh, babe, I couldn't ask you to do that. I mean I wouldn't want to put you out."

"No, it doesn't put me out. I mean, it's just floating you the money for a couple of weeks. That's no worries."

"Oh, wow, babe, that would be such a big help. That's great. Can I just e-mail you through my account details, and you can do an online transfer?"

"Yeah . . . sure. Yeah, that's fine. Do that."

"Okay, thanks so much. That'll make things much quicker and easier. Talk to you soon. Bye."

As I hung up, I couldn't explain the twinge of uncertainty I felt. I shook it off. *I'm sure he's genuine. Everyone needs a bit of help every now and then. Of course, I won't be able to tell anyone in my family about this. They wouldn't understand. They would freak out, I'm sure. I know him though. I know it will be fine.*

My sister was the only one who really knew what was going on between the two of us. I didn't feel like I could tell anyone else. I confided in her. I could only imagine anyone else saying negative things about the budding relationship.

Even home started feeling like a fishbowl. Everyone was so concerned about me. They just wanted to look out for me and the boys. But I wanted space. Space and privacy and room to try to find my footing. I wanted to push them all away. I was spontaneous and impulsive. I made decisions on a whim. I took trips. I did whatever I felt like in the moment. I was in a spiral. Going in every direction but getting nowhere. My emotions, uncontrollable. Especially when the grief waves hit. I couldn't be normal. I couldn't act how I normally act because I wasn't normal. I felt an expectation from people that I should stay home. Wearing black. Cry for months on end to prove how much I loved Dean. I was so sick of crying. I was so sick of being sad. *I'm twenty-seven years old for goodness' sake. I'm young. I want to have fun.* And so I made up my mind. The alcohol continued. It became a regular part of my life. Especially wine at night at home. I loved its soothing presence and the calm it brought.

I mentioned Cazador to my parents. I was afraid of what they would think or say. Dean had only been gone for a couple of months. They were cautious but tried to be supportive and encouraging.

A few days after the money transfer, he called.

"Babe, I'm gonna need you to come out here," he said matter-of-factly.

"What do you mean?" My heart gave a thud.

"I still have my California driver's license, which is now expired. I never got a New York one because nobody drives here. It's going to take forever to try to get one organized, and I won't be able to rent a removal truck to drive across the country unless I have a driver's license. Come out. I'll pay for your ticket. Come out here, and we'll drive back to Cali together. It'll be fun! C'mon. Say yes." His tone turned playful.

I was hesitant. I knew my family would be worried. *Me? Fly to New York? This is going to sound crazy. I'm flying to New York to drive back to California with some guy?* I could already hear my family's protest. *Who is this guy?*

I wanted to go. It sounded like an adventure. It sounded like fun. *I've so been wanting to have fun. It's crazy, yes. But why not? I've been cooped up in hospitals. I've been strangled by circumstances for years. I should do it.*

"Okay. Let me talk to my parents. Let me think about it. I want to. It sounds like fun." *I was trying to think of how I could word this to my family so they wouldn't think I've gone completely mad. They should be happy for me. I'm a grown woman for goodness' sake. I can make my own decisions. If I want to go on a trip to New York, what's so bad about that?*

"C'mon, babe. It'll be great. Drive across the country together. We'll be able to talk the whole way. What a great thing to get to do together. You can spend a day here in New York. I'll take you around to see some of the sights. You'll love it. I need you, babe. I really need you to do this." *Is he asking me or telling me?* I wasn't sure.

My heart and head seemed to say two different things but spontaneity won out. I went to speak to my parents.

"No, Cass." My dad was adamant. "Don't do it. If this guy wants to see you, let him get himself here. He needs to get his stuff together and figure it out and find a way to get here. If he can't do that, something's wrong. You just flew across the world. You just made it here all the way from Australia. He can't get from New York to California without you holding his hand? Come on… " Daddy wasn't impressed.

It made sense. I couldn't argue with him. I called Cazador.

"I don't think I can come. My parents don't like the idea. I don't think I'm going to be able to help you out."

"What? Why? Cassi, you're a grown woman. You're not sixteen years old. You should be able to make your own decisions. You don't need your parents' approval. You know me. You understand the situation. Your parents don't get it. That's all. They just don't understand how hard it is to organize a driver's license here. I'm not gonna be able to come out there if you don't do this. You have to come. Come on, babe. I really need you. Don't you want to follow your heart? When you're an old grandmother telling stories to your children, don't you want to tell them how you followed your heart?"

Well, yes, I do. What he said was true also. *What do I do? I'm so excited about spending time with this great guy. On the other hand, what my dad said made sense . . . I don't want to disappoint my dad . . . but my impulses are agreeing with Cazador. I mean, all I've done for years and years is what I have to do. Can't I do this just because I want to? Is it that wrong? I'm helping my friend. What's wrong with helping my friend?*

I called my sister. To my surprise, she was siding with my dad, telling me not to go. In fact, she was in conference with her husband and my parents, and they were all in agreement that it would be a mistake for me to go. Sides forming. On one hand, was my family, on the other, this man I had grown so attached to. *What do I do? Why won't my family just support me? Why won't they just love me? Can't they just let me live a little? Even if I do make mistakes? Aren't they my mistakes to make? Aren't they my decisions to make?*

Aloneness came again. The sense that no one understood me. That I needed to self-sacrifice and be responsible as I had always been. I had a bad feeling. I wanted to go. *I want to go to New York. I'm sick of always being so damn responsible.*

I left the boys with my mom and her husband. I got on a plane. I went to New York.

And it set me on a course of events that would be devastating.

LA to New York and Back

August 2010

When I got off the plane in New York, Cazador wasn't waiting for me. I called him.

"Hi, I'm here. Where are you?"

"I'm at home. Get in a taxi, and I'll text you the address. See you soon."

Weird. Okay. I got in a taxi and gave him the address. It was about four or five in the morning as I had taken the red eye. The sky was just starting to light as we pulled up. The first thing I noticed was the horrible stench. There were trash bags sitting out on the streets everywhere. *Oh my gosh. This is not romantic at all.* And not only that, but the air was humid and thick. Unlike anything I'd ever felt before.

When I saw him, he looked different. His eyes weren't those pools of young hope and spark. They were tired. His face was puffy. His brow was furrowed. He was only twenty-five but looked ten years older. *How odd. What has aged him so?* We walked around the docks and looked at the water as the sun rose. We talked. I felt shy. Unsure of being there. *But, hey, I'm in New York for a day. This is going to be amazing.*

We went and got some breakfast at a little café. I was enamored by the charm of NY's old buildings. Fire escapes. Alleyways. And architecture. Around every corner, I was delighted with her appeal. The smell of the rubbish had started to subside. *This is so different to*

California. It was like being at an amusement park. I couldn't help but smile at everyone I walked past. I looked on with the fascination and intrigue of a child as we passed along the buildings of Wall Street and the other streets of Manhattan. *What an incredible place. From Australia's outback to NYC in as many days.* Like a good tourist, I took photos on every corner. I couldn't hide my girlish bubbly pep.

We went to the truck removal place as soon as they opened and rented a truck with my license, under my name. Drove the truck back to C's place. We got some lunch at a pizza place downstairs. *WOW. Fabulous pizza.* I was enthralled with it all. C, on the other hand, seemed gloomy and brooding. *There is something mysterious about him. Something almost . . . dark? Was it?* It was something I didn't remember him having in earlier days. Something acquired. Something let in. Still, if I looked close enough, I saw the boy I had so much affection for.

We walked a couple of blocks down the road to visit one of his friends. We went inside to a clean and stylish little apartment. A solidly built, fiery, bartender with a mouth for language invited us in. He and C started talking about work and drama. This person and that person. I was in my own world with my rose-colored glasses on. Filled with delight and amusement. I was lost for words when he brought out a huge bong. I had never even seen one like that before, but I knew what it was. He lit it, and the two passed it back and forth. *What am I doing here? How did I get here?* Surreal. We left after a short visit and walked back to his apartment.

His place was dark. And hot. There was no AC. There were things haphazardly placed all over. It looked like it had been nicely decorated at one point but had been neglected for some time. He hadn't packed yet. We had a lot of work ahead of us. We were busy well into the night. Hours going up and down the stairs, loading up the truck. Covered in sweat and exhausted, I fell asleep on the couch in the early hours of the morning.

We had to leave at eight in order to get to California on schedule. I would have to drive the truck out of the city, just in case we were pulled over. It was rented in my name.

So here I was. Driving a U-Haul through peak hour traffic in the middle of Manhattan. Something I never thought I'd do. I mustered up all the courage I had to navigate a truck I'd never driven through streets I'd never traversed, full of New Yorkers who aren't particularly obliging. There were some scary moments, but miraculously, I managed to get us across the bridge and out of the city with no accidents or tickets.

It took us three and a half days to drive across back to California. There was some lovely scenery, but mostly, it was just an exhausting drive. The truck was uncomfortable. At some of our stops, C would smoke marijuana from a small bong he kept in his pocket. It appeared to be a regular habit. I was gracious. *He just needs love. Love and Jesus.*

I greeted the boys happily on my return. They hugged and kissed me. Their love, unconditional. But everything had changed. When I saw my dad, something about him was different. He seemed stressed. On edge. My sister didn't want to talk to me. There was a rift. A rift in my family.

Once C came into my house, it became impossible to get him out. I tried to make him go home to his parents' house at night.

"Babe, it's fine. I'll just sleep here on the couch. You want me to get in an accident? Can't you see how tired I am? Stop acting like a child." *Was I being a child?* My insides quaked. Anxiety riddled and coursed through me. *Why doesn't this feel like the sweet romance I was promised?*

It was still so engrained in me to take care of everyone. Keep quiet. Make everyone happy. Keep the peace. Avoid conflict. I was still scarred. It was so raw. I was trying to create the reality I wanted. I was trying to fill the void in my heart and my life. I could see Cazador had some pretty serious character flaws I was unaware of. The drugs. He was a pretty heavy drinker. He seemed to have a fairly short fuse. This all became fairly evident in the first week or so. I needed time. I needed time to sort out what I thought of him. Time to figure out who he was and what to do.

I threw a party for Maddox's fifth birthday. We did small and simple with cake at the park. My sister's husband refused to allow their children to come. He said he didn't want his children around someone of my character. Another arrow in my heart.

Tensions grew as my parents were not happy with C and that he had pretty much moved into my house. He had not yet found a job. It all came to a head as e-mails began to circulate within the family. I don't know exactly what they said. Everyone giving their opinion. Disapproval. Approval. Drawing their lines in the sand. Taking sides. Slinging insults. I only read parts of them. My world was spinning. And I felt lost. And very misunderstood. A whirlwind of anxiety and uncertainty. I wanted to be okay. I wanted to be happy. I wanted to do the right thing. I wanted to have fun. But all around me, problems formed and swarmed. The upheaval and chaos going on in my heart and mind made me incapable of facing conflict. Any turmoil without only heightened and strengthened the quakes and tremors within. Made the avalanche thunder louder. I could feel the crumbling snow hit the backs of my legs. *Run. Run. Run. Hide. Run. Hide. Get away. Get safe.*

I clung to C like a life raft. I had put all hope into this relationship. This was my happily ever after. This was my Promised Land. *Why is it all unraveling? Why is it falling apart?* I curled up against the wall and put my head in my hands. *I can't do this. I can't do this. Why is everyone mad at me? I just want to be happy. I just want to have fun. I just want the nightmares to stop.* The adrenalin coursing through my veins. Nauseous. *I need some wine. I need some sleep. I don't know what I need. I'm so tired. I don't want to think about Dean. His frail body. His yellow face. His yellow eyes. His broken bones. I don't want to think about it anymore. I just want to move on. I just want a normal life.*

I couldn't settle. Couldn't find Peace. I begged for her. I begged her please come. Sit with me. Push Anxiety away. Tell Insomnia to leave. But she evaded me. I grasped for her, but she was out of reach.

Things came to a head. My dad and C got in an argument. Their faces contorted with anger. The yelling. The awful yelling.

I couldn't face it. Couldn't cope with the conflict. I didn't know what to say. I didn't know how to fix it or make it better.

So I ran.

RUNNING

I packed a bag for me and one for the boys. We left the apartment my parents had set up for us. We went and stayed at a cheap hotel a couple of towns over. C came with us.

Peace. I want Peace.

"Fuck 'em, babe. They don't want to support you or let you live your own life. That's what family is supposed to do. We'll get a place. You, me, the boys, and my parents. We'll get a house together. You can live with me. It'll be great. We'll find a great school for the boys to go to. Don't worry, babe. It's going to be fine."

His words were supposed to be reassuring, but all I felt was dread. It sounded nice. A house. A nice school. I could cook and clean. That's what I knew how to do. I knew how to be a wife and a mom. *I don't know how to be a single, working mother. I don't want that.* I looked at C. *If I just love him enough. If I show him what real love looks like, he'll change. My family will eventually learn to like him, I'm sure. It'll blow over. It's just going to take some time.*

I got more money out of my savings. C's parents needed to get their things out of storage. So I rented another truck, and we made a trip a few hours north to do that. I put a deposit on a nice four-bed-room, two-story rental not far from my parents'. The neighborhood had that sterile, track home, Stepford wives thing happening. Pretty but eerie. Lacking in character. Color. Warmth. There was a school a few blocks away. It lacked personality but had that fresh look of a newly built school. I thought of Australia with her turquoise sea and red dirt. A pang of sorrow followed.

We moved in. C, his parents, me, and the boys. The boys shared a room. C and I had a room, and his parents had a room. The house was quite lovely inside. *This will be good. We can settle here. We can make memories here.* We went to Ikea to get Cazador everything he needed for a new home office. He set up in the garage.

"Cassi, you have to be very strong." C's mother would speak to me in her thick accent. Offering her advice on all areas of life. I mostly enjoyed our conversations. She was a fiery Hispanic woman. Her face was lovely but weary with lines of battle fatigue. We talked for hours about love, life, men, and housework. She was pedantic about housework. Not long after I moved in, I realized most of my days would be spent cleaning.

"If you use the oven, you must clean it."

"The benches must be wiped and cleared at all times."

"The floors must be swept."

"The banisters must be wiped and dusted individually."

"The bathrooms must be immaculate. No drops. No drops of water."

"The toilets must sparkle."

The washing. The windows. Emphatically, she went through every area of the house with me, showing me how it was to be cleaned. If there was a drop of water left on a bench or the bathroom sink, she would call me over to wipe it down. It was "unacceptable." I tried to embrace it as good training. But over the days and weeks, I became a slave in my own house. She made all the rules while I was still paying the majority of the bills. Rent, utilities, groceries, and so forth. I walked on egg shells trying to do everything right. Trying to keep the house up to her immaculate standards.

C came to church with the boys and me. I hoped something said would penetrate his hardened heart. I silently prayed for God's intervention. I noticed he was texting on his phone quite a lot during the service. I was wrapped up in emotion, and he looked bored. "We've got to make a stop on the way home, babe. Do you have fifty bucks?"

We stopped at a quaint neighborhood nearby where he exchanged the money for drugs in a mailbox. *God, I can't do this.*

Most of my family was estranged at this point. My mother and her husband, Brian, were the only ones I was really in touch with. I felt forsaken by almost everyone. *Where were all the people who supposedly cared about me? Or the boys? Why didn't anyone care? Why didn't they reach out?* There were only two friends I kept in contact with. They were life to my veins.

C would spend all day in his "office" looking for a job. I had to knock and be invited in before entering.

"C?" I knocked.

Nothing. *What is he doing in there?*

"C?" A little louder this time.

"Come in. What is it, babe? I'm working." His tone was short. As though he were inconvenienced by my visit.

He would be in a pair of basketball shorts, no shirt. Sitting in his office chair in the dark. The only light coming from his computer screen. A haze of smoke encompassing his desk. Half-empty bottle of whiskey on the left. Small bong sitting on the right. The smell of marijuana hung hot in the air. An open bag of sunflower seeds next to the mouse. Its shells scattered across the desk and floor. His leg was shaking. He always had a nervous, shaking leg. *What was that about?* He looked up at me with a dazed, vacant, somewhat annoyed expression. "What do you want, babe? I'm working."

You're working? I wanted to be supportive. I was spending hours cleaning every micro millimeter of the house. My back was sore, and my hands were dry.

"How are you going with finding a job?"

"It's hard, babe. The economy isn't very good. I've put my resume out to every job offer that comes up on Craig's list. I'm doing my best, babe. It's gonna take some time."

My patience was wearing. "Well, I can't keep spending my savings paying for rent. One more month. That's it. I'm done."

"Fine," he said flatly. With a tone that said he didn't believe me.

I stood there looking at him. *Was he even hearing me? Was he actually looking for jobs? Is he an alcoholic? What does he do in here all day? Why doesn't he want to spend time with me? Why does he look so empty?* Even through this pathetic exterior, I could see a glimpse of the ambitious and playful young man I had grown so fond of in my young years. I had so hoped my unyielding respect and affection would make an impact. Make a change. *Why hadn't it?*

New York. He let her ruin him. He gave in to every carnal desire. Every fleshly appetite. He didn't deny himself any of her indulgences. He partook of all her snares. All her seductive vices. And now here he was. Bound. Chained. Chewed up. Spat out. Cynical. Skeptical. Addicted. Empty. A shell. It had cost him his soul.

God, what am I going to do? God, show me what to do.

Thanksgiving came around. I came downstairs, smiling. Wearing one of my favorite dresses. It was something I felt pretty in. Determined to find gratitude where I was. I was met by the disapproving eyes of C's mother, shaking her head.

"Go change, honey. You don't want to wear that. You don't want to show all of that. Go put on something appropriate."

Dejected, I walked up the stairs. Slow tears stinging. Any joy I had was gone. *I can't even wear what I want.* Heckled by her words of shame, I sat on the floor of my closet. Cried into my hands. Hurting. Alone. Lost. Broken. *God. God. Help. God, what do I do?* Crushing weights pulling my heart down. Down into an abyss.

SWIMMING TO SHORE

W e'd been living in the house with C and his family for a number of weeks now. Fighting became a normal part of life. C's parents would start shouting at each other in Spanish. I had no idea what it was about. C and his mom fought too. Screaming in each other's faces. I had my fair share of disagreements with mine, but never had I seen family look at each other with such hateful disdain. Sometimes I tried to mediate. I soon realized they didn't want to stop fighting. The angry binge put a venom in their veins, and they loved the high.

I found joy in my children as I always had. In their innocence and playfulness. There could be darkness all around, and they would find the light. Dance in it. And they would lead me to it. I hate yelling. I hate shouting. I despise it. It makes me sick. Nauseous. When the shouting would ensue, I would take the boys into their room and play with them. I would play music and talk to them, trying to distract them. Forced to retreat to a sequestered corner for safety. Hiding in our home. The home we paid for.

"Mom, why are they yelling? Why are they fighting?" Asher was looking at me with those big brown eyes. Pools of innocence where there is no gauge for hatred between family members. *Oh, my love. My love, I'm so sorry. I'm so sorry we're here in this house with these people. I don't even know what we're doing here. Jesus, help me. God, help me. What do I do? I don't even know what to do.*

"Sweetie, sometimes grownups disagree on things, and it makes them mad and they yell. Let's build some train tracks. Why don't you show me how?"

Panic flooded my body. My heart on the roller coaster. Skipping a beat. Pause. THUMP. Rush of adrenalin. This became my normal. Incessant. Over and over. The roller coaster. Dozens of times per day.

At nights, I looked forward to being held. C had his many faults, but at least I had someone. Someone to love. Someone to lie with. Lie next to. Enjoy. We watched a movie together one night, and I showed interest. I craved touch. Affection.

He was preparing to go "work" in his "office."

"Don't go." I gave him my cute pleading face. "Stay here with me." I tried to pull him onto the bed by his arm.

He shook free. "You've got a vibrator. Use it. I've got to work." His tone was indifferent. He wasn't even trying to be insensitive or hurtful. He didn't have to try. He just was. And he left the room. All I had done. All I was putting up with. Was so that I could have companionship. Affection. And after all I'd given. Forsaken. And spent. Still, I had it not.

Tension mushroomed in the house. C hadn't found a job yet. My patience with his mother was waning. Her intentions may have been good, but I felt like her slave. Cooking. Cleaning. Constant. I was spending money like water. Paying all the bills. Money that was supposed to be for me and the boys. I knew I had to put a cap on it before it was all gone. C's drug and drinking habits were getting to me. There was something dark about him. I was getting glimpses of it. Suspicion grew in me. It was a sensation I hadn't felt before.

One morning, in usual fashion, an argument broke out amongst C's parents. The boys got caught in the crossfire. I was in another room. I overheard something and went to see the boys. They were in their room. They told me C's mom had yelled at them and sent them to their room.

That's it. As far as I am concerned, these boys are paying for this house, and no fiery, Latina woman is going to yell at them and shove them in a bedroom. I put the boys in the car and drove to McDonald's up the street.

I was in tears. Almost hysterics. No matter how much I run from Conflict, he corners me. *Is there any escape from this drama? Drama after drama.*

I called my mother. The one link to my family I still had. I recounted the events of the morning to her. She could tell how upset I was.

"Cassi, you get you and the boys in your car, and you drive straight here, you hear me? Don't even go back to that house. You come straight here." She had that firm "mom" tone.

So I did. I got the boys in the car and drove the hour to her house in Cardiff.

"You can stay here with me and Brian, sweetie. Don't you go back to that house. Those people who yell at you and treat you that way. No, you stay here with us. You'll be safe here. We'll get the boys enrolled in school here, honey. It's going to be okay. You just needed to get out of there."

I called C.

I told him what had happened that morning. He had been in his dingy hideout.

"Oh, babe, oh my gosh, I'm so sorry. My mother had no right to do that. You're right. It's too hard all of us living together. You know, I really want to help them, but . . . I tried. I did my best, and sometimes things just don't work out. This will be better, babe. I'll find a job closer to San Diego. We can get a place over there. It'll work out, babe. Don't worry. I'll pack your things and the boys' things and I'll drive to your mom's house. I'm so sorry, babe."

My doubts over the relationship grew daily. *What do I do?* I had been so hopeful about it. It all seemed like it would work out so well. This was going to be my happily ever after. *How did it all go so pear-shaped? I don't know. God, help me please? Is this man supposed to be in my life? Lord, if this man isn't supposed to be in my life, please show me. Show me, God.*

I had started talking to God a little bit again. I wasn't ready to fully let Him in, but I knew I needed guidance. I was making a mess of everything.

His whispers still followed me.

THE BEST IS YET TO COME.

C came to my mom's with our things.

"We can stay here, babe. I'll set up my computer here, and I'll start looking for jobs first thing tomorrow." More promises. My confidence was waning.

We set up beds for the boys in my little brother's room. My mom still had two children at home. My half-siblings, Gaetano and Izzabella.

There was a small family room just off from the living room. We put a blow up mattress on the floor in there for me to stay in and C when he was there as well.

What a day. I welcomed sleep, but I tossed and turned. Battling my demons. The memories. Dean. Chasing me. Running after me. Me, terrified, running away. *I knew it would never end. I knew he would never die.*

Christmas was a few days away.

"Babe, there are some excellent job opportunities in Texas. I mean the economy in Austin is just booming. I have filled out some applications, but I really think I should make a trip down there to interview for some of these jobs in person."

Texas? Am I supposed to move to Texas with this man?

"Um, like now? Before Christmas?"

"Yeah, babe, if I leave tomorrow, then I can be gone and come back before Christmas. I can stay with my friends in Austin. I just need money for gas."

"Oh. How much do you need?"

"I don't know, probably eight hundred dollars should be enough."

All I had was eight hundred dollars. I didn't know what to do. So I gave it to him. "Okay. Yeah. Alright."

That night, we decorated the Christmas tree at my mother's house. I still hadn't spoken to my dad, my stepmom, or my sister. It had been months. It was agony. My family torn apart. Dean dead. *I'm sleeping on an air mattress. God, help me. This is bad.*

We were all spending time together doing Christmas-y stuff. C was nowhere to be found. I went and found him playing video games in the bedroom.

"You should come out. We're having fun. We're decorating and watching movies."

"Not right now, babe." He was in an alternate reality where he was saving the planet from certain destruction.

What? This man doesn't even want to spend time with me? Does he even love me? Does he even love himself?

All night, he stayed in that room. All alone. Captivated by a screen.

This is not what I want.

The next, day he left for Texas.

Anxiety was my constant companion. Nausea came with her. Heartbeat. Heartbeat. Pause. BOOM. Flood. It felt like a drug. *I need some wine.*

I Skyped with Sue and Karen. It was so lovely to see them. They seemed a million miles away. It felt like years since I'd seen them. I tried to keep my composure, but my efforts failed. "I'm trying . . . I'm trying to do the right thing. I don't know. We might move to Texas. I'm not sure. I really want to do the right thing." I was fighting a losing battle against tears.

Karen did most of the talking. They were emotional as well.

"Cassi, we just want you to know. We are so happy Dean married you. We have no expectation of you at all. We just love you."

Her words were honey from heaven. *Love. I feel loved. They really love me. In spite of everything. Wow.* The tears streamed. Karen showed me the love of Jesus. *Thank you, Jesus. You don't judge me. You aren't mad at me. You love me, Lord. You love me.* All I could do was cry tears of awe of the profound love of God. I had been feeling so much shame and condemnation over my decisions. So judged by people. By Christians. By people who I thought were my friends. Other's thoughts, opinions, and labels as bags that I'd willingly chosen to carry. Karen's words were that of unconditional love. This unconditional and undeserved love gave me wings. And cleared my mind. They gave me wisdom to know what to do and the strength to actually do it. This love. This love empowered me. Love and grace gave me *power* over my sin. I felt strength flood my heart. Not like the

---

ferocious waves of grief. This was different. This was a river of life flowing into my parched soul.

My mom sat down with me.

"Cassi, are you giving him money?"

I squirmed in my seat. *Well, yes, I am giving him money, but . . . well . . . how do I excuse that?*

"Uh . . . yeah."

"Listen to me. That stops NOW. If this man is for real and he wants to take care of you, then you sit back and see if he can do that. You don't give him one more cent."

She looked intently into my eyes.

"Cassi. Not one more cent, you hear me? You watch how fast this relationship comes to an end when you stop. You just watch."

I felt good about that decision. It seemed right. It was put to the test sooner than I thought. He called that afternoon.

"Babe, I need some money."

"Oh, you do? What do you need money for?" He blew through that fast.

"For gas, to get back to California."

"Oh. What happened to the eight hundred dollars I gave you?"

"That's all gone, babe. I just need it okay? Can you put a deposit into my account?"

I paused. Courage. *Be strong, Cassi.* "Um, no. No, I can't."

"What?" He sounded hurt. "Why? How am I supposed to get back?"

"I'm sorry, I can't do that. I don't know. I guess you'll have to figure that out."

I hung up. I smiled. *Wow. That actually felt really good. I can be strong. Being strong feels good.*

AND THE SPELL
WAS BROKEN

C got back Christmas morning. He was looking less and less appealing. He looked dark. Empty. Angry. *What was he so angry about? God, please help me. Show me what to do God. Show me Lord.*

A couple of days after New Year, I woke up. C was asleep next to me. We were on the air mattress in my mother's house. As I stirred, he woke up.

"Good morning." I smiled at him.

"Morning." He yawned. He looked bored.

"I'm gonna go have a shower. Do you wanna come?"

"No, babe. You go. I think I'll try to go back to sleep."

I walked down the hall into the bathroom, trying not to be disappointed. The house was empty. *Mom must have taken the kids to the park or something.*

I didn't turn on the light. The light coming in from under the door was just enough. I ran the hot water and breathed in the steam. I got in, finding therapy in the heat and sound. I hung my head under the water. *Jesus. Help me, Jesus.* The tears came. *God, I need you. God, help me. I pray for this man, Lord. Show me what to do. If this is not the man you have for me, then show me what to do. Help, God.* I leaned my forehead against the tiles. The hot water gliding down the nape of my neck and down my back. I soaked in the moment. The quiet. The hot. The dark. The solace. *God, I need you. Help me, Jesus.* After a long time adrift in a sea of thought and prayer, I turned the water off.

175

Grabbed my towel. Dried off. I wrapped my hair in one towel and wrapped another around me. Opened the door and walked down the hall. I went into the family room that was my "bedroom" with the air mattress and C's computer. He was sitting at the computer. I looked up at him sitting there. He didn't look back. Not noticing I had walked in. His computer screen caught my attention. *What are those pictures of?* It looked like something odd. He was scrolling down. Slowly. Carefully. Studying the images. *What is that?* Intense panic surged through me.

He clicked on one and a video started. It filled up the screen. A woman got up. My heart was pounding so hard it was jolting my whole body. She had no clothes on. C pulled down his shorts and started to play with himself. *Oh my God.* I couldn't think. I couldn't speak. I was horrified. Mortified. I can't watch anymore. *Lord. Oh my Lord.* I took a step forward and touched his shoulder. My stomach sick. He swung around, shocked and startled. He got up.

"Cassi! Oh shit!" He started mumbling. He started apologizing and excusing. I felt like I was going to throw up. I couldn't look at him. He reached out to touch me, and I shuddered. I finally saw him. I finally saw him for the man he really was. Depraved. Perverted. Disgusting. Completely given over to evil. What's worse is he preferred that image on a screen to a woman in the flesh. Me. I wasn't satisfactory. I felt complete betrayal.

And then, the spell was broken. In that instant. Any love I thought I had for him was gone. The illusion was shattered. I sat down numbly.

He was looking at me. Grabbing my shoulders. Shaking me. Making promises. Making vows. Giving excuses, saying sorry. Talking. Talk, talk, talk, talk, talk. In fact, I think that's all he ever really did. Talk. And look at porn. And drink. And smoke marijuana. *How could I be so stupid? How could I be so blind?* I was amazed at my own naïveté. *How could I possibly think I could change this man? How could I love this man? How could I want him to be a father figure to my children? He's not a role model. He's weak. He's a sick, weak, pathetic, man. My dad was right. Everyone was right. He was nothing compared to Dean. He wasn't half the man Dean was. He wasn't a shadow of the man Dean was.*

What I didn't know, was at that very moment, my dad was being led by the Holy Spirit to forgive C. He had been fighting his own battles and had been so angry at C for the way he was using me for money and taking advantage of my vulnerability. At that very moment he was on his knees saying, "God, I forgive. I forgive Cazador. I choose to forgive."

I sent my dad a message.

"You were right, Dad. You were right about everything. He spent my money. He used me. He's a bad man. I'm sorry, Dad."

Something Mended, Something Broken, and Something Unexpected

T he rift was mended. My parents wasted no time being reunited with the boys and me.

I told C to leave. I told him I needed a week. A week to think. A week to get some clarity. And then I cried. I cried for a day. Over my mistakes. Over the rift in my family. For my boys. For the death of my fairy tale. My dream that I had love in my life again. My dream of having a companion. Reality had given me a good, hard slap in the face. And then I thought. For the next six days. I cried, and I thought. And at the end of the week, I knew. It was over.

I called him and arranged to meet. We sat in my car. I was calm. I told him. It's over. I explained why. You're a liar. You're an alcoholic. You do drugs. You're not employed. There's no trust. There's no love. I used him to fill a void in my life. It was wrong. The relationship was wrong from the start. I needed something. Something to escape my pain. He was a great distraction. A fantasy. And that was over now. It was done.

He begged. He pleaded. I was insistent. I made up my mind.

The following weekend, my siblings and their spouses and the boys and I all went to my parents' for a visit. My sister and I were on speaking terms again, for which I was beyond grateful. My period was four days late. It was playing on my mind. *Surely not. I'm surely not.* I wanted to get a test though, just to have the peace of mind that

I wasn't pregnant. I told Naomi I wanted to go fuel up the car and asked her if she would come along. She agreed. On the way there, she assured me, "Yeah, Cass, I agree. I don't think you are. Let's just do a test though, and then you'll know for sure."

I took a deep breath. *Yes, that peace of mind will be good.* We got some fuel and then went into the drugstore. Found a test. Paid for it.

"Let's just do it while we're here. There's a bathroom at the back of the store." She pointed.

"Good idea."

We went into the girl's bathroom. It was a rather large room with a toilet in the corner. Florescent lights and white tiles. A typical commercial bathroom. It was stark but clean.

Being sisters, there was no issue with her being in the bathroom with me while I took the test. I squatted. Peed on the stick. And set it down on the floor. I pulled up my jeans and wriggled them back on. I looked at Noni.

"Are you okay? It's gonna be fine, Cass."

I couldn't wait any longer, it had only been a minute or so.

I picked up the stick.

Two lines.

I collapsed. All I could feel was the cold tiles underneath me. Pain like a tidal wave crushed me. *I've ruined my life.* Pain. *Oh my God, I've ruined my whole life. No, no, no, no, no. This can't be. Oh my God. This can't be. What have I done? What have I done? Dean's family, my family, what will they think? Oh my Lord.* Thoughts bombarded me like a barrage of bombs. Hundreds, all at once. Wreaking havoc in my mind. Anxiety. Dread. And Panic swept over me. I could feel my sister next to me. She was trying to comfort me. I was in a world of my own though. A world of regret, pain, panic, and despair.

Naomi helped me off the floor.

"Okay, Cassi. Listen. Let's just go next door to Applebee's, get something to drink, and talk this through, okay? Do you think we should let C know what's going on?"

That guy. Oh my gosh. How can I have a child to that man? It sounded like a life sentence. A life of fighting. Like his parents.

Screaming matches. Bitterness. Hatred. Blaming. Resentments. *Oh my Lord. Oh my Lord. Help me, Jesus. Help me, Jesus.*

I sat down at Applebee's with Naomi. She had a way of making light of any situation, for which I was most grateful at that moment. We got in touch with C. He seemed happy. *Yeah. This is just great. Did this man possess any foresight? Do I try to make a relationship work with him just because I'm going to have a child with him?* I couldn't figure out if that sounded right or wrong.

We got back to my parents' house a number of hours after we left. I don't know where they thought we must have got to. I was exhausted. I was pregnant. *Pregnant! Sweet Jesus. Since when is this my life?*

Bed. *I need sleep.* Bed.

Over the next week, I cried. A lot. I would sit in my car looking out at the ocean and weep. And weep. The idea of bringing a new baby into my situation was beyond comprehension. *I can hardly take care of myself and the kids I do have, let alone a new baby.* Anxiety pumped through my body. Whoosh. Adrenaline. *Why do I have to be so damn fertile? Damn those Irish genes. God. Oh my God. I'm going to have two kids to a dead guy and another kid to a deadbeat guy. Who will want me then? Any man would have to be insane to want me with that package. Oh my Lord. What am I going to do?* Tears, tears, and more tears. *I'm so sick of crying. When will it ever stop? When will it stop?*

I told my mom and Brian. They were compassionate and supportive.

"Well, if we're gonna have a baby, then we're gonna have a baby. We'll just make it work. Worse things in the world have happened." Mom comforted me as the tears flowed. I was grateful for their help.

That weekend, we went to my dad and Ginny's house again. I knew I had to tell them. There are some things that . . . there's just no easy way to say. I know. I've tried to find one. There's no easy way to say you're pregnant. Six months after your husband's death. With a man who is an absolute mess. How do you say that? Other than, say it. Some things are just hard. There's no way around it.

I sat my parents down in the living room. My sister was there.

"Guys, there's something I have to tell you . . . " Pause. "I'm pregnant."

They were quiet. Thank God they are the beautiful and gracious people that they are.

"It's been rough, Cass. We never wanted this for you. We never wanted you to have to go through what we went through." My dad was referring to the visitation, custody, child support, blended family business that we were all too familiar with.

"We're here for you. It's going to be okay."

I spent the rest of the day there. I had a sort of relief now that they knew. I wasn't shouldering the burden so alone anymore. I had my family with me. And for me.

The boys were enrolled in school now. I had gotten a job at Starbucks just a few blocks away. There was beginning to be a sort of rhythm to life. The days were okay. I had something to get me out of the house, I had the boys to tend to, and family at home. It was the nights, when everyone was asleep, that Torment came. I was fraught with worry over my baby. Over my relationship with C. Over my future. Panic and Anxiety came over and over again. Assaulting me. Taunting me. I was so lost. *I'm sleeping on my mother's floor. My kids are sleeping on the floor.* I was grateful for a place to stay where there was Peace and we were provided for, but it was so transient. *What am I going to do?* I filled my blankets with tears in the night. Fearful that Grief and Agony would swallow me. Their jaws, a death grip. Trying to hold them at bay. Trying to fight them. Push them down. Run from them. Ignore them. But they won out. And I caved to their bidding. And so in the quiet darkness of night, I would sob my heart out. Weeping over Dean. Crying over my regret. Worrying about my future. Desperate to figure out how I would care for a new baby. And how I would deal with the other half of that baby's family. Eventually, exhaustion would overcome me, and I would fall into haunted slumber. Where Trauma and Fears would take shape and hunt me down in my sleep.

I went to see a pastor at a church I'd been attending fairly regularly. I sat down with him in his office. I told him everything. I told him about losing Dean. About the relationship with C. Finding him with the porn. Breaking it off. And finding out about the baby.

"I've made such a mess of everything." I was surrounded by tissues. My voice distorted by the suppressed emotion trying to escape.

He listened. His expression soft and concerned. He was patient. "Your mistakes do not define you, Cassi. When you look back on your life, this circumstance will be a complete anomaly. This is not who you are."

He believed in me. He saw me. Not for my sin but for who I really was. He gave me a book about God's grace. And sent me away. His words were ointment on my wounds, and I soaked in the balm. His words sang in my ears. *This isn't who I am. It doesn't define me. Thank you, God.*

THE BEST IS YET TO COME.

I told a few close friends about my pregnancy. My two very close friends were absolute gems. Kellie and Leah. I could tell them anything, no matter how crazy, and they would just listen and encourage me. There was never an ounce judgment or criticism. Just love and acceptance and grace. They were a spring of life in the desert for me. A place of refreshment and hope. Friendships that revived me. They reminded me of who I was when I had forgotten. They believed in me when most others walked away. They never gave up on me. I will never be able to repay that debt, but I will endeavor to try.

I wasn't looking forward to telling Dean's parents. But I knew I needed to, and I knew I wanted it to come from me. So I sat down and wrote an e-mail. Daddy is right when he says doing the right thing is usually the hardest.

To my surprise, Sue responded with the kindest and gentlest words. She responded better than anyone. I praised God for her.

I was out with my sister and my cousin one day. We were shopping. Our mood was bright and bubbly. We got to talking about kids. Both my sister and cousin have two boys, like me. As we were chatted away, the girls decided what a wonderful idea it would be if we were all pregnant together.

"We could all try for a girl together!" We gushed and giggled. "And we could be pregnant and get pedicures together!"

The idea sent us into a frenzy of excitement. I was delighted with the idea of having companionship in my pregnancy, especially seeing as I was doing it on my own.

SUBMERGED IN
BLACK WATER

March 2011

C had moved to Vegas. He found a job there and decided to go. We kept in touch. I gave him updates on the pregnancy. We decided we would go to the doctors for the ultrasound when he was in town.

I was about ten weeks along when he drove over for a visit. We went to a small clinic. It was exciting. I was letting this little life in my heart. Your child is your child, regardless of the circumstances. A mother's love is a mother's love, and I was going to love this baby. Even if it meant things were tough. Even if it meant I was a struggling single mom with three kids.

The nurse went about doing the sonogram.

We waited. The boys were there as well. On the screen, we could see the outline of the baby's body.

"Okay. Yep . . . " She wasn't saying much. "Are you sure you're ten weeks along?"

"Yes." *Of course, I'm sure. You don't have to have a degree to count to ten.*

"Hmm, okay. Your baby looks a bit small. I'm just having a hard time finding the baby's heartbeat."

Something's not right. I felt it. In the pit of my stomach. *This isn't right.*

We left. I had mixed feelings. Seeing C again. It was even more evident to me that this was not the man I want to walk alongside in the journey of life. He left the next morning. I told him I would keep in touch.

About a week later, on a Sunday afternoon, I was working at Starbucks. I started feeling some cramping. Like period pain–type cramping. *That's odd. I don't remember having cramps when I was pregnant with the boys. Hmm. Weird.* I went to the bathroom, and there was the slightest spotting. Fear swept over me. *Something isn't right.*

When I got in my car, I called Naomi, who is also a trained doula. I explained what was happening.

"Okay. Yeah. Listen. Go home. Put your feet up. Get some rest. I'm sure everything is going to be fine. See how you feel in the morning, okay?"

I went home and tried to relax. It was harder to relax without having any wine.

I put my feet up on the couch. The cramping continued. Just the slightest sensation. I had another fitful night's sleep. I woke up to worse cramps and more spotting. *God, no. No, no, no. Something's not right.* Shaking, I called my sister.

"Calm down. Okay, I'll come down to mom's house. You stay there. Keep your feet up. We'll take you down to the clinic just to make sure everything is fine."

I was trying unsuccessfully to hold back the tears. "Thank you, Noni."

I called in to work and told them I was sick. Naomi came to get me. I was walking ever so gingerly. Afraid of making abrupt movements. We got in her car and drove to a clinic. They turned us away saying we needed to go to hospital emergency.

So we drove to the hospital where they admitted me. They got me into a hospital gown and laid me down in a bed. It was awful as most emergency rooms are. Sterile. Florescent. Devoid of color or life. Once again, I was grateful for my sister's ability to make me laugh in any situation. She took time away from everything else to be with me. My heart squeezed. *Thank you, God, for my sister.* We chatted and giggled over inside jokes and funny movies. Trying to lighten the seriousness and uncertainty that weighed in the atmosphere. I laughed outwardly but was quivering inwardly. The doctor came in. It was a female doctor. She asked me a few questions and then gave me a quick internal exam.

"There's some blood there. It's not a lot of blood, but there is some blood. We're going to send you up to ultrasound to get a scan and see how your baby is going, okay?"

"Yes, okay, thank you." I felt grateful.

A little while later, someone else came and put me in a wheel chair. They wheeled me to the ultrasound room. A woman did my scan. She didn't speak to me while I was there. Then they wheeled me back. I was grateful to have Naomi at my side again.

After some time, the doctor came back.

"I'm sorry to have to tell you, your baby is not alive. It looks like your baby stopped growing at about eight or nine weeks. You are going to have a miscarriage. Now, if you like, you can have a DNC done, which is a procedure we do here at the hospital where we basically vacuum and clean out the uterus. Or you can go home and have your miscarriage naturally. At the stage you are, about half the people would have the DNC." Her tone was sympathetically matter-of-fact.

I couldn't hold back the tears. Naomi was crying. She was holding my hand. *My baby is dead. Grief gripped me hard.* I was trying to maintain some sort of composure so I could respond to the doctor. "I think I'd like to go home and miscarry naturally."

"Okay, yeah. I'll prescribe you some pain killers. It will be pretty painful, so just be prepared for that."

Your baby is not alive. Her words echoed in my head. *My baby is dead. My baby. My precious little innocent baby.* My mind raced. I thought about all the nights I lay awake, crying and sobbing. The stress. Anxiety. My body probably thought I was too stressed to carry the baby. I was too distraught.

"Cassi, how can you go through so much?" Naomi was crying at my side. She'd been so strong. She'd been so reassuring. The doctors were gone now. It was just me and Noni. Crying. Pain. More tears. More pain.

We had lunch together. I wasn't very hungry. We talked. I tried to process it. The cramps were slowly intensifying. Eventually, she had to go home to her kids. I went home, already feeling emotionally drained. I was trying to wrap my head around what was happening. I had made phone calls during the day so that most of the family were aware of what was happening. I called C.

"The baby died. It stopped growing a couple of weeks ago. I'm going to have a miscarriage." I said somewhat despondently.

"Oh my gosh, really? Oh no. Babe, listen, I'm going to come out there as soon as I can. Call me whenever you want. I'm here for you."

Yeah, but you're not here for me. Whatever.

I went to the drugstore to get my prescription filled. A line started forming, and I started feeling painful pressure. *I need to sit down.* I sat down, and someone took my place in line. I tried to explain to them I was uncomfortable and needed to sit down, but I was actually in line. They weren't interested. Others formed in line behind them. The pain was mounting, and I couldn't wait any longer. Defeated, I went home without meds.

It'll be like really bad period cramps. I'll just have to grit and bear it.

Everyone went to sleep. I tried to lay down in bed, but the pressure was getting too intense. I drew a hot bath for myself. As hot as I could stand it. Got in.

Alone.

The cramps were becoming unbearable. I grabbed at my stomach and tossed and turned in the bath. Crying. *I had no idea it was going to be this bad. Oh my god. Oh my god. I can't take this!* I clenched my fists and teeth. I tried to swallow my sobs. I fantasized about someone coming in with a baseball bat and knocking me unconscious.

The worst physical pain I have ever endured. Matched by the excruciating emotional pain I was in. *My husband is dead. My baby is dead.* The finality of death and the pain of loss overwhelmed me. I looked down into the water. It was black. I was surrounded by death. Immersed in death. Death. I could feel my heart as it was breaking. My insides being slowly torn out at the same time. Alone. So alone.

Dean. My husband. My baby. My angel baby. That I'll never hold. My darling baby. My precious baby.

I got my iPhone and played the Alison Krauss song, "Baby Mine."

"Baby mine, don't you cry. Baby mine, dry your eyes. You are so precious to me, sweet as can be, baby of mine."

I wept and I wept and I wept.

I picked up my phone. I called C. *I need someone to talk through this with me. I need to talk. I need to distract myself from this pain. God, it's more than I can bear.*

He answered. "Hey, babe, how are you?"

"I'm in the bath. I'm in a lot of pain. It's happening." I could hardly think straight. I felt a wave of nausea.

"You are? Oh wow, that's bad. Listen, do you mind if I call you back in just a minute? Just in a moment."

"Uh, yeah, okay."

He never called back. I rang him, but he didn't answer. *Bastard. Help me, God.*

I called one of my closest friends in Esperance. I didn't know who else to call. She answered. I fought back the tears to try to explain where I was and what was happening.

She paused and then gave feigned empathy. "Oh wow. Gosh, Cass. Well, maybe you'll do that differently next time."

Her trite and insipid tone were salt in all my wounds. Making the all-enveloping death darker. Stronger. More powerful. It stole my breath. *How can she be so cold? I never want to be like that. I never want to be that person.* The conversation ended shortly after. And I felt I'd lost yet another friend.

DESIRE GIVES BIRTH TO SIN, AND SIN GIVES BIRTH TO DEATH.

That's me. I'm literally giving birth to death! Oh my Lord. My God. Look at this mess I am in. This world of pain and hurt. This is so bad. This whole situation is bad. It looks so hopeless! Like the part in the movie where everything is so bad, and you can't possibly see how things could work out. You're the only one, Lord. You're the only one I know who can take broken and impossible situations and turn them around. Turn them into something good. I'm sorry I've been running from you, Lord. I'm broken.

I could see it all so clearly then. I'd been running. Running from my pain. Making decisions out of brokenness. Living out of brokenness. Unable to see past my pain. And I was going to keep making a bad situation worse and worse until I let God heal my heart.

I'm ready, God. Oh it's going to hurt so much, and I'm so scared to face my pain. I feel like that avalanche will crush me. But, Lord, there's no way around it. There's no way around my pain but through it. I'm ready, Lord. Heal my heart. I want you to heal my heart. You can have my life again. God, you can have it all.

And right there in that bathtub, lying in a pool of death, in a world of pain, with a broken heart, I surrendered it all to God again. I reached for Light. For Hope. And I asked Him to come. *Come, Lord. For I am weary. I am faint. I cannot do this. My Lord, you will have to because I cannot.*

After four hours in the tub, I felt a gush. Relief. The placenta. It was a bit bigger than my palm and an inch or so thick. I let out the blood water and dried myself off. It wasn't over, but it was a reprieve. I carried myself on shaky legs to bed. Weak. Exhausted but not alone. God was with me. Sleep.

The next day, I mostly stayed home to rest. I was having some light cramping but nothing bad. I had the good sense to go back to the drugstore and fill my prescription for pain meds. When the next round hit, I would be ready. It was the following morning, about six. Pain woke me up.

I got up and took two of my Vicodin and laid back down, trying to mentally prepare myself for the ensuing torture. I was squirming in bed and moaning. The pain was gradually getting more and more intense. I hadn't passed the baby and the sack yet. I knew that must be happening now. My mom came in. "How are you, honey?"

"It hurts, Mom. It hurts so much." The tears were running across my temples and into my ears. Lying still was too painful. I was rocking around and rolling in bed. The Vicodin made me nauseous. I asked Mom to bring me something to eat. Thankfully, she was there to help the boys get ready for school and drop them off. I got up and drew a hot bath. *Heat. I need heat and water.* The Vicodin didn't seem to be touching the sides. I sat up and banged on the wall. "DAMMIT!" I stood up. Leaned my head against the wall. Let out a bellow. "God. Oh my God. Oh my God. Oh my God." My mom came back and sat in the bathroom with me. Having someone there somehow helped. Someone to witness my torture, even if they couldn't stop it. I banged against the walls and shouted. I got out of the bath and back in bed. Writhing in the pain. I took two more Vicodins. Still no relief. I took two Advils as well. I continued to toss and turn. Crying. Moaning. Mom kept me from getting hysterical. My fists clenched, I punched the pillows. So angry. So frustrated. So overwrought. *Dean. Dammit, Dean. Why Dean? C. You fucking asshole. God. Oh my God. You're supposed to have a baby at the end of all of this pain. My baby is dead. I'm going through all of this pain, and I don't even get a baby at the end of it.* I thrashed in bed and swore. Once again, I wished someone would give me a good hard hit in the head to knock me out.

Four and a half hours later. In the bath. I felt something between my legs. The sack and my baby. Before I thought about it, I flushed it down the toilet. *My baby. Oh my God. I flushed my baby down the toilet.* A flood of tears came. The cramping was gone. I went into the living room and lay on the couch. I could feel the effects of the Vicodin now. The woozy, cloudy high. *I'm empty now. Baby's gone now. My angel baby is with Jesus. I'm sorry, my little baby. I'm so sorry. I'm going to miss you. I'm sorry I never got to meet you. I'm sorry. I love you. I'll see you in heaven one day. Angel baby . . .* I drifted off. Sleep.

FACING THE AVALANCHE

"Ruin is a gift. Ruin is the road to transformation."
—*Eat, Pray, Love*

The next day, I sat on my bed. I knew it was time. Time for me and God to sort things out. It was time to face Pain. The avalanche. The tide. I felt like I'd been grieving for so long. I didn't want to grieve anymore. I didn't want to cry anymore. But it was the only way. I knew Pain was still in my heart. I knew I was broken. *I have to work my way through it. Through it is the only way past it. There's no going around it. There's no ignoring it. There's no drinking it away.* I crossed my legs and sat still. In the quiet, by myself.

I'm ready, Lord. I looked within my own heart. The avalanche of pain I'd been running from. I stopped. It took all the courage I had. I stopped running. I turned around. And I faced the avalanche. I faced Pain. I was expecting to get flatlined by a torrent of emotions. Swept up in Pain's avalanche where I would be pummeled, beaten, and buried.

Instead, slow tears came as I felt God put His hand on my heart. It wasn't an avalanche. It was gentle drops of healing oil. I cried while my Heavenly Father poured His love on me. With the skilled hands of a surgeon, He began to mend my broken heart. I was a little lamb. A little lamb with a terrible injury. Running around the paddock in pain. Bumping into things. Making it worse. The Shepherd wanted to pull me into his lap so He could fix me up. But whenever He came close, I ran away. *Don't touch it! It hurts too much. It hurts too much. Just leave it. Leave me alone!* But the little lamb was ready now. Ready to lie in the Shepherd's lap. To let Him put His hands on the sorest places. Trusting that, as much as it may hurt, He is going to make me better. If I just let Him. And that, when the time is right, He will send me bounding back into the paddock again. All healed up.

Four weeks grief settled over me like a gray sky. Incessant tears. Not like the waves that would come to drown me. Like steady winter rain. There's a time to grieve. And I was grieving. The song "It Is Well with My Soul" brought me much comfort. I sat, staring out the window. The clouds and rain echoing my heart's melancholy, listening to the precious words of hope. Hope beyond brokenness. That my soul is well. Despite the loss. The suffering. The trauma. The pain. Death. *It is well.* The tears welled up in my eyes and fell down my cheeks. Dripping off my chin. Then more would well up and fall. Rise and fall. Rise and fall. *The only way past it is through it.* I was lost at sea. In a boat. Feeling the water's rise and fall with its gentle ebb. Unsure where I was headed. But trusting that God, my rudder, would guide me back to port. Eventually. That was me. Sitting. Staring. Weeping. My weathered soul's lament. *My baby. I love you, my baby. I'm sorry, baby. Mommy loves you, baby. Dean. Dean. I miss you, sweetie. Gone. You're gone. Can't get you back. Alone. I'm alone. Won't see you. Not in this life, I won't.*

Not long after, my sister and my cousin got pregnant. Both with girls. The news stung.

My *baby is dead.*

My *husband is dead.*

OUT OF THE ASHES

After my four weeks of tears, something started to happen. Something changed. A strength. A strength I had never felt before rose. Determination. Out of the ashes, the phoenix rose. That was me. I don't know how. God. He's the only One who could have done it. I felt iron in my bones. Where I had felt the shakes, quakes, and quivers. I was immovable. Undeterred. Resurrected. Determined not to give up. *I am not going to curl up with a bottle of whiskey. Fuck no. I am not going to give up.* Leaving the house to go work at Starbucks. Walking out to my car. *Fuck no, I'm not giving up. NO!* I had been in the fire, and everything had burned away. All that was left was made of steel. *If I can bury Dean. If I can let go of my angel baby. I can do anything.* To the powers of darkness: *You cannot have my smile. You will not take my joy. It is mine. I'm going to keep smiling and keep laughing and keep loving.*

I made a decision. Any negative thought I had or sensed from anyone else, I'm going to turn it into joy. And love. And hope. With light and everything good. I loved my days at work. My objective was to make people smile. To spread cheer. Especially to those most determined to resist its compulsion. I loved it. And I succeeded often.

One morning, at church, I was sitting in my seat just after the service had ended. It was heavy in my heart and thoughts that I was sitting alone. Most people were sitting with their husband. Their wife. I was alone. *God, I am so broken. This looks like a happy families' gathering. I don't even feel like I belong here. I'm barely holding it together. I'm so broken. Oh God. How is it that I'm so broken and everyone here looks so strong? Alive. Together. Whole.*

CASSI, WHO WOULD BE HERE TO ENCOURAGE YOU IF THEY
WERE AS BROKEN AS YOU ARE NOW? WHO WOULD BE HERE
TO BE OF STRENGTH TO YOU? OF HELP?

I hadn't thought of it that way. *Blessed. I'm blessed there are those who are not in this season. Those who are strong and able. Able to give. Able to encourage.*

I felt a woman scoot toward me, settling in a chair next to me. I looked to my left, and there was a roundish woman with kind, twinkling eyes.

"Hello," she said with warmth.

"Hi." I wondered what she might say.

"Can I tell you something? I just really feel something for you."

"Sure." I was open.

"I feel like you're going through a relationship issue. Are you going through a relationship issue?"

You could say that. I nodded.

"Yes. Well, I feel God is saying that as you give that to Him, you are going to blossom." She beamed her beautiful smile at me.

Her words spoke to the cry of my heart. "Wow. Thank you for saying that."

I walked back to my car. *Give it to you, Lord? You want me to give it to you. To trust you with it. Let you bring things about in your time. Your way and your time. And in the meantime, I will blossom and grow. Okay, Lord. I hear you. But this is going to be hard . . .* And it was.

A couple of months later, I found an apartment available for rent a few blocks down the road. It was close to work and school. I took a look and signed a lease. *A little bit of independence. Just me and the boys. This is going to be good.*

My family helped us move, and we settled quickly. It was two bedrooms with an open living and kitchen. It was small, but we didn't need much. It only felt cramped for the lack of paddocks and cows. Sigh. *We're not in Esperance.* There was a community pool. It would have to do.

Dean's one year anniversary came around. I organized a party. His freedom party. At my dad's house. A gathering of friends and family to celebrate and honor Dean's life. The impact he had on us all. And the love we had for him. I wanted to celebrate him on this day, not mourn him. We made his favorite food. We told stories. It made him come alive. He felt close.

The boys finished school. Asher, kindergarten and Maddox, Preschool. That was hard. Watching them celebrate with their classmates. Watching them achieve. The beginnings of so many achievements. And Dean not there to partake in the pride.

THOSE WHO SOW WITH TEARS WILL REAP WITH SONGS OF JOY.

Dave and Sue came out to California to visit for a month. I was both excited and apprehensive. When I had left Australia, it was a whirlwind of intense emotions on everyone's part. My choices when I came back to the States were hard on everyone. I wasn't sure what to expect. They had the idea of renting a van and driving across from California to Arkansas and back again so we could all visit my grandparents. The trip was a time of healing and reconciliation. The boys loved seeing their grandparents again. Our time spent was making memories. Games. Cuppas. Teasing. Good Aussie humor. I felt their love. And they took so much joy in spending time with Asher and Maddox. For them to have peace of mind. Seeing we were settled. Seeing we were okay.

At one point, Dave took me out for a coffee. He looked like he had something on his mind. Something he wanted to talk about. I was a bit worried. I wasn't sure if I was in for a difficult discussion. I felt a knot in my stomach. I fidgeted with my paper cup, looking into his face for clues of the topic of conversation. His expression was serious and focused.

"Cassi, I've prayed with a dozen or so girls over the years." He paused and looked away. He seemed reflective. I was still holding my breath. "That God would bring along a husband for them."

Oh. Oh wow. Oh, this wasn't what I was expecting . . .

"We would make a list. A husband list. And, most of the time, got a man who came along who was pretty close to exactly what we asked for. Ya know. Now I'd like to pray for God to do that for you as well." I was completely taken aback. I would never have imagined this is what Dad wanted to talk to me about. *Wow. Oh my gosh. Dad wants to pray for a husband for me? How redemptive. How completely remarkable. How blessed am I? Lord. Oh my Lord. My heart was singing. Praise you, God.* It felt SO good to have my heart's deepest desire validated by Dean's father. I was overwhelmed. What an enormous blessing. *Yes. Yes, please.*

We took an hour or so and made a list of all the attributes I was looking for in a husband and father. Then made another list of the characteristics I would aspire to as a wife and mother. Sue joined in toward the end of the conversation, and we filled her in. She approved very matter-of-factly. My heart swelled with love for them. *Wow, God. You really never cease to amaze me.*

MAKING ENDS MEET
WITH HANDS

Summer was upon us again. I was putting one foot in front of the other. We had Asher's birthday and a July full of barbecues, beach days, pool swims, and family gatherings.

The primary question on my mind was how would I provide for me and the boys financially? I was living off the money Dean and I had made when we had sold our house in Australia. That wasn't going to last forever. My grand wage of eight dollars an hour at Starbucks wasn't going to pay the bills. I worked there more for my mental health and enjoyment. It was somewhere to go. Somewhere to be. Something to do. It got me out of the house and interacting with people, which meant I wasn't at home in bed being a wreck. And I genuinely enjoyed interacting with customers.

One day at work, I was rubbing my friend's sore shoulder. I was always touching everyone. Massaging. Rubbing. It's just in my nature. I soon got the nickname "Magic Hands."

My friend looked at me out of nowhere. "Cassi, have you ever considered becoming a massage therapist?"

Lightbulb.

"Actually . . . no. I've never thought of it."

Why hadn't I thought of that? It seemed so obvious. I had contemplated nursing, but considering the length of schooling and long shifts, it didn't seem conducive to my single-parent family situation. Massage was a similar job. Where compassion and empathy are paramount. But the training was reasonably short and allowed for a flexible schedule.

I looked into massage schools the following week. I found a school fifteen minutes down the road. I sat in on my first class before the end of the month. And I was en route to my new profession.

I was busy. Working at Starbucks four days a week on early shifts. Going to school Monday, Wednesday, and Friday nights from six to ten in the evening. I was paying my sitter more for babysitting in one night than I was making in a day at the coffee shop. It didn't make sense, but that's just how it was.

My day started off with getting the kids ready and to school. Then serving hundreds of people coffee. Coming home to do housework. Getting the boys from school. Getting them their snack. Organizing homework and dinner. Then going to massage school for four hours at night. I was dog tired on coming home. But still sleep eluded me. I would lie down, wide awake. A deep need to talk to someone. To connect. Text my sister. My brother. My best friend. During the day, I could distract myself from Loneliness with the busyness of life. But at night. At night, there was no escape. The Loneliness would come with a wrathful vengeance. I would get up and pour myself a large glass of wine, trying to drown out the sound of my own silent suffering. Quell the emptiness. Fill the void in my heart long enough for me to fall asleep. Learning to sleep alone. Only the lonely. Only the lonely know what that's like. The desire for companionship. The need for affection. It becomes extreme. And you become desperate. Willing to compromise. Making decisions you wouldn't usually make. Exceptions. Oversights. Loneliness blindfolds then suffocates you. Can't breathe. And you're going to die unless you get some air. Unless you get love. Love. Words. Affirmation. Touch. An embrace. To experience that craving. That need. And be deprived. It's torture.

Wine, Lies, and Envy.

I had a box in the closet of some of Dean's things. His Bible. A few shirts. A couple belts. Some other bits and pieces. At this point, the waves were getting further in between. They would come about once a month and last three or four days. But they hit hard. Thankfully, the boys had each other to play with and things to do at home. I would try to cry somewhere they wouldn't be able to see me. Screaming into my pillows or the carpet. Rolling around on the floor. Overcome with missing Dean. Picturing his face. His hands. His smile. The sound of his voice.

Everyone loved Dean. Everyone.
It should have been you.
Dean would have done a better job than you.
You're a fuck up.
You're a mess.
You can't get your life together.
Dean was a better person than you.
A better parent.
A better Christian.

The thoughts came like a plague of ticks. Burrowing themselves into my head. Embedding themselves under my skin as I howled and heaved.

I poured myself a glass of wine one night and got into a scalding bath. The adrenaline rush from the heat helped calm the anxiety.

I reclined. I partook of the dark elixir. Crying. Wondering. Hoping. Trying to picture a future. That somehow, somewhere, everything would work out. One day. *Maybe we'll have a two-story house. Maybe a dog. The boys will have a stepdad. Someone nice. Someone who likes to play sports with them. Someone strong and kind. And we'll laugh a lot. And we'll go on trips together. And the boys will be happy. And I will be happy.*

Once the bath was too cold to be comfortable, I got out. Relaxed and woozy from the wine and heat.

Dean.

Tears. A rush of emotion. The floor. Crying. Sobbing. *Dean. Dammit, Dean. Dammit, Dean!* Punching the ground. Hitting the ground. Can't breathe. *Lord, help me, I can't breathe. I can't do this. It's too hard. It's too hard. I want to be a good mom. Help me be a good mom. Oh, Dean. Why did you leave me? Look at me. Oh my God. Help me do this.* I remembered the box in the closet. I crawled over to the closet. Pulled the door open. Dragged out the box. *You're more than a box, baby. You aren't just a box. I love you. I need you. I miss you. Why aren't you here?* I ripped it open, pulling everything out. *His T-shirt.* I put it up to my face, inhaling deeply. *Baby, oh my love, my love.* I put the shirt on. *Baby, I need you. Come to me. Come to me. Darling. You're not just a box. You're more than a box. Baby, I'm sorry.* Crying. Sobbing. Travailing. *Scream into the pillow. So the boys can't hear you. Don't let them know. Be strong for the boys. You have to keep going for the boys. Dean. I miss you, honey.* Tears. *I miss you. Babe . . .*

Exhausted.

Asleep.

Seven o'clock came way too early. My eyes, red and swollen from the tears. I felt sluggish from the two glasses of wine as well. *Ugh. Okay.*

"Mom! I want breakfast!"

"What cereal do we have?"

"I'm doing show and tell today. I need to bring a book about my favorite animal. Okay, mom? Mom! Do you hear me?"

"Where's my shoes?"

"What am I having for lunch?"

"I don't want the vanilla yogurt in my lunchbox. I want the strawberry one."

The morning routine. Accosted by the boys with their thoughts, requests, complaints, plans, and questions. A whirlwind as I tried to surface. Trying to be patient. Trying to be organized. Trying to understand. Trying to be helpful. Trying to show love.

Alone. I'm on my own. I fucking hate doing this on my own. I fucking hate it. I wished somehow I could put their lives on hold. Call a timeout. I could gather myself on the sidelines for a while. Regroup. Get a plan. Get an award-winning motivational speech by Denzel Washington. Then I could come back pumped. Ready to win. This was the only childhood they were going to get. And I was off balance, off guard, off sides, out of bounds, and recovering from injury.

Off to school.

I had determined long ago I would never be a single mother. I had a single mother growing up. It was bloody hard. We were always late. Unorganized. The house was a mess. We were all falling apart most of the time. It was an existence I said I would never replicate. But try as I might to avoid it, here I was. And all around me, all I could see were happy families. Whole families. Beautiful, healthy, thriving families. *I should be happy for all these people. But I'm not. Why? Why am I not happy for these people?* I was unable to drown out the sound of the searing pain of my own loss long enough to experience joy on another's behalf.

ENVY. YOU ENVY THESE PEOPLE.

The truth hurts. *I'm envious? Yes.* I had to admit it. It was the truth. I was envious of lots of people. Including my sister. She had the husband, the beautiful home, new cars. She got to stay home with her kids. She had the two boys, and now she was pregnant. With a baby girl.

I was living in a moldy two-bedroom apartment. Working my ass off. Struggling. In almost every area of life.

You're the eldest, and your whole life is in shambles.

Everywhere I looked, I saw what I didn't have. Stability. Wholeness. Joy. Peace. Lives of blessing. Seasons of abundance. I was a tree in winter. No leaves. Bare. Cold. Gray. Still alive. But no signs of life.

We met at my sister's house for Thanksgiving. Everything was perfect. Everyone was happy. Everyone else had their spouse. The house was warm and clean and beautiful. My sister cooked most of the meal. We brought some side dishes and desserts. As I sat in the house that evening, I felt a giant, gaping wound in my chest. Salt poured into it. Naomi, with her beautiful pregnant belly. The house. The family. It was all so beautiful. And taunting me. Everything I longed for in my heart. Everything that had been taken from me. Stolen. *Robbed. I'm so robbed.* I could barely hold the tears back. *Does my family know how I feel? Do they know how much pain I'm in? I'm so broken.* The tears kept threatening, but I didn't want to ruin the evening. Everyone was so happy. *Alone. I'm alone. This evening will end. Everyone else has someone. To talk to. Snuggle next to. I go home alone. I sleep alone.*

Cardiff had its perks. It was often perfect weather. Sunny and warm but not overly so. The hillside was a beautiful haphazard array of beach houses. Some old. Some new. It was an expensive place to live but was cheerily confident in its eclectic and unassuming charm. I was walking one morning. Wrestling with God. Talking to Him. I still wasn't talking to Him a lot at this point. But I was always keenly aware of His presence. I knew He was close. I just kept Him at a distance.

This envy issue was troubling me. As long as I can remember, I never found it difficult to be happy for people. Friends. Family. Whoever. I hadn't really struggled with insecurity or jealousy or envy before. I felt so ripped off. *Why, God? Why couldn't Dean and I just live in Australia our whole lives? Raise our children. See our grandchildren grow up. Live our lives. I would have been content with that. Why did that not happen?*

I feel so ripped off! I'm so angry. It isn't fair. It's not fair. Why, God? Why?

CASSI, YOU RESENT YOUR CIRCUMSTANCES.

Yes. Yes, I do.

YOU'RE PUSHING THEM AWAY.

Yes, I am.

CASSI, YOU ARE A SINGLE MOM, BUT IT DOESN'T HAVE TO BE
THE WAY IT WAS WHEN YOU GREW UP. IT CAN BE DIFFER-
ENT. YOU ARE PRIVILEGED, CASSI. YOU HAVE BEEN GIVEN AN
OPPORTUNITY THAT VERY FEW PEOPLE GET.

I have? I suddenly remembered I had always had the desire to do ministry. Especially women's ministry.

IF YOU LET ME, I WILL WRITE AN AMAZING STORY WITH
YOUR LIFE. EMBRACE IT, CASSI. EMBRACE YOUR CIRCUM-
STANCES. EMBRACE YOUR LOSS. ALL OF IT. DON'T PUSH IT
AWAY. DON'T RUN FROM IT. DON'T RESENT IT. EMBRACE IT.
AND LET ME SHINE THROUGH IT. I WILL DO AMAZING THINGS
IN YOUR LIFE IF YOU LET ME.

Lord. Oh Lord. Yes, Lord. Change my heart. Change my heart, God. Mold me. Shape me. Make me the woman you want me to be.

And there was a shift. I chose to embrace it. To trust that God would do what He said. Look at this as a privilege. Let Him shine through my life. Only He can turn this into something amazing.

And so I trusted Him.

The nightmares had stopped. I had a good dream about Dean. I was walking in the sunshine, and I looked up and saw him standing next to me. I looked into his face, and I was so happy and relieved. I hugged him. I told him I missed him.

A few months later, my sister went into labor in the middle of the night. I got the text and hopped in the car to drive the fifteen minutes to her house. She was giving birth to her baby girl at home. On the drive down, my heart was heavy. *My baby is gone.* I knew I had to make a choice. To be there for my sister. To celebrate with her. To usher in this little one with joy. Even as my own heart swelled with grief.

It was a wonderful and powerful experience, being at my sister's side as she labored. Seeing my beautiful niece as she gracefully entered our family as her own little person. And I was grateful I didn't let my own pain get in the way of being there that night.

I joined a Bible study with some ladies at the church I was going to. We did a Beth Moore study. There was one week in particular that spoke unmistakably and directly to me. "God uses our biggest pain for our biggest ministry. He doesn't let one tear go to waste. Not one. He will use it all. For something good."

Tears. The other ladies could see it too. That God was speaking to me. He was speaking to all of us. But particularly to me that day. It confirmed in my heart everything I had felt for so many years. There was something. Something that would make it all worth it. Something I couldn't see. But there was a purpose. A purpose in all of it. *If all of this pain and suffering is going to be used for something good, I want to be ready. I want to be ready when the good part comes. When God is ready to say "Okay Cassi, let's turn this all around and do something amazing," I want to be standing in front of Him, ready for my instructions. Not distracted. Not wandering. Not wallowing. Not passed out. But ready. Lord, make me ready. Help me be ready. Help me not be distracted. I want what you have for me, Lord. I want it more than I want anything else. Use me. Use me, Lord. I want the good part. The promise.*

The days went on. God continued to make His presence known to me even though I didn't pursue Him. He spoke to me in dreams. The song "What a Friend We Have in Jesus" followed me. It was playing everywhere I went. Every time I turned on the radio. Even the grocery store. He followed me. He pursued me. He never gave up on me.

I wasn't playing the guitar at all. I didn't paint. Or draw. Or sing. Or dance. I didn't do any of the things I loved. I was that tree. Dormant in winter. Alive. No signs of life. No leaves. No fruit. People told me I should paint. I should play guitar. I wasn't ready.

I understand seasons well now. It wasn't the season.

Sleep was still a problem. The wine helped some. Going to bed alone was a death march to a pool of Loneliness. After mustering up the courage, I would enter. Then slowly sink into it. Until my head was submerged. Once my head was under the water, I was held down, unable to resurface. The suffocation would start. The struggle would ensue. Slowly at first. Then more intense. Violently trying to surface. Gasping for air. Oxygen. The oxygen of companionship. The oxygen of relationship. But there was none. Just the struggle. Tossing. Turning. Sobbing. Wishing there was reprieve from the agony. The agony of Loneliness who was strangling the life out of me. I would fight it until I could no longer. Slowly. Weakened. My strength ebbed away. The struggle would subside. Sinking. I would surrender to my slumber in the pool of Loneliness.

The coffee shop was still a great place for me. Being around people. Talking to people. Charming them. Making them laugh. One of the things I loved to see was the men who would come in to order a drink for their lady. Some had the order all written out with its specifications. Others came in with it memorized. *I wonder if I'll have someone like that one day. Someone who knows exactly what I drink. Exactly how I like it. And bring it to me without being asked.* One of our regulars came up and ordered his and his wife's drinks with me.

"I hope one day I have someone like you who will come to Starbucks and order a drink for me," I said smiling.

He paused. "You don't have anyone?" he asked seeming puzzled. The look on his face was so sad my heart squeezed and tears swelled. A lump blocked my throat. All I managed was to shake my head.

"Oh, wow. You seem like you have so much to give." He looked into my eyes. "You know what, God is preparing someone for you right now."

The words sank deeply into my heart as a promise. I couldn't hold back the tears. I smiled. Unable to speak. Grateful for his kind words that were life to my deepest desire. I headed to the back to dry my eyes and breathe through the wave of overwhelming emotion that surfaced. *You're preparing someone for me, God. You are.*

I was still grieving the loss of lots of friendships. I was like the man lying on the side of the road. Stripped and beaten by bandits.

Robbed. Half dead. Bleeding out. A mess. A broken mess. To my dismay, as many of my friends learned of my plight, they didn't help me. They turned away. Crossed the street.

"Maybe you'll do that differently next time."

Abandoned in my hour of need by those I thought friends. The amazing network of people who were so supportive when Dean was sick evaporated. Maybe if I hadn't made mistakes. Maybe if I mourned the way people thought I should. *Is a friend not supposed to love at all times? People are going to have an opinion about what I should do? Shouldn't do? Judge me? Criticize me? From their steady jobs. Comfortable homes. Happy marriages. Healthy families.*

They have absolutely no idea. Silence. From so many. Nothing. And I resented it.

I resented the idea you would only offer love and support if you *like* what someone is doing. *How is that love? That is not love.* And I silently resolved. *Lord, I pray I would not be the callous Christian. Whose love is conditional. And abandons those who are most in need. Help me, God. Help me be the kind of friend who loves at all times. Especially those who are hurting. Broken. Lost. Abandoned. Robbed. Cheated. Lied to. Through their struggles and their trials and their mistakes and failures. I want to move in close, get down on my knees, and whisper in their ear, "I'm here." Help me love like you love.*

And so I became grateful for my mistakes. Grateful for my trials. Grateful my friends had abandoned me. So God could show me. He could show me exactly how it feels. To know what it's like. And to learn how to love people.

LYING SPIRIT, COME OUT

I was reading my devotional one morning. "The work God does in you is a hidden work, and others will often not see it until much later."

Relief. *I don't need to prove myself. I don't need to chase after people to be my friend. I don't need to carry whatever label they have for me. Whatever judgments they've made for me. God is working in me. He's working in my heart. That's what. If other people can't see it or don't notice it, it doesn't matter. It's not about them. It's about me and God. Him and me.*

God was doing something in my heart, and I cherished it. I started to lean into Him again. I treasured the moments when I knew He was close. I began to recognize the people who knew Him. The ones who knew Him well. Because they were like Him. They weren't condemning and discouraging. They believed in me. They spoke life into me. They loved me.

He never left me. Never once. Not when I pushed Him away. Not when I ran away. Not when I ignored Him. Not when I disobeyed. Not when I was drunk. Not when I was completely disinterested in Him. Not only did He not leave. He pursued me. He showed His love for me. He brought people to encourage me. He provided for me. He showed me He was close to me. He comforted me. He showed me He is so good. And so faithful. In my faithlessness, He was faithful. In my wickedness, He was good. In my indifference, He was kind and merciful. What an amazing God He is. That I do not deserve His love. There is no way I ever could. Yet He lavishes it on me… even when I don't want it. His love never runs out. Never dries up. Never gives up. It never fails. It really doesn't. And I began to learn that it really is Him that's good. It's not me. He alone is good. It is only Him in me that is good. *You alone are good, my God. Let me not forget. It is not me who is good but you.*

THE BEST IS YET TO COME.

I had another dream about Dean. I was sitting in a chair in a living room. He was sitting on a couch adjacent. Lying on his back. He had Maddox in his arms. He was blowing raspberries on his neck. Maddox was giving the most delightful belly chuckle. Laughing loudly and wildly. Giving squeals of pleasure. In my dream, I knew I was dreaming, but I wanted to enjoy it. Stay as long as I could. I drank in the sound of my son's joy. Relishing each detail of the blissful encounter. How long it had been since I reveled in such a beautiful moment.

On Valentine's Day, I was sent a single red rose. Anonymously. With a ribbon. In a box. Along with a scripture. I lay on the floor holding it. Weeping and weeping. Sobbing. For longer than I can remember. *God loves me. God has promised good to me. He sees me. He knows me. He cares about me. He loves me.*

At church, pastor spoke about the Israelites. They were on the move, and their enemies came upon them. They had put their instruments by a tree. They laid them down. The message was that our worship is a weapon against the enemy. And we must not lay it down. It's time to take up your instruments. Worship God. Take back the things in your life that the enemy has stolen.

It was time for me to pick up the guitar again. To worship the Lord the way I used to. It had been so long. But it was time. And I wrote this song:

He watches over me
He leads me beside still waters
He makes my enemies bow
At my feet
I need your loving kindness

208

Without it there's only blindness
Change my ways, Your Highness
Set me free
Clothe me in purity
Wipe these tears away
Take these scars make me lovely
For I belong to thee

My massage course was coming to an end. I would be a work-ing massage therapist soon. I was still living off the money I had in savings. And that money was running out. My lease at my apartment would be up in July. I needed to decide if I was going to sign for another twelve months. I wasn't sure I would be able to afford it. In March, I started praying hard. *God, show me what to do. If I move, where do I go?* I knew I didn't want to bounce around from one place to another with no real sense of purpose or direction. I wanted to go somewhere with the sense that we would be there to settle and stay for quite some time. *Show me, Lord. Show me what to do.*

I petitioned Him daily for direction. The move, the job, pro-vision. Being a single parent has many challenges. Not the least of which is learning how to make massive decisions on your own. People can give their advice. But only you actually live in your house with your kids every day. Those other people don't. Family, friends, pastors, whoever. I've never been very a particularly confidant deci-sion maker, so this was a massive challenge for me. My first concern, as it should be, was the boys. *What's best for them? Where do I want them to grow up? Who do I want them spending time with? What do they need most?* The questions swirled as I pondered and prayed.

I went to a prayer meeting at Dad and Ginny's house one night. Their home was folded in orange groves. Owls. Horses. Gravel roads. There was room enough to find yourself and space for thoughts to be set to order. It was tranquil. A welcome contrast to the frantic frenzy rampant elsewhere.

That afternoon, I sat on the small pond deck in a wooden recliner made of large planks. I soaked in the sun's life like an iguana who had been buried in a pile of snow, silently praying for the Shepherd to still the waters within.

Don Abshere led a small group of us in prayer that night. He's a jolly-looking man. Tall and broad with stark white hair and beard. His voice boomed as he imparted wisdom and strength. Toward the end, we prayed for each person individually. Ushering them into the middle of the group. Listening intently to the Shepherd's whisper to impart to that person. Words of life and hope. Confirmation. Encouragement. Upon my turn, I walked toward Don and stood next to him. He lay his hand firmly on my head, saying loudly, "Lying spirit, come out." Before I had time to think, I threw my head back and let out a scream. I couldn't recognize my own voice. It sounded so different to any other scream I'd cried out. At once, I collapsed on the ground. The group surrounded me and lay their hands on my limbs and back. The first thing I noticed was Peace. My thoughts, quiet. For so long, my thoughts were a jumbled tormenting mess. And now . . . quiet. Still. Peace. *Thank you, Jesus.* By evicting the disturbing intruder, He had stilled the waters within.

By mid-June, I still didn't know what to do. All the options were on the table. Moving in with family. Perhaps my sister or my mom in California. My brother in Colorado. My dad and Ginny. My grandparents in Arkansas. My prayers were daily. Nearly hourly. And were getting more and more fervent. I wanted to do the right thing.

Dean's second freedom party came quicker that year. It was a brilliant day, and as it had done the first year, it helped me immensely to turn it into something fun. We had an Australia-themed party and held it at my dad's house again. Sausage rolls. Meat pies. Pavlova. There were less people this time, but it was no less joyous.

By the end of the night, we were gathered around in the living room watching old family movies. Footage I hadn't seen since it had been taken. My dad and I had rummaged through some boxes and found them. Everyone else had fallen asleep where they sat or lay. Bodies lay across the couch and floor, limbs going in every direction. The tapes played on as I watched intently. Every time Dean appeared on screen. Watching him move and speak. His playfulness. I still remembered him so vividly. Some of the things he said on tape I had forgotten about, and I had a fresh giggle at his cheeky jokes. His relentless teasing of me. At one stage, there was some footage of us out on a bush track. As I was looking at the Australian landscape on the TV, I heard Him.

AUSTRALIA. GO BACK TO AUSTRALIA.

My mind raced. Everything I want for the boys. Everything I want for them. Is in Esperance. Family. Community. Stability. Safety. Support. Church. Beauty. Things to do. Country lifestyle. Resources for us, which means spending more time at home with them. It all made so much sense. Perfect sense. And it became clear. *I know what to do.*

The next morning, I went upstairs to speak to Daddy. I always talked with him about big decisions. I told him about the home movies and what God said. He agreed straight away that Esperance was a good option for me and the boys.

With that confirmation, I set about making phone calls. Dean's parents. They were supportive of the idea. Really excited, actually. And they said they would be willing to help us when we arrived. The difficulty would be telling my other family. I knew some wouldn't take the news well. It was hard enough on them having the boys and me away for five years. Telling them we were going back wasn't going to be easy.

Over the following week, I had conversations with each of them. My mom and my sister took it the hardest. There were tears. There was some heated conversation. But my compass was set. I knew. I knew without a doubt what I was hearing.

GO BACK.

Moving back to Esperance was going to be the easy part. The hard part was getting there. The flight. That bloody airplane. I started tossing and turning in my sleep thinking about it. The familiar anxiety that plagued me constantly came in big echoes through my chest.

I could feel myself break into a sweat. *Help me, Jesus, help me. Lord, help this feeling to go. I want Peace, God.*

REPENT.

What? Repent? But what am I repenting of?

YOU DO NOT TRUST ME. YOU DO NOT TRUST ME TO KEEP YOU SAFE.

There it was. The truth. I was trying to trust in pilots and engines. Pilots can err, and engines can fail. Tears streamed down my cheeks. I didn't trust God the way I wanted to.

Forgive me, Father. I'm sorry I haven't been trusting you in this. I put my trust in you. I choose to put my trust in you. Not a pilot, not a plane, but you. Just you.

And then it came. Peace rushed over me, in me, through me. Sleep.

The boys and I made the most of our last months in the States before going back. We did Disneyland. Beach days. Park days. Soaking up everything California had to offer us. Everything we wouldn't see for who knows how long.

Somehow, I made it through the security check. Onto that long flight to Sydney. And then on the next one to Perth. I held on. Anxiety was still there but not as excruciating. I set my sights on Esperance. And all that waited for us there.

RETURN TO ESPERANCE

September 2012

And then there I was, driving down that dusty red road again. Dave and Sue came to pick us up. Sprawling farms. That big outback sky reaching out in every direction. And the familiarity grabbed me. All at once. The memories. Dean. Me. The journey. The first time I came to Australia. The first time I laid eyes on those farms. His eyes. The joy. His laugh. His arms. The pain. His family. Camping. Playing. Trips to Perth. Seeing doctors. Dinners. The beach. Him well. Day trips. Him sick. All the memories came like a flood over my senses. The beautiful ones. My favorite ones. The horrible and awful ones. The heartbreaking ones. The deliciously sweet. The terribly bitter. All at once. And all I could do. Was soak it all in. And cry.

My Dean. Oh, my Dean. God, I miss you. I miss you so much. Why did you leave me? Oh God, why did he have to leave? Oh, I miss you. I wish you were here. I wish we were living on the beach in Esperance. Watching our boys grow. I could cook. You could wrestle with them. I could do a beautiful boring life. That sounds so lovely. I'll make cookies. You can tease me and irritate me and try to get a rise out of me. I don't mind. I want you to. And all the dreams I once had of a future with my beautiful husband stared me in the face. Vivid. Beautiful. And utterly out of reach. *God, help me. God, help me do this. Oh, it hurts. The tears. Oh my God, the tears. Will they ever stop?* And my eyes stayed on the horizon. This beautiful setting. The place of most glorious joy and most excruciating agony. The tears came as a steady stream until we pulled into Dean's parents' home. And the memories continued to invade my thoughts. Everywhere I looked, was him. He was everywhere. All the things in Mum and Dad's house. They were things he'd sat on or touched or fixed or stood by. All around the house. In every room. I felt him. I felt him all around me. And I saw him all around me. *You're here, darling. I can feel you here. I feel your presence here. And I love it. Oh, I love it. Because I love you. And I wish you were here. I wish you were here. Oh God, it hurts. Come back, my love. Come back. How do I do this without you? Oh God, how do I do this?* Tears. Tears. Tears.

We unpacked the car and got somewhat settled in. That night, amazingly, I didn't have trouble sleeping. Peace accompanied me. *I'm here, darling, I'm here.* I heaved my tired body into bed. Sleep took me. For the first time in two and a half years, sleep came easily without wine.

The very next morning, we went to a church called Hope of God. The pastors were friends of ours for years. Steve and Helen Wallace. I had the most incredible sense of home and belonging going to their fellowship that morning. *I'm supposed to be here.*

Steve has the heart of a true pastor. Helen is inspiring in the way she does everything. I knew that at this church, I would get the love and encouragement I was going to need as God continued to heal me. The first two or three months, I was up at the front regularly for prayer after service. God turning my heart inside out. One woman specifically prayed in regards to suppressed grief. She held me tightly as I cried into her bosom. I felt the dormant grief rise. A colony of bats disturbed from the home they had made in the pit of my belly. Flapping their wings wildly as they were ushered from their resting place.

God deals with things in layers. The first layers of grief were dealt with. The last remained. It was deep. And dark. And powerful. Anguish. The claw.

God brought me back to Esperance to heal my deepest parts.

I joined a ladies' Bible study. We met at the old farmhouse where Dean and I had lived. I had painted most of the inside of that house. It had many memories. On every wall, room, and corner. Stepping inside it was stepping back in time. Looking around, there was someone else's furniture and someone else's photos, but all I could see was the house as we had it. I could see Dean sitting in his brown leather chair near the fireplace looking up at me. I could hear the boys playing in the other room. Running down the hall. I tried to concentrate on the teaching that night. But I was bombarded with memories. Memories that were so sweet. Birthday parties. Breakfasts. Movie nights. Winter nights by the fire. Prayer times. Hanging the washing. My walks to see the cows. The boys outside on the trampoline. It was all so fresh in my mind. But it was a lifetime ago. *We lost so much. Oh God. My children lost so much.* This house that I had loved. The longest we had ever lived anywhere was here. And now it was someone else's. It was theirs to build memories and plant their family. But I wasn't done. I wasn't done grieving it. I was in a room full of women, but I was a thousand miles away from them all. I was having a lazy afternoon with my family four years in the past. *I feel so ripped off, Lord. I feel so ripped off. Why, God, why?* I left feeling like I had failed. So close. Memories so near. A past almost within reach. *Can I go back? Can't I reach into that time and change the outcome? Can I live there for a day? So I can crawl into Dean's lap again. And listen to his heartbeat. So that we can be whole again? Even for just a day.*

At random moments. Random places and times. Deeply. Intensely. Anguish would dig in his claws. His giant hand would reach up from my belly, tear through my heart, grabbing me by the throat. It would happen suddenly. I had no time to prepare. Unable to breathe. Pain. The kind of pain I ascribe to Anguish. Gripping. Can't escape. Can't wriggle free. And no one around me knows. That there's a monster with his hand around my throat. I don't know if I should tell anyone or try to pretend it's not happening and I'm okay. For me, it was a seven-foot man coming into the room. Throwing me on the floor. Wrapping one hand around my neck. And putting a dagger in my heart with the other. That is Anguish. A stronghold of pain. Disabling. Debilitating. Agonizing. Pain. All around me, I see beautiful, whole families. Beautiful women caring for healthy husbands. Happy children, growing up in stable, established homes. *Why don't my kids get that, God? Why? Here we are, starting again.*

From scratch. My kids don't have a dad. They don't have a school they've "always gone to." A street they "grew up on" or a "set of friends" they always had. Alone in my grief. No one could understand how I felt. And so Anguish continued his assault.

God's provision is amazing. Everything just came together. Within a week of arriving in Esperance, I was settled at Mum and Dad's, the boys were in school, I found a church, and I joined a Bible study.

I was desperate to visit Dean's grave. The last time I was there was the day of the funeral. Today was similar. Cloudy and cool and threatening to rain. I had gone halfway around the world and come back again. I needed to sit on his grave and tell him I came back. That I'm okay. That the boys are okay. That I love him. That I miss him. That I think about him every day, and I want to be close to him so much. On the drive to the cemetery, I felt the emotion welling up. *Dean. Dean. My Dean. I need you, my sweetie.*

I pulled up and parked. I walked briskly. Passing through all the old pioneer graves to get to the back of the cemetery where the more recent ones were. I got to the recent graves and started walking to the back toward the gazebo where I remember the funeral being. *Wait, this is different. There's more graves. Of course. It's not the same as when we buried Dean. That was years ago. Oh Lord, where is he?!*

I looked helplessly across rows of headstones and unmarked graves. We didn't have a headstone for Dean yet. *Oh my Lord.* The tears welled. *Dean, where are you? The date. Of course. Go by the date.* Dean died June 17, 2010. So I started down the rows and skipped across to where I found 2010. I walked along. *Dean, my darling. I've come all this way. Where are you, my honey?* And finally I found an earlier in 2010 and a later in 2010 with four unmarked graves in between. My eyes blurred. *Oh God! Help me! I'm here, and I don't even know which one is his! My darling. Dean. Oh, Dean. Where are you, sweetie?*

It started to drizzle in soft, nearly weightless, tiny droplets. I looked around desperately for someone who could help me. There was a house on the grounds. The groundskeeper probably. *Surely they could help me.* I quickly walked in that direction. Tears and light rain falling on my hair and face. And this terrible longing in my heart to lie on my lover's grave. *Please. Please let me have this. Let me have this moment with my darling.* As I walked toward the house, I saw no car, and it looked very quiet. *Oh God. Help me. Oh Lord.* I turned in a few circles, looking for help in any direction. Suddenly, a ray of hope. Down one of the paths fifty meters or so, I saw a little brown structure that said DIRECTORY.

Praise you, Jesus. I ran toward it. Under a little roof was a binder full of paper on which were names and grave numbers. I started to scan it, looking for Dean's name.

And there it was.

Dean Mack.

My sweet husband. Here. Listed in a grave directory. The reality hit me all over again, and the grief welled in my throat and with it more hot tears.

Now, knowing his grave number, I ran back to the four unmarked graves. And found Dean's. *My love.* I laid myself across the wet grass, over the top of his grave. *My sweet. My darling. I'm here. I came back. I miss you. My love, I miss you so much. Oh, my sweetheart. I miss you. I love you.* Tears rolled off my nose and onto the grass. It was a strange comfort knowing his earthly body was below me. Separated by wood and soil. In separate dimensions. I was still bound by time and mortality. He was already outside of time, clothed with the immortal. *My husband. My lover. God, I miss you. We miss you. The boys. Oh honey, you would be so pleased. You would be so proud. They are so amazing. They miss you. They miss you so much.*

After I poured out my heart in tears, I rolled over onto my back. Peace with me. And I just lay. Looking at the clouds. Watching the soft whispers of rain make their gentle cascade to earth. The landscape echoed the winter in my heart. *Dean.*

RUNNING IN THE
WOODS WITH JESUS

“There's someone here who needs to know God is going to pay you back for the years the locusts have taken.” A wall of a man with a South African accent had taken the mic at the front of church one morning. He had a shaved head and goatee and had large tribal-looking tattoos. He reminded me of the machine gun preacher. I was standing in the back, feeling particularly fragile. The words stirred hope inside me, and I broke.

He continued authoritatively. “You have been robbed. You have been wronged. God wants you to know He is for you. He is with you. He will contend for you. He is going to set things right. And He is going to bless you abundantly.”

I couldn't dry the tears. I couldn't see. They poured. And poured.

Oh, Lord. You are for me. You will repay for the years the locusts have taken. Thank you, Lord. Thank you, God.

The nights were still the hardest. When the day was done. The boys were in bed. The house was quiet. And it was me again. I had grown more accustomed to my own company. But still I had to contend with Loneliness. Sometimes he was like a dark pool. Sometimes like a strong man. Sometimes like a python.

He would coil himself around my chest. Slow enough as not to draw attention. And then commence the arduous torment in which he took such delight. Into my ear, he would whisper his lies.

You are too old. No one will want you.

The adversary that plagued me. The hardest to defeat. So clever with his lies. And Pity let him in. She would open the door for him and prepare me as his meal.

I sought to find contentment in my singleness. Find a place where the yearning for companionship ebbed away to something tolerable. To somehow find joy in it. Peace in the aloneness. To embrace its season for me.

Every now and then someone would come along. Words. It was always the words that drew me in. Conversations would lengthen. Then deepen. Compliments exchanged. Trust given. The seed was planted, and hope would blossom. Love. A conception of combustion. Two hearts lit by the same undying fire. An embryo of Possibility and Future. And Future would look so bright. The struggle that ensued in Darkness was going to cease. Decisions. Life. Sleep. Finance. Time. Discipline. Encroaching on the Promised Land. The desert behind me. To be desired. Someone to share in all things. Someone who could look at my scars without flinching. And willing to show me theirs.

And out of nowhere, still in the budding stage, Hope withered. The embers cooled. The Promised Land, a mirage. A flare. Burning bright and hot at the start but left with nothing but smoke and a signal of distress.

I didn't guard my heart enough. I didn't make them earn it. Or prove it. I didn't wait it out. To see if they were who they said they were. I believed what they said. I trusted too easily. The broken heart propels itself into romance, seeking the high. Without first reading the label:

Long-term side effects: bitter disappointment
WARNING: Not a cure

A dog trainer. A fisherman. A teacher. A musician. A chiropractor. A coast guard.

Each relationship a rush of euphoric flight. Followed swiftly by more broken pieces. Another shattered dream.

But in the wake of the devastation, a miracle. With each relationship. Each devastating heartbreak. I found myself closer to Jesus. More reliant on Him. More focused on Him. More determined to live passionately for Him. More alive in Him. More at peace in Him. More free in Him. What an amazing God. Who could take my missteps. My mistakes. My weakness. My pain. And turn it into an ever-deepening relationship with His invisible self. The invisible force who guided me. The force of love and compassion I discovered was deeper, richer, and more beautiful than I had ever imagined.

In January 2013, the fisherman and I were engaged. My elation was cut short when he broke it off five weeks later.

Crushed.

Devastated.

The morning that he broke up with me, I was supposed to be singing one of my songs at church. For the first time.

I wept the whole way to church as my heart was reeling from the shock. I tried to dry my eyes. I tried to muster some semblance of adequacy as I walked through the back doors. But as I was greeted by Pastor Helen, the facade evaporated. She held me as I sobbed. Despite her not being much of a hugger. *Abandoned. Again. Alone. Again.* As I sat in my seat, there was no damming my flow of tears. But I felt the peculiar sensation of quiet strength grow in my heart. *I have to sing. I have to sing my song. Especially now. In God's strength. Lord, be glorified. God, be magnified. I'm going to sing your praise. As broken and defeated as I feel. Nothing will stop me from singing your praise.* This is what I had trained for. To praise at all times. To worship in all times. To overcome. This is what I was made for.

I got up to play guitar. As I walked forward, it seemed surreal. A stillness came over me. I had always struggled with stage fright. Always got tight, nervous, and jittery playing and singing in front of other people. Even at church. I only ever felt truly at ease and free when I played on my own. But as I strummed that guitar, I looked up. Toward the back of the room. I was looking at a white wall, but I saw a forest. And Jesus was there. I started to play and sing. And it was as if no one else was there. They all disappeared. My arm was loose. My breathing was easy. My voice was bold and steady. I was free. I was with Jesus. We were running and playing in the forest. I sang my heart out to my God. And His spirit completely filled me. I was free. Totally. Free.

God took my broken, heavy, hurting heart that day. And turned it into my moment of greatest victory. I did nothing. I just chose Him. That's all. He did everything else. So, at thirty years of age, the prophecy spoken by John Paul Jackson over me as a fourteen-year-old came true.

"I see you singing."

Yes. Yes, I am singing. And I am free.

RETURNING TO THE BATTLEFIELD

After I left the hospital on the day they flew Dean home to die, I swore I'd never go back. I hated all of it. Except the nurses. The nurses I liked. I hated the elevator. I hated that awful sanitizing gel. Horrid stuff. I hated the lighting. I hated the curtains. The buttons and buzzers. The vials and tubes. The cold floor. The pastel color scheme. And all the awful things that took place there. Where they poked and prodded my love. Where they pumped him with poison. Where they told us he was sick. Where they told us he would die. I hated that woeful place. And I couldn't wait to never lay eyes on it or step foot in it again.

One of the ladies at church got sick. Ronnie, a small, gentle-spirited Filipino woman. She had breast cancer. She fought it for years. It spread. She was hospitalized. They prepared the family. It was almost three years after Dean had passed away. I wanted to visit her. I wanted to take my guitar and go play to her. *Can I go in that place? Oh God. I want to see Ronnie, but I really hate that place.* Love propelled me. My friend Timmy and I went together. We both brought our instruments. Timmy and I lead worship at church together, and he loved her also.

I took deep breaths as I headed to the front doors. The Esperance hospital was much smaller than Perth, which helped somewhat. I gathered my courage as I walked into the entrance, grateful I wasn't alone. We got the information we needed from the receptionist and followed the hallway back. The smell. The smell of mashed potatoes mixed with hand sanitizer and God knows what other chemicals. Nausea. *I hate this place.* Anxiety came with his over familiar greeting. I spotted her room number. *God, I don't know if I can do this.*

As soon as we entered, we saw her two daughters sitting adjacent one another. Her husband sat in a chair looking at her. His face was flushed, and I recognized the myriad of agonized emotions in his expression. Joy came like a flood. Pure joy. I greeted him and hugged him. *This is where I'm supposed to be. I'm supposed to be here.* Ronnie laid in bed. A bandage wrapped around her head. She was sleeping. Timmy and I pulled out our guitars, sat on chairs either side of her, and started playing worship songs. We didn't stay too long. She woke up briefly at one point and saw us there. We said goodbye to her family as we quietly left. Transferring as much strength and courage through a hug as we could. I left with wings. I left with purpose. *Yes, God. This is where I'm supposed to be.*

The beautiful Ronnie passed away that week. Tim and I sang at her funeral. We all wore bright colors in commemoration. We knew where she had gone.

Getting back into the same social circles Dean and I were in was harder than I thought. I had expected a change of sorts. Becoming single, I quickly learned you lose most of your married friends. They still might keep in touch. Exchange pleasantries. Give you the odd call every now and then. But for the most part, married people don't want to hang out with single people. I started having issues with some of the women. Women who felt threatened, I suppose, by me. I always have been puzzled by that. When I was married to Dean, I didn't have many issues with women. I was married and downtrodden. I guess that made most happily content that I wasn't after their husband. Now that I was single though, and coming alive again, jealousies stirred. Insecurities surfaced. It didn't help that I was a massage therapist. It added fuel to the gossip. My outgoing, friendly "American" personality didn't bode well for me at this point.

The wife of Dean's best friend asked me not to call. Or visit. Ever. That was a blow I struggled to recover from. I was giving Dean's brother a massage when, halfway through, I was accosted by his girlfriend. I was forced to oblige her barrage of unwelcome monologue and questions. Treating me like a deviant being paid for sexual favors. There were women at church too. With their "concerns."

I went to one of my favorite older ladies to help me navigate the choppy seas of drama and gossip. She was someone I had leaned on over the years. She offered a shoulder, wisdom, and cuppas. I relayed to her the issues I was having with various women.

"Well, you are a flirt, Cassi. You are inappropriate with men. And it's not just one person who says that. There are numerous people who say that. It was so sad to hear about what happened to you having that miscarriage when you were in America. Did you have sex with the other boyfriends you had?"

Her words shocked me. I expected to be met with empathy and understanding. Instead, I got judgment. As though Esperance had made up its mind about me. "Lock up your husbands, Cassi is on the prowl." The ridiculousness of the notion made it hard for me to process or even think through. I had known coming back to the little town would have its challenges. The way talk spreads. The gossip tree offered mouth-watering and irresistible confections. I knew everyone would have heard about my rebound relationship and subsequent pregnancy. I expected gossip. But some of my closest friends? People from church? This I did not expect. And it grieved me deeply.

I went to an event one night. A mother's social night. Food, drinks, pampering, and what-have-you. The evening was pleasant enough. One of the women struck up a conversation with me. I didn't know her well. She went to one of the other churches in town and was quite close with Karen. We had crossed paths at the odd meal and such. She asked me about Dean. About coming home and the weeks before he died.

I candidly responded, "The days and weeks before Dean died were brutal. It was too much for me. I pushed him away toward the end. It was more than I could bear."

"I remember. I was there." She said as she raised one eyebrow. Her gaze was cold and almost amused at the sting of her remark.

I stood agape. Not knowing what to say. Her expression showed she had made up her mind about me.

And things were similar in many of the people I saw and places I went. The hardhearted. People who wouldn't look me in the eyes because of the talk they'd indulged. Some avoided the subject altogether. Others insisted on reminding me of my past. In case I had forgotten. And although I hadn't forgotten, I had dealt with it. I had suffered the grave consequences. I had repented. I received the grace, love, and mercy of my Father in heaven. Who gives without measure. I had left my past where it belongs. In the past. But these supposed Christians carried my past around with them. Insisting on keeping its memory alive. Did we read the same Bible? Mine says "As far as the east is from the west, so far has he removed our transgressions from us" (Ps. 103:12).

I went home that weekend, still living at Dave and Sue's. My shoulders and heart heavy. *You're a flirt. You're inappropriate with men. I remember. I was there.* Their words echoed in my mind. *I'm a widow with two kids, and I've just moved countries. You'd think people would want to help me? Is that what you think of me, God? Is that who I am? Am I a flirt? Out to get my hands on married men? Am I just a slut, and I don't realize it? Who am I? Who do you say I am, God? What do you say?* The loss of more dear friends. Friends I'd hoped would continue to share in our lives. Make memories. Especially now that we had moved all the way back from the other side of the world. We were minutes away yet living separate lives. I swallowed sobs in my sheets. Wishing I had my own house so I could release them in loud heaves.

YOU ARE MY PRINCESS.

Lord?

YOU ARE LOVED. YOU ARE MINE. YOU ARE MY DAUGHTER.

His whisper came.

I DELIGHT IN YOU.
I MADE YOU.
YOU ARE RIGHTEOUS.

YOU ARE PURE.
YOU ARE HOLY.
YOU ARE BEAUTIFUL.
YOU ARE PRECIOUS.
YOU ARE LOVED.
I LOVE WHO YOU ARE.
I LOVE THE WAY YOU TALK.
I LOVE THE WAY YOU SING.
YOU ARE MY DAUGHTER.
YOU ARE MY PRINCESS.

I smiled widely. Relishing Daddy's words. His affection. His wonderful affection for me. Tears still streaked my cheeks, but now I laughed loudly. *That's who you say I am? Yes.* I laughed. *Yes. That is who I am.*

"But even greater is God's wonderful grace and his gift of righteousness, for all who receive it will live in triumph over sin and death through this one man, Jesus Christ" (Rom. 5:17).

His gift of righteousness. *Righteousness is mine. Given to me by God. No one could take that away. Doesn't matter what they say or think. What I have or haven't done. I am righteous. God says so. I am not going to dim my light so others can feel better about their darkness.*

And I walked freely from then on. Unhindered by the handcuffs of judgment. Unfazed by the gossip's nectar of venom. Unaffected by the rejection of those I loved.

The joy of the Lord became my strength.

A Temporary Home and Love's Pillars Therein

Dean's auntie and uncle, the Florrisons, offered to rent us a little house. The rent was affordable, so we moved in with eager excitement. It was fully furnished and only two blocks from the ocean. It felt like a holiday home, which it was most of the time. Behind the house was a park with some play equipment but primarily a large grassy field. It was empty most of the time, so the boys enjoyed it as if it was their own backyard. I loved the freedom. Once again, I could walk my heart to the ocean, finding solace in the glory of God, which was so aptly displayed at all times of the day. Double rainbows. Silver clouds with gold lining. The water reflecting the sky's many hues of pink and orange, unashamed in its own vibrant shades of turquoise. God adorning the horizon with luminescent extravagance for me alone to behold. My love letters to Him were in prayers and praise. His to me were written in light on the elements.

I still had complaints. I made a cuppa for myself one afternoon, deciding to make them known to God. *God, I'm grateful for this house. I am. It's cute and beautiful and furnished. But . . . I want my children to have* roots. *None of this furniture is* ours. *These photos on the walls are not* ours. *It feels like we are living in someone else's house.*

CASSI, THEIR ROOTS ARE IN ME.

Their roots are in you? In you . . . Okay. I drank in His whisper. *Yes. I can live with that. But God, I want to be settled. I don't feel settled here. I want . . . I want . . .*

WHAT DO YOU WANT?

I want a house. Like a proper house. Like other people have. Where we can feel settled. A home.

YOU NEVER WANTED THAT, CASSI. YOU NEVER WANTED THE WHITE PICKET FENCE. DO YOU REMEMBER WHAT YOU WANTED?

And as a flash, it came to me. Me as a child. Daydreaming. Sharing dreams with my sister. *I do remember. I remember my sister always wanted the house and the white picket fence. But not me. That was never what I wanted. I wanted adventure. I wanted the horizon. I wanted the unknown.*

YES, CASSI. THIS IS WHAT YOU WANTED.

Tears welled as I realized He'd already given me what my heart had desired. Adventure. Memories. People. Places. Travel. These things, I had.

The snow started to melt, and so began the year that spring blossomed in my life. I was singing at church regularly now and had determined to build my life and time around the things I loved. Singing. Dancing. Art. These became my pillars. Around and on which everything else was structured. Timmy and I were playing regularly at church. We took a weekly gig at a restaurant in town and played here and there at various pubs around the place.

I joined a dance class. It had been fifteen years since I put on jazz shoes and leggings. Surrounded by women in their twenties to forties, we danced and giggled like schoolgirls, and I was much the better for it. The exercise did me wonders. Feeling my body stretch and move. Leap and turn. It cured the amnesia left by the haze of tragedy and adulthood. My muscles' memory awakening to former seasons of youth. Before cesareans. Sickness. Death. And years of stress.

I started to paint. I did a painting for my friend, Mary's, birthday. And then I did another. And another. Painting the pictures God had sown in my heart along my journey. Pictures that brought me understanding. Hope. Healing. They'd been marinating in my heart for so long. After years of gestation, they were ready to be born. And so I painted. And painted. The dormant tree suddenly had signs of life. Leaves sprouting. Beginnings of new branches. My living room was scattered with tubes of paint. Brushes. Buckets of water. An explosion of creative chaos. It bothered some. But I loved it. It was birth. It was messy. It was life to me.

God continued to speak, and I continued to learn. We had visitors from a church in New South Wales. Dave and Jen von Blanckensee. They spoke at our church. I was deeply moved by their humility and understanding of spiritual things. They shared of their many experiences of seeing miraculous physical healing through prayer. Many testimonies.

Dean's death left me scarred. My once full faith was fractured and depleted. I knew God was real. I knew he could heal. I just knew it didn't happen all the time. And I didn't have it in me to pray for healing for others. When preachers would get up to preach on healing, I would usually walk out of the service, preferring instead to sit in the car.

This was different. What they shared. The tone. It was insightful. Encouraging and inspiring. *God. Give me faith. I want the faith to believe for healing again. I want to pray for people. I want to see miracles.* I lay on the floor at church. As God bathed me in faith. The faith that was faltering. He fortified it. He reinforced it. Anchored it. And grew it.

And I felt it.

My singleness had become an issue again. I would come to a place of contentment. Thinking I had dealt with it. That Loneliness had been slain. But he would slither back in again. Refusing defeat. To temp and trap me. Catch me unaware. The tears would come again. The crushing sensation.

God. I just want a decent man. Hardworking. Honest. Is it that hard? I just want what so many other people have. It doesn't have to be amazing. Just average. I'll be grateful for that.

CASSI, I WANT THE BEST FOR YOU. WHEN ARE YOU GOING TO WANT THE BEST FOR YOU?

Gulp. *Oh wow. Gosh.*

I didn't think of it that way. Well. If I've had to wait this long. Then, I suppose I would rather . . . wait for the best. For your best for me, God. Your person. In your timing. I thought of all the truly remarkable marriages I'd seen. The kindness. The willingness to work together. The oneness. *Yes. I want the best for me.* Tears.

IS THAT WORTH WAITING FOR?

Yes. Yes it is.

And Peace came.

Pity opens doors. She lets Loneliness in. She lets Grief stay too long. She enhances the effects of Pain. Pity lays me down in a paralytic state so the monsters can have their way with me.

But thankfulness. Thankfulness drives her away. I started learning Thankfulness. To be thankful in all things at all times. And so I started to thank God. Slowly at first. Quietly. Then louder. Stronger. More. And He prompted me to thank Him for EVERYTHING. Even all the hardest, worst things. And my spirit rose.

Thank you God! Thank you that you love me. Thank you that you never left me. Thank you that you followed me into the wilderness. You never left my side. Thank you for my children. Thank you that I am a single mom. Thank you that I had a husband with cancer. Thank you that you brought him home. Thank you for years of pain and suffering. Thank you for all the many ways in which you are good. Thank you for my struggles. Thank you for my failures. Thank you for the anxiety and the sleepless nights.

For you have used it all. To mold me. Shape me. And turn me into the woman you have called me to be. You have made me strong. You have made me humble. You have made me compassionate. You have made me steadfast. You have made me reliant on you.

My thanks grew and grew. And so did my smile. My hope. My spirit. And so did my faith.

I started working as a massage therapist alongside an established therapist in town. I loved the flexibility it gave me, and I found great reward in the work itself. In the early afternoons, I would settle in on my couch with a cuppa, my Bible, and a journal. Ready to read. Ready to listen. He was near again. I felt Him with me all the time. I felt His love. His attentiveness. His presence. His nearness. His wonderful closeness.

Anxiety had decreased immensely. I was no longer on the heartbeat adrenaline rollercoaster. It was only in my sleep, halfway between the worlds of physicality and dreams, she would come for me. Come like the haunting presence of the Invisible Beast. Seizing my heart. Accelerating its tempo.

The beast is coming for you.

He's coming for your children.

My breath would quicken in the darkness. *God, help. No. No. No.* Fear.

You can't stop it. He's coming.

God didn't stop him from taking Dean. He won't stop him from taking you.

I tossed and turned as I fought the lies, battling them in my half-slumbered state. Fear painting images of the beast. Skulking in the shadows of my room. I wrapped my arms around myself. Clutching onto my flesh. Pulling myself into a ball. Trying to hide from his ambush.

With the morning sun and a new day's tasks, Fear would evaporate. It was only in my half consciousness that he wielded his power over me.

A scripture God had spoken over me many times, many ways, through many people was the double portion of Job. That God also had a double blessing for me. That my latter days would surpass the former. It was a promise I held onto fervently. I decided to read the passage in full. I had missed something in all my previous readings of this.

After Job had prayed for his friends, the Lord restored his fortunes and gave him twice as much as he had before (Job 42:10).

After he prayed for his friends. The friends who had misrepresented God. The friends who had made his sufferings harder. The friends who had offered him no comfort or solace. *Those* friends. And God brought to my mind the flood of faces who had so disappointed me. Who had hurt me and let me down. Gossiped about me. Betrayed me. Been cold toward me. Judged me. Those who never called. Those who turned their backs. C. With his lies. All the lies. There were so many. So many hurts. So many unmet expectations.

PRAY FOR THEM.

Tears welled. *Oh the pain. The rejection. Yes, Lord. I know. I know what I need to do.*

And so I listed them. One at a time. Each person. Each instance. Each hurt. And I forgave. I blessed. Praying for God's goodness over their lives. For abundance for them and their families. For their heart's desires to be met. And I wept. And I continued to pray. And I even prayed for C. That God would free him of his many chains. That God would give him a heart of flesh and not of stone. I forgave him for lying. Taking my money. I forgave him for his indifference and his inability to love. And I asked God to bless his life. And I wept. And strength entered my heart. A new strength. A new peace. Hurts as ropes around an eagle's wings. Suddenly cut. Wounds as weights on her feet. At once, lifted. And I stretched them. My unbound wings. And I danced on my weightless feet.

THE MIGHTY PEN AND A LITTLE PLACE CALLED TEXAS

G od brought me friends. Deeply compassionate, vivacious, fun women. Some were married. Beautiful families that invited us into their adventures. Fathers who included my children in time with their sons. My infinite gratitude could not be measured. Most of my friends though were single. Other single moms. Single without kids. Other wonderful misfits. We did movie nights. Dinner nights. Girl nights out. And in. We went dancing. We supported each other. Friendship bloomed. Sisterhood blossomed. And I was truly blessed.

The boys continued to be my purpose. My heart's beat. I took advantage of our time. We read together. Did movie nights. Pizza nights. Ice creams. Bike rides. Trips to the beach where we swam in our clothes. Often stayed up too late. Played in the rain. The mud. Where I saw an opportunity for a moment of joy, I reached out and grabbed it. Took hold of it. For them. Giving them moments of joy, this was my endeavor.

At one of the boys' sports days, I was helping out. Organizing kids and teams and such. A woman came up to me. I had known her here and there over the years. She was sweet and uncomplicated. A mother of a large family.

She said, "Cassi, you shine so brightly. God just loves being your husband. I'm sure you will get married one day, but for now, God just loves being your husband."

Joy. That God would love to be my husband. My provider and protector. And I remembered the scripture Daddy had given me after Dean's death.

"For your Maker is your husband—the LORD Almighty is His name—the Holy One of Israel is your Redeemer; He is called the God of all the earth" (Isa. 54:5).

Yes, Lord. I am blessed. My heart fluttered. *I am yours.*

Dave and Jen von Blanckensee came back to Esperance. I was delighted. I had wanted to send them a card letting them know how God amazingly restored my faith for healing at their previous visit. I was able to spend some time speaking with them before service began. Dave asked me, "Has anyone come along? Has God brought a man into your life?" I teared up slightly, as the subject often made me do. Someone acknowledging my heart's greatest desire.

"No. No, He hasn't."

"Cassi, God has a ministry for you. And it's yours. And once it is established, then your husband is going to come." His words were confident and breathed new life into my future.

I received them and hugged him. Grateful. *God. Oh God. You have a ministry for me. You are going to use it. You're going to use everything I've been through. All the tears. All the years of agony. It's not been for nothing. You have a ministry for me and a husband for me. Thank you, Jesus. Thank you, Jesus.*

Another dream. Heaven's song. I saw the riches of heaven being poured out on Earth, veiled by a curtain. I walk into a room and shout. "The power of death be broken over me in Jesus's name!"

Small, ugly batlike creatures fell off my back and onto the ground. Awake.

Dean's four-year anniversary came. I wrote a post on Facebook:

It's been four years since Dean left this world and went on to the next. My life was

turned upside down. I was thrown into a spiral of grief. Layers of emotion I couldn't process or understand. Haunted by nightmares and memories. It was like anguish was a gnarled claw that tore through my chest and gripped my heart. The long nails cutting deep. And this realm of pain, this deep pit of agony and anguish I had never known, opened up to me. An abyss of brokenness. Where there is no peace, no joy, no solace. Just pain. Deep, horrific, inescapable pain. I felt like a crumpled up heap on the side of the road. It was hard to see anything other than the rubble and carnage that surrounded me and the anguish claw's death grip. Shattered. Shattered within. Shattered without. Shattered dreams. Shattered hope. Shattered life. Hardly recognizable. Just a broken me surrounded by the broken pieces of my broken life. And then, from this deep place of the deepest blackness I've ever known, I called out to God. "God, I'm a broken, shell of a woman. You're the only one who can change that. Take me, Lord. Take my broken heart, and make me whole again!" I would like to thank the people who stood by me when I didn't have the strength to stand, believed in me when I didn't believe in myself, hoped in the best for me when they saw the worst in me, supported me when I was falling, encouraged me when I would have given up, were generous to me in my greatest need, and loved me when I would have died without it. It is because of your love and friendship that I am where I am now. I will never forget your kindness toward me. To those who judged me, criticized me, gossiped about me, and turned their back on me, I would

like to thank you. Because of what you did, I have become stronger than I ever imagined, and I now know who I really am and to whom I belong. All I have for you is love and gratitude. Four years later, I can stand and tell you my heart is WHOLE! My life is beautiful! I have so much joy! I live a life of abundance and blessing! My children are happy, driven, amazing young men! I do the things I love, I have amazing friends, but my heart, oh my heart, my heart is not broken. The claw of anguish has been removed, and its power over me is shattered! I don't have nightmares. I have hopes and dreams! I love my life. A life restored. Thank you, Jesus!

After posting, two women I greatly admire and respect commented to say I should write my story. "There's a book in you, Cassi, that will bring others hope." And so, I started. I started to write the memories, letting them sweep over me. Vividly, they came. And with them, the emotions. The longings. The pain. The love. All their bitterness and sweetness combined. In the telling of my story, I found healing. Healing tears. Tears that made an ocean where I could set the memories free. Taking each one off the dock. Setting it in the water. And letting it float away. Freed of its weight. Of its burden.

I had to fight for time. Against distraction. Against my own laziness. Force myself to submerge into the past. Feel its extent. The great expanse of highs and lows. Letting its tide come and take me to days gone by.

Two years in Esperance went quickly. I could feel change in the air again. I was feeling the itch for a visit home. I spoke to my dad frequently. He and Ginny were living in Texas now, and in speaking to them about their work there, my heart stirred. I started praying. We would need four thousand dollars to make the trip. I could barely afford groceries most of the time. So I prayed. I continued to write. Continued to dance. And sing.

Write. Dance. Paint. Sing. Repeat.

I started to see signs as I sought God for answers. For guidance. I walked into a random pub outside of Esperance where they had a huge Texas poster. Then my massage client was watching the Dallas Cowboys. There were others. One after another, I was seeing Texas. In the Esperance night club, ads for Texas hold 'em circulated the screens. In awe, I stared at them.

A Christian magazine sat on my dining table for months. It had been given to me, but I had avoided it. The commercialization of Christ. *God, if I'm supposed to visit Texas, then I'm going to see Texas in this magazine.* Thinking how unlikely that would be. I opened it. Page 1, 2, 3, 4. Nope. Page 5, in large print:

BE RIGHT WHERE GOD IS RIGHT NOW.
FORT WORTH, TEXAS

I couldn't believe my eyes. It was some sort of conference or something. It was undeniable. *Okay, Lord. I guess you're taking me to Texas.*

Weeks later, my mother called me. I was walking along the beach, as was my custom. Soaking in the coastline. Beauty, the soul's medicine. She informed me she and her husband had decided to buy the boys and I tickets to come and visit. Prayers answered. *I'm going home. Thank you, Lord. Provision.*

I was thinking the trip would be months away, but in looking at ticket prices, I saw it would be cheapest for us to leave in six weeks' time. I called my mom to give her the news, which she met with much enthusiasm.

I knew I was going to have to step onto an airplane. Facing Fear. Again.

I went about making arrangements for our trip. The most important of which was getting some good quality fun time in with my besties. We went out dancing. At one point, Mary and I were talking about my trip.

She stopped and looked at me deeply. "That's right. Because you might not come back."

The music and lights faded in the background, and it all became clear. In that moment. As soon as the words left her mouth. *I'm not coming back. I'm going to stay. God's moving us there.*

The following morning at church, a woman approached me after service. She seemed to know who I was, although I never remembered meeting her. Many people knew of me because Dean was so well known. She asked me about my life and what God was doing. I explained God had done a lot of healing in my heart in coming back to Esperance, but I was planning on flying home to visit and perhaps stay.

"As you've been speaking, I saw the Israelites as they walked through the desert. And when the cloud would stop, they would stop and rest. And when it would continue, they would move forward. God brought you to Esperance to stop and rest, and now He's going to move you again." She was confident and encouraging. The weight of her words hit me as the confirmation I'd been looking for.

Provisions were made. Each day had its tasks and preparations. Packing was fairly easy, as none of the furniture was ours. I set aside things to give away and things we would try to keep. It felt good to pack again. Be on the move. Onto whatever God was calling us to in America. Telling Dave and Sue we were leaving and most likely wouldn't be returning was hard. Telling Matt and Karen was difficult as well. The boys were such a joy to them. A piece of Dean that brought some comfort in his absence. Saying goodbye to Timmy and my girlfriends was emotional. They were all so precious to me, and my love for them had grown so much.

We took advantage of the time left. I had a party at the boys' school for them where they bid their mates goodbye in a frenzy of lollies, hugs, farewells, and laughter. I struggled through bittersweet tears to get good photos. And that's how life always seemed to be. The bitter in one hand and the sweet in the other. Each taking turns outweighing the other. And figuring out how to carry them both and keep moving forward.

People asked me where we would be living. Where I would work. Where the boys would go to school. How would I get around. And so forth. None of those questions had really occurred to me. I just knew I was supposed to go and God would have some sort of plan. In my response, I would laugh and give a puzzled expression. "How would I know? Ask God. He's the one who knows."

They prayed for us at the front of church the Sunday before we left. My gratitude for Steve and Helen's love and pastoral leadership over my life was beyond measure. As they prayed for us, a dear friend of mine, Kylie, said, "Cassi, God brought you here because you've been in heart surgery. He needed to heal your heart. And now it's time to go. It's time to leave the hospital." I was given many words of hope to give me strength when I would need it. With warm and teary embraces from them all, we left.

Spreading My Wings

March 2015

And so we bid farewell to the land we love again. The boys were going to miss her. The way only those who have their heart in two places can. I felt it too. The rising tide of the Southern Ocean. Her ebb and flow on my heart's shores. Sometimes a gentle rise and fall. Others, a furious pounding. The desperate swells of a deserted lover.

We spent a month in California and then drove to Texas. We were welcomed to stay as guests in a beautiful and grand southern style home with friends of my parents. Within days we were given a car and I was offered a job. God's promise of provision came to fruition at every turn.

I continued to write my story. Continued to battle distractions and my own flesh. Beseeching God daily for the strength to finish such a monumental task. A mountain I was scaling but struggling to conquer.

I also sought direction and leading. In work. In destiny. In all things, really. Praying for signs. Doors. Favor. For His plans to come about for me and the boys.

My wedding anniversary came around again. I reflected. No one else remembered. Why would they? But I did. I knew what day it was. I contemplated verbalizing my bittersweet reminiscence. And I heard His whisper.

LET GO, CASSI. YOU CAN LET GO. YOU DON'T HAVE TO CARRY YOUR PAST AROUND WITH YOU. YOU LOVED DEAN. YOU LOVED ESPERANCE. YOU WILL LOVE NEW PLACES AND NEW PEOPLE. YOU CAN LET GO.

I smiled. Yes, Lord. It's time. And so, I turned my face toward the sun and exhaled. The palms of my memory relinquished that tether. Leaving me feeling free. Arms wide for the future. *I love you Dean. But I'm letting you go. I'll always remember. Thank you for loving me.*

I continued to wonder why God had brought me here. Here to Texas. As the months went on, I felt a stirring in my heart. One completely unexpected. A beckoning to the place I said I would never return. The place of my deepest suffering and moments of torment. The hospital. I wanted to go back. Back to the battlefield. The place where I had fought. The place where I had bled. The place that nearly broke me. The place that I fled from. The place that became deplorable to me, I now wanted to run towards. Run to with open arms. I could hear the cries of her inhabitants, in that underbelly of darkness. Where brave soldiers fight invisible beasts of all kinds. I wanted to be the voice in the darkness saying, "Don't give up! Stay strong! You will live! And you will not die!" Combating the lies that Fear and Anxiety feed to the downtrodden and the injured. That is where my heart is. It is with those who suffer. And those that love them and are forced to watch.

God. Take me there. Make a way. Make a way for me to reach those people. Equip me. Open the door.

I went to a meeting one night at a home church in Midland, Texas. The pastors were dear friends of mine. He started speaking about God's Kingdom and those who are called according to His purpose. Those that He calls to minister on His behalf. He then looked in my eyes and said, "Cassi, do you answer to the call?"

He held papers in his hand. I was shaking all over. I felt relief and elation and overwhelmed all at once. I wasn't exactly sure what was happening.

I managed a quiet, "Yes."

"Stand up." He said in his thick Texas accent. The eyes of a warrior chief.

I stood up. I was surrounded by people laying hands on me. Praying. Speaking in tongues. *Lord. Oh my Lord.* The presence of the Holy Spirit was on me so intensely, I could hardly stand. All of my limbs were shaking and my heart was pounding out of my chest. My fingers felt swollen and tingled. But it wasn't Fear. It was Love. Overwhelming Love. Calling me by name. Singling me out.

Saying, "It is time! It is time, Cassi! Arise and shine!"

I felt electric syrup being poured over me. And I felt like I was soaring. Like I'd been waiting on the edge of the cliffs for so long. Longing to spread my wings. And I could feel my spirit. My spirit open wide and free. With His wind all around me. *Jesus. I feel you, Jesus.*

Pastor then anointed me with oil on my forehead and my hands. Saying that they are ordaining me as a minister of the Gospel of Christ. Bearing witness to what God is already doing in my life. They spoke words over me. Words of my calling and future and what God would have me do. To pray for the sick and comfort those who suffer and mourn. I shook all over and cried from deep within. *Yes, Lord. Yes.*

"It's time for you to soar with the Eagles now, Cassi."

THE BEST IS YET TO COME.

Epilogue

The boys and I have been in Texas for two years now. We live with my Dad and Ginny as we continue to await the fulfillment of God's promises in our lives. I am homeschooling them which is a blessing and a joy. Asher is twelve and Maddox is eleven. I am amazed at their joy and zest for life despite all that they have been through. They love God and they know him as Father. We go to a large thriving church here that is a constant source of blessing, relationship, and encouragement. I await with expectation, the man that God will one day bring into my life. Now you know my story. You know my love. You know my torment. My cries. My weaknesses. My struggles. The seemingly insurmountable obstacles. The debilitating loss. Betrayed by friends. Deceived by men. I've battled the Invisible Beast and his comrades relentlessly. Defeating each one. By putting my eyes on Him who saves. Letting Him replace the lies with Truth. Letting Him speak to my heart. Taking up the tools He gave me to overcome and defeat my enemies. Until I grew in strength enough to break the chains.

I am still amazed God has healed my heart. Restored my life. I laugh. A lot. I am surrounded by His goodness. Daily reminded of His faithfulness to me and the boys. He has carried us. Provided. Protected. Healed. Delivered. Strengthened. Encouraged. Prepared. He made me bold. As I had prayed He would, He has molded and shaped me into the woman He has called me to be. And I am so grateful. I would not change it. I would not uncry my tears. I would not trade my suffering. For in it, I found the depths of His love and the certainty of His mercy. I look back on it all. I see how much

He's loved me. How much He loved Dean. What if Dean and I had never gotten married? He would have had all those years of sickness on his own. Instead, God brought me to him. And gave him two amazing sons. And though our journey was painful and at times very dark, it was so blessed. So seasoned with His grace. With His affection. I could see His love for the boys. That He has kept them. Protected their hearts. He has become so real to them. He brought people around us to carry and cover us. I see His unfailing love. I see His immeasurable goodness. Toward us all. He brought me into the dessert that I would find the treasures there. That I would share them with those who are parched and weary as I once was.

I now sleep through the night. Anxiety no longer stalks me. The Invisible Beast no longer haunts me. The shadow of death has lifted. Fear no longer grips or mocks me. The claw of Anguish has been shattered. I have learned to forgive those who gossiped about me. Who judged and forsook me. The waves of grief no longer pound or drown me. Loneliness cannot strangle me. I no longer welcome Pity. I do not usher her in.

The King of Light and Love has dispelled the powers of darkness over my life. He reigns over me. He gives me Peace. He gives me rest. He has made me whole again. He has poured His Joy over and in me. He has given me Purpose. Strength. He holds me. He lifts me up.

And He will do the same for you.

Dean and Cassi's Wedding July 2003

Dean and Cassi October 2003

Dean and Cassi - Pregnant with Asher November 2003

Dean during first round of treatment in Perth with Cassi's
Dad, Steve, and friend, Mitch November 2006

The boys playing on the beach in Esperance November 2007

Dean, Cassi, and the boys 2007

Dean (in Remission) and Cassi December 2007

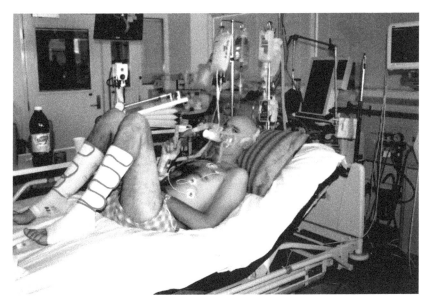

Dean in ICU fighting lung infection 2008

Dean with Steve in King's Park April 2009

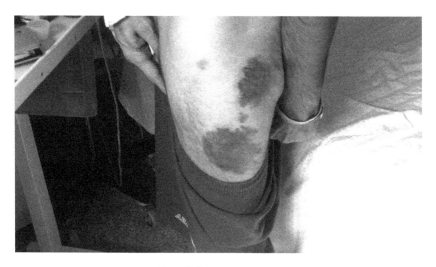

Dean's bruising 2009

Dean September 2009

Dean's Funeral June 24th 2010

Cassi and the boys back in Australia, the end of 2013

ABOUT THE AUTHOR

Cassi Eve. Mother. Painter. Writer. Worship leader. Born and raised in a broken family in Southern California. At the age of twenty, she married Australian born Dean Mack. Three years after they wed, her husband was diagnosed with leukemia. She cared for him for five years.

She has found joy and purpose out of the things she suffered and now helps people who are enduring the horrors of cancer. Grief. Widowhood. And the struggle of single-parenting.

She currently resides in Lewisville, Texas with her two sons. You can find her creative and kingdom exploits at cassieve.com.